A Case for the Case Study

A Case for

the Case Study

Edited by

Joe R. Feagin,

Anthony M. Orum,

and

Gideon Sjoberg

The

University of

North Carolina

Press

Chapel Hill

and London

© 1991
The University of
North Carolina Press
All rights reserved
Library of Congress Cataloging-in-
Publication Data
A Case for the case study / edited by
   Joe R. Feagin, Anthony M. Orum, and
   Gideon Sjoberg.
      p. cm.
   Includes bibliographical references
and index.
   ISBN 0-8078-1973-5 (cloth : alk.
paper). — ISBN 0-8078-4321-0 (pbk. :
alk. paper)
   1. Sociology—Research—
Methodology.   2. Social sciences—
Research—Methodology.   3. Case
method.   I. Feagin, Joe R.   II. Orum,
Anthony M.   III. Sjoberg, Gideon.
HM48.C37   1991
301'.01—dc20
90-27036   CIP

The paper in this book meets the
guidelines for permanence and
durability of the Committee on
Production Guidelines for Book
Longevity of the Council on Library
Resources.

Manufactured in the
United States of America
04   03   02   01   00
6   5   4   3   2

THIS BOOK WAS DIGITALLY MANUFACTURED.

Contents

Preface

    This is a collection of essays about the nature and use of the case study in sociology and the other social sciences. We have put together this collection of important articles because we believe that social scientists need to make much more use of the case study approach to studying social life. With the advent of modern quantitative techniques and the wide-scale use of these techniques in the social sciences, we have experienced in the United States the regrettable result of a neglect or a downplaying of research that employs the methods of case studies. We feel that the case study remains an extraordinarily useful and important strategy for social analysis. Here we provide major examples of case studies by prominent social science researchers in a number of substantive fields, together with a reasoned rationale for the case study approach. We seek here to help bring these issues back into the social science forum, and we expect that the contents of these articles will prove stimulating materials for our fellow scholars in the social sciences.

    This collection of essays provides a wide range of information on the nature of the case study. In the introduction we set the case study in the broader framework of methods available to social scientists, and we refer to a number of important examples to illustrate our claims. Then the first essay of the collection, by Gideon Sjoberg, Norma Williams, Ted Vaughan, and Andrée Sjoberg, examines the issue of methods in the social sciences from a broad philosophical perspective and provides a firm rationale for the independent significance and widespread use of case study methods by social scientists. Together with the introduction, this essay provides the methodological foundations for the essays that follow.

Beginning with the essay by Howard Bahr and Theodore Caplow, three pieces examine and illustrate case studies of cities. The Bahr and Caplow piece reports on their follow-up research on the classic Middletown studies of Robert Lynd and Helen Lynd, studies conducted more than a half century ago. Next, Anthony Orum and Joe Feagin report on more recent case studies of two different southwestern cities—Austin and Houston—and provide a detailed comparison of the similarities and differences in their methods and substantive work. Then David Snow and Leon Anderson report on their case study of the homeless, work that represents an in-depth case study treatment of a major segment of the urban poor.

The essays that follow illustrate the wide variety of contexts in which case study methods have been fruitfully applied in the recent intellectual pursuits of social scientists. R. Stephen Warner reports on his case study of a single church in Mendocino, California, a piece of research that provides insight into changes that have occurred in recent decades in American religion. Gilbert Geis discusses a wide variety of case studies in the field of crime, some of them ranking as classic examples of case study research. Christine Williams describes her ingenious deviant case studies of gender, using two contrasting cases to unearth new insights into the operation of gender roles in the United States. And Gerald Handel offers a description of the use of case study methods in the study of families, particularly in his own field research. Each of these essays, then, furnishes an illustration of how case study methods may be applied to the social life-world and also of the reasoning and research that went into the particular site for investigation.

In sum, we have provided readers with a broad and diverse set of essays. We believe that all interested readers will find them to be a useful introduction to case study research and that social science students in particular will find them helpful in promoting ideas about what to study in the social life-world and how to study it.

A Case for the Case Study

Anthony M. Orum, Joe R. Feagin,

and Gideon Sjoberg .

Introduction

The Nature of the Case Study

Who studies single cases any more? This question was posed
to one of us recently in an effort by the interrogator to belittle an extended research project in which the author was engaged. Today most
social scientists do not study the single case, nor even a handful of cases.
Is this because the single case is an anachronism, a primitive research
method used by social scientists in the early days? Should we dispense
with the single case altogether and rely primarily on masses of information about hundreds or thousands of individuals? We will argue that both
questions must be answered in the negative. The study of the single case
or an array of several cases remains indispensable to the progress of the
social sciences. Several years ago, at an annual gathering of American
sociologists, the three of us presided over a roundtable about the case
study. To our surprise, the attendance at our session was large and the
interest voiced in the case study by those in attendance very enthusiastic.
As we talked to more and more fellow researchers about our concerns,
we discovered a reawakened and growing interest in case study research.
This concern led to our decision to provide these essays. We hope to use
this collection as a way of instructing the uninformed about the nature
of case studies, as well as a means for providing case study enthusiasts,
like ourselves, with references and illustrations for case study research.

To say we are excited about the prospects today for case study research in the social sciences would be to understate the matter. Many researchers will need to turn to the case study as a way of making a serious investigation of some mystery about the social world. The case study offers them the opportunity to study these social mysteries at a relatively small price, for it requires one person, or at most a handful of people, to perform the necessary observations and interpretation of data, compared with the massive organizational machinery generally required by random-sample surveys and population censuses. Because so little has been written about case studies in recent years, our discussion will assume the form of an argument for the merits of case studies. We do *not* think the case study is the only method for conducting social research, but it does represent a significant methodological tool and strategy for the social scientist.

Qualitative and Quantitative Methods

Let us begin with a straightforward definition of a case study. A *case study* is here defined as an in-depth, multifaceted investigation, using qualitative research methods, of a single social phenomenon. The study is conducted in great detail and often relies on the use of several data sources. This definition is intentionally broad, and we do not argue that it is unambiguous. For example, some case studies have made use of both qualitative and quantitative methods. And some of our best research studies have involved a small number of case studies conducted in a comparative framework. In case study research the nature of the social phenomenon studied has varied. It can be an organization; it can be a role, or role-occupants; it can be a city; it can even be an entire group of people. The case study is usually seen as an instance of a broader phenomenon, as part of a larger set of parallel instances. (Compare this definition with Black and Champion 1976, 89–94; McCall and Simmons 1969; Nachmias and Nachmias 1976, 42; and Yin 1984.) Now, since just a single instance of a phenomenon is under investigation, there is the further presupposition that certain kinds of data collection procedures will be employed, procedures that will permit the investigator to examine the phenomenon in great depth and detail. These are usually termed *qualitative methods* and are contrasted with *quantitative methods*.

QUANTITATIVE METHODS

Most quantitative social science research studies fall, generally speaking, into two types. There are surveys, which are methods of collecting data from large numbers of people who represent a population or a random sample of a population. Random-sample surveys and population surveys (called censuses) rely on the administration of a standardized set of questions. The general U.S. census is conducted once every ten years and employs a set of standard questions designed to gather basic information about the American people. The census attempts to survey the entire U.S. population in regard to its most fundamental questions, and it surveys samples of that population in regard to other basic social and economic questions. A census survey attempts to portray features of an entire population of people living in a particular society. Another major category of surveys is the opinion survey, which typically makes use of random samples drawn from a larger population. Opinion surveys may focus on practically any type of question, from sexual behavior to voting preferences.

Second, there are experiments, typically conducted by psychologists and social psychologists. Experiments are typically done to test specific hypotheses about purported causal relations between different phenomena. Before the experiment, the researcher predicts what people think or how they act. Then she or he administers the particular experimental condition and compares the results on the experimental group with the group that has gone unexposed to the experimental condition. The difference between the quantitatively assessed scores of the two groups is said to be the product of the experimental condition.

Although these two data-collection procedures differ, each furnishes information that is quantitatively manipulated, often in sophisticated ways. Precision in the form of statistical procedures is emphasized. Typically, certain hypotheses are proposed, they are examined with the data, and then some firm conclusions, rendered in the form of probabilistic statements of likelihood, are set forth by the researcher (see also Bryman 1988, chapter 2).

QUALITATIVE METHODS AND CASE STUDIES

There are several types of qualitative research that have been termed, or linked to, case studies. The first of these is ethnography, or what is sometimes called field research. An ethnography represents a detailed study of the life and activities of a group of people. It typically relies heavily on firsthand observation of their ways of acting, believing, and feeling. Anthropologists are the professional group of scholars most likely to undertake ethnographies. Typically, anthropologists observe a single group of people, such as a particular clan or tribe, over a long period of time. They spend months, perhaps even years, observing how the people go about their daily routines and how they celebrate special occasions. The term *participant observation* is sometimes used to refer to this brand of research because investigators often can acquire a rendering of the activities only by participating in those activities. In sociology, William Foote Whyte's classic research study on street-corner life in East Boston (1943) is an ethnography; it could not have been conducted without the tools of participant observation. Then there is Stack's (1974) ethnography of black families in a ghetto community, a study that challenged with inside information much accepted wisdom about black families. Stack lived with and learned from the people she studied. In the articles that follow, Warner provides an ethnographic study of a church, and Handel discusses ethnographies of families.

A second type of qualitative research procedure, which, again, may take the form of a case study, is the examination of life histories, or partial or total biographies of individuals. We mean here biography not in the conventional sense of the term, such as the biography of Franklin Roosevelt, but rather the sociobiography of a particular social type or social role. There have been life histories of hoboes (Anderson 1923), of black domestics (Rollins 1985), of alcoholic selves (Denzin 1986), and of middle-class blacks (Feagin 1991). Primarily using in-depth interviews, the social biographer seeks to understand the nature of the role and to do so by constructing the (partial or whole) life histories of the role-occupants. The researcher may use one particular role-occupant—as Anderson (1923) did in the classic example—or, as more often happens, the researcher may examine a number of people to capture the richness associated with the occupancy of a particular role. A brilliant example of this is Rollins's (1985) study of black domestics and their white employers in Boston, a study that revealed the persistence of racial "deference rituals" in white middle-class areas of a major city. The research of Williams on gender roles and of Snow and Anderson on the homeless, discussed later in this volume, followed this strategy of data gathering.

A third type is the social history of a social group or collectivity. Social histories that qualify as case studies are those conducted on the past experience of a group and that seek therein to elicit discoveries and insights that can illuminate the experience of other, similar groups. Here it is worth noting that the historian, as compared with the social scientist who conducts such histories, usually operates with a different set of implicit assumptions about the meaning of historical data. The historian is apt to assume that the study of a particular event, let us say the American Civil War, is unlikely to illuminate a parallel event, let us say the civil war in Vietnam in the 1970s and 1980s, because, supposedly, the world consists only of singular events. One event, the historian assumes, possesses its own concatenation of actors and institutions, and these simply are similar to those of another event in only the most abstract and general way. Social scientists, by comparison, will relax the assumption of singularity somewhat and will look for parallels between historical events (see also Tilly 1981; Stinchcombe 1978). What makes this revolution similar to that one, for example? Why is the history of this city in the Midwest similar to the history of that city in the Northeast? Nevertheless, it will be a difference of degree, not of kind. Both sorts of researchers will seek to construct a record of the past and seek to tell a story of the life and times of a specific group of people. Further, both may be interested in the matter of historical continuities and changes, searching for ways in which patterns remain the same or vary over time. In our volume the research reported by Orum and Feagin and Bahr and Caplow falls into this category. It should be noted that numerous qualitative studies have used elements of these various case study approaches in an eclectic fashion.

Some Advantages of Case Study Research

Consider the influential and timely case study of Muncie, Indiana—called Middletown—by Robert Lynd and Helen Lynd (1929).

This social history research provided important information about the range of customs in a middle-sized American city, knowledge about matters as diverse as the magazines that people read and the ways they go about making a living. This case study has suggested numerous theoretical generalizations used by two generations of subsequent researchers to guide both qualitative and quantitative research. So too did Floyd Hunter's study (1953) of Atlanta. Hunter was interested in the nature and display of power in Atlanta and set about in a novel way to uncover its dimensions. His was the first major empirical work to reveal the structure and networks of urban power and to demonstrate how social and governmental policies were implemented through this structure.

Sociology is not the only social science to rely on the case study for fundamental insights. Political science has enjoyed considerable acclaim because of its detailed analysis and because of such major works as that by Robert Dahl (1961) on New Haven. Dahl's classic study, in part a reaction to Hunter's earlier study, became the basis for constructing a theory of urban polity and for much methodological debate over the best way to do research on urban power structures. Note too that psychoanalysis had its own beginnings in the case studies done by Josef Breuer and his young colleague Sigmund Freud. Their studies of individual patients, such as Anna O., gave rise to such revolutionary ideas as the subconscious and to the cure of physical distress through patient-doctor dialogue and the use of catharsis in the patient-doctor relationship. These studies have in turn influenced several generations of social science researchers and theorists.

Research studies such as those of the Lynds, Hunter, Dahl, and Freud provide a richness and depth to the description and analysis of the micro events and larger social structures that constitute social life. There are several fundamental lessons that can be conveyed by the case study:

1. It permits the grounding of observations and concepts about social action and social structures in natural settings studied at close hand.
2. It provides information from a number of sources and over a period of time, thus permitting a more holistic study of complex social networks and of complexes of social action and social meanings.

3. It can furnish the dimensions of time and history to the study of social life, thereby enabling the investigator to examine continuity and change in lifeworld patterns.

4. It encourages and facilitates, in practice, theoretical innovation and generalization.

We can expand each of these points.

THE STUDY OF PEOPLE IN NATURAL SETTINGS

Consider first that case studies enable the investigator to ground the observations and concepts with which she or he works. The detailed and rich data offered by the well-crafted case study permit the analyst to develop a solid empirical basis for specific concepts and generalizations. Much quantitative work in modern social science deals with brief survey questions and answers and large numbers of disconnected respondents; indeed, such work often does not involve original data collection. As a result, the flesh and bones of the everyday lifeworld is removed from the substance of the research itself, thereby diminishing the usefulness of the research for subsequent investigations. In contrast, a principal argument for case study research is that it provides a way of studying human events and actions in their natural surroundings. We have noted numerous examples of this, from Whyte's classic study of a Boston gang to Stack's study of black families in a ghetto. The case study lies at one end of a continuum, with the experiment posed at the other. Whereas the case study enables an observer to record people engaged in real-life activities, the experiment is an artificial construction of life.

An experimenter may wish to examine how one particular variable, let us say exposure to a film, affects the way people think about some phenomenon. So he or she assesses people's beliefs before the film, exposes one group of them to the film, and then afterward compares beliefs of the exposed and the unexposed sets to determine whether exposure made any difference. Although such an experiment provides an elegant method of uncovering something about how people's beliefs are shaped and modified, it is usually conducted in such a way as to remove people from their daily circumstances of living. Earl Babbie has noted: "The greatest weakness of laboratory experiments lies in their artificiality. Social processes observed to occur within a laboratory setting might not necessarily occur within more natural social setting" (1975, 254). Somewhere between the experiment, with its artifices, and the case study, with its bold naturalness, lie the census and the opinion survey. These latter methods are generally based on observations of people taken out of the context of their daily lives, though both, especially the opinion survey, can be so adapted as to come closer to the natural qualities of the daily setting than can the experiment.

All of this is to make another point often put forth by researchers who engage in case study research. The argument is made that such analyses permit the observer to render social action in a manner that comes closest to the action as it is understood by the actors themselves. Here the observer wishes to make claims that are grounded in the claims of those who make them. In contrast, an experiment creates an artificial social setting in which the experimenter manipulates the participants (see the classic illustration reported in Milgram 1974). A random-sample survey also relies on questions created in advance by the survey researcher to measure dimensions of belief or action reported by decontextualized respondents. Yet if one assumes that belief or action removed from its immediate (personal and social) context is, in one sense, no understandable action at all, then one must turn to the tools of qualitative research and the case study. (For one of the original arguments on behalf of this claim, see Thomas and Znaniecki 1918–20.)

HOLISTIC STUDIES OF COMPLEXES OF ACTION AND MEANING

A second common feature of case studies is their holistic approach. Since the case study seeks to capture people as they experience their natural, everyday circumstances, it can offer a researcher empirical and theoretical gains in understanding larger social complexes of actors, actions, and motives. The organismic approach has been defended by case study advocates for many decades. Cooley (1930, 314) pointed out that the statistical approach does not take us very far in understanding human beings in some wholeness. Whereas a random-sample survey can permit some understanding of how respondents relate to one another, the typical survey assesses people as though they lived, acted, and believed in isolation from one another. A survey of voting behavior, for instance, may assemble considerable information on the voting preferences and on the social and political characteristics of people, for example, their educational attainment or family income, but it typically assembles no detailed information on the array of partners, colleagues, relatives, and friends with whom the voter interacts on a frequent basis. Yet social scientists know from a few detailed studies of voting contexts that social networks are of vital significance to shaping the timing and form of voting decisions. In addition, we should note that in recent years the number of quantitative analyses of social networks has increased dramatically. This specialized work shows a clear recognition of the importance of the integrated social complexes often missing in random-sample survey research.

A case study, in contrast, can permit the researcher to examine not only the complex of life in which people are implicated but also the impact on beliefs and decisions of the complex web of social interaction. Studies of tribes permit the observer to discover how systems of kinship networks develop and operate; studies of the occupants of individual roles enable the investigator to discover how the definition of a role emerges out of interactions between role-occupants and others; and studies of organizations permit the researcher to discover social interaction patterns that occur among employees or between employees and clients. An example of this can be seen in Hunter's work on Atlanta, where he argued that there existed a structure to the distribution of power in that city such that certain individuals from widely disparate settings were intimate associates of one another and that they routinely fashioned the important public decisions of the city. He then proceeded to demonstrate the validity of his assertion by displaying the specific patterns of friendship and interaction among key figures, along with materials on how these figures formulated particular policies.

More generally, a case study of a single phenomenon, let us say a city's public decision making or an organization's informal operations over a long period of time, allows the observer to examine social action in its most complete form. The investigator is better able to grasp the total complex world of social action as it unfolds. For someone who is interested in how people act in organizations, and how daily routines influence their work, such a gain can be quite considerable. Peter Blau (1955), for instance, examined the way office work was conducted in two different federal agencies. He found that informal norms, and everyday social relationships, had an impact on how people carried on their work within the organizations. More recently, Rosabeth Moss Kanter (1977) studied gendered roles and the informal norms that channeled jobs by gender in a major electronics corporation.

Case studies permit researchers to discover complex sets of decisions and to recount the effect of decisions over time. Political scientists probably pay more attention to such phenomena than other social scientists primarily because they believe decisions tell much about the character of power and influence. One important instance comes from the research of the political scientist Robert Dahl. Dahl's theory of American politics claimed, among other things, that the exercise of power is a distinctly differentiated activity: Politicians, rather than wealthy capitalists or leading socialites, exercise power, and they do so through the control of specific decisions. Dahl went on to show how in the case of three particular arenas of public decisions in New Haven, different groups and individuals sought to exercise power. He found that the one individual who seemed to exercise control over the most decisions was the mayor, Richard Lee, not some wealthy local businessperson. This was an observation consistent with Dahl's general portrait of power in the city. The vivid materials used to portray the patterns in New Haven, along with the lucid manner in which Dahl linked his generalizations to the empirical reality, enabled later investigators to seek to duplicate his work in other urban settings. Moreover, it also enabled another student of power in America, G. William Domhoff (1978), to redo Dahl's New Haven history and to come up with data that challenged some of Dahl's original claims about the impotence of business elites.

The study of total complexes of social action is indispensable for certain sorts of social research. To a cultural anthropologist, for instance, action and belief are not very meaningful unless observed in the immediate context. The distinguished cultural anthropologist Clifford Geertz has written: "In order to follow a baseball game one must understand what a bat, a hit, an inning, a left field, a squeeze play, a hanging curve, and a tightened infield are, and what the game in which these 'things' are elements is all about" (1983, 69).

Holistic case studies can also involve the study of complexes of social meanings. A good case study can provide a full sense of actors' motives that eventuate in specific decisions and events. The student who uses the case study can see human beings up close, get a sense of what drives them, and develop claims of how their personal as well as collective lives have been created. For example, John Dollard's case study (1949) of racial relations in Birmingham, Alabama, some decades ago involved studying a group of residents in some depth. By weaving together their motives with the social history of that southern town, he gained a clear sense of the personal motivations that underlay southern race relations. From a series of in-depth interviews, coupled with observational and historical data on the city, Dollard showed how, to take one example, sexual motives lay just below the surface of local black-white relations. Among other things, he concluded that "any move toward social equality is seen on its deepest level as really a move toward sexual equality, that is, toward full sexual reciprocity between the castes." More recently, Arlie Russell Hochschild (1983) examined the emotional and the emotional management sides of the occupational roles of flight attendants and bill collectors. Using in-depth interviews, she described the commodification of the "smile" and other emotional expressions on the part of flight attendants and the relationship of this emotion management to gender roles in the United States.

Another illustration of how a case study permits insight into human motivations is provided by Kai Erikson's award-winning study (1976) of the Buffalo Creek flood. The flood tore apart an Appalachian mining community. Erikson showed that the physical disaster produced significant personal and social upheavals as well. It had left people without a sense of who they were, destroying their sense of time, space, and family. More important, Erikson showed through a series of close interviews with survivors that the disaster had fundamentally disrupted the social fabric of the community, undermining its norms and way of life. Before the flood, members of the community, for instance, had strongly relied on the custom of neighborliness among one another, helping out in times of need, providing support to friends and family; the flood was so traumatic, however, that it literally destroyed this general social support system and with it the sense people possessed of a common way of life.

A related point here is that the case study permits an investigator to examine how humans develop "definitions of the situation." Erikson's study of Buffalo Creek casts the "definitions" in terms of the neighborliness among Appalachian mountain folk. Another classic example is the in-depth study of the Balinese cockfight by the anthropologist Clifford Geertz. Geertz (1973) revealed how the cockfight in Bali is an event that discloses a whole host of meanings. Men treat the cocks quite literally as their sexual organs, preening and caring for them with excessive attention: the more handsome the cock, the grander his master. But Geertz went beyond that titillating claim to suggest that the intensity of the fight increases as those who engage in it become more the social equal of one another. The sign of the intensity lies not merely in the emotion and animation displayed during the course of the cock match but most especially in the wagers placed on the respective cocks and the masters' identification with them. When the masters are of relatively equal social standing, they are more likely to closely identify with their cocks. It would be difficult to see how any method other than the in-depth case study could provide insight into the various *levels* of social meaning associated with the Balinese cockfight. Note too that there is a type of precision here that is more substantial than the quantitative analysis. The precision is in the recording of social life as a meaningful whole, not as the sum of lifeless quantitative units.

A SENSE OF TIME AND HISTORY

Third, the case study can enable a researcher to examine the ebb and flow of social life over time and to display the patterns of everyday life as they change. A case study thus permits the analyst to uncover the historical dimension of a societal phenomenon or setting. One example is the Muncie study conducted by the Lynds. The Lynds' first research was done in the mid-1920s, and in that work they traced the history of the city as well as explored the various dimensions of everyday life. The volume they wrote was received with considerable enthusiasm by sophisticated readers. When misfortune intervened, and the Great Depression arrived, the Lynds returned to Muncie to see how circumstances had changed the residents' ways of life. The rich detail of their earlier study, coupled with an equally intense probing of Muncie during the mid-1930s, permitted the Lynds to discover the many ways in which the depression and poverty had disrupted the lives of local residents. Moreover, they were able to see social and political change at work: for example, over the course of the decade between the first and second studies, banks failed, businesses were disrupted, and one family, the Ball family, came to be increasingly wealthy and politically dominant in the town. The close observations of the wealth and influence of the Ball family became the foundation for other studies that sought to link together social stratification and the distribution of political power. In addition, the detailed analyses and descriptions by the Lynds permitted Bahr and Caplow, many years later, to return to Muncie to study the changes that had occurred over half a century. They discuss this follow-up case study research later in this volume.

Another illustration of how the case study provides special insight into time and its ramifications for social life is the monumental research of Anthony F. C. Wallace (1978) on the origins and unfolding of the industrial revolution in Rockdale, a small community on the edge of Philadelphia. Wallace was particularly interested in how industrialization had reshaped the life of an American community, and he set about to examine such matters as how new machinery was introduced into the nature of production in Rockdale. What he found was particularly rich data on changes over time, data that he used to reassess the arguments of Max Weber in *The Protestant Ethic and the Spirit of Capitalism*. In particular, Wallace watched the making of a class of manufacturing capitalists among landholders, and he documented how they used their Christian principles to justify their mercenary attitude toward fellow townspeople, those who had become their industrial laborers. The data—on everything from the nature of industrial machines to the diaries of the capitalists—are lush, detailed, cumulative, and comprehensive.

THEORY GENERATION

A fourth virtue of case study research, like other qualitative research, is that it lends itself to theoretical generation and generalization. Theoretical generalization involves suggesting new interpretations and concepts or reexamining earlier concepts and interpretations in major and innovative ways (Yin 1984). Case studies have been particularly important in the generation of new ideas and theories in social science. Certainly one can develop significant new theoretical innovations and generalizations from good quantitative research, but in practice this has been less likely than in the case of qualitative research. Indeed, most quantitative re-search has been concerned with offering low-level generalizations or with extending, all too often in very small ways, inherited theory. Quantitative research has pioneered in accenting the natural science method, in the language of verification: "hypothesis and proposition testing," "tenta-tiveness," and "proof." Although the corroboration or falsification of in-herited theory is a legitimate social science enterprise, it has often been framed in this hypothetico-deductive verification language, in excessively rigid natural science terms. This verification framework has led to an overemphasis on statistics and refined quantitative techniques, overshad-owing the important enterprise of theory generation. At its most rigid, this verification method has taken the form of "positivism." Developed in the long tradition of Giddings, Ogburn, and Lazarsfeld, this American positivism is characterized by a preoccupation with statistical techniques and a research instrumentation imitating the natural sciences. At its cen-ter has been the hypothetico-deductive verification rhetoric.

Statistical generalization has been of much greater concern in quanti-tative research than has theory generation. Statistical generalization de-velops out of statistical measurement and involves the extrapolation of findings from one set of data to a larger set of data. Quantitative research often involves this type of generalization, whereby one can extrapolate within certain statistical parameters to a larger population from a small random sample. When it comes to statistical generalization, a case study represents the investigation of but a single instance of some phenomenon and therefore limits the degree to which the researcher can claim that her or his findings hold in like instances (see too Bryman 1988, 88–91, 92, 100–101; Black and Champion 1976, 92). In raising this legitimate con-cern, however, we must make certain distinctions to properly understand what is being generalized. If, for example, you are studying a social pro-cess, such as "recruitment to a fundamentalist religious movement," then it is the population of such processes, not a population of people, to which you will generalize. Presumably, you would need to identify how many fundamentalist religious movements engage in some form of re-cruitment in order to know the boundaries of the population. The answer to that question may be that the relevant population is considerably smaller than you first thought. If a researcher is dealing with social units, like organizations, the population may not be so large as is first imagined.

And there are other considerations too. Some case study researchers demonstrate precisely how representative a particular case is of some larger population to which they generalize. The Lynds (1929), in their research on Muncie, argued that the city was representative of midsize American communities and that therefore its social and economic patterns could safely be generalized to the population of such places. Likewise, Becker and his associates (1961, chapter 4) went to great pains to argue that the University of Kansas Medical School, where they conducted their research into student culture, was similar to other medical schools in the United States. Hence, they argued, even though they were studying only one such school, claims about its student culture should hold true in other American medical schools. In general, then, we may conclude that the nature of the phenomenon that one studies is the true gauge of the population to which one seeks to generalize. It is not merely a question of how many units but rather what kind of unit one is studying.

Some of the most frequent critiques raised in regard to case studies have to do with how or whether such studies can cast light on propositions derived from prior research and on variable interrelationships (see, for example, the discussion in Nachmias and Nachmias 1976, 42). The argument—which stems from the natural science model—runs something like this. To make claims that two separate phenomena are related to one another, the researcher must examine a number of different instances in which both phenomena are present, and further, she or he must be able to demonstrate that the connection between the two is real, not artificially induced by some other variable or variables. Some quantitative methodologists wonder how a single instance, even one where the two phenomena may both be present, can ever cast light on covariation, much less on the matter of whether two phenomena are related in time, the one as cause and the other as effect. Here a single case study has some limitations, as seen from this perspective. Quantitative assessments of many related variables are not possible. However, the case study may suggest that two phenomena are related to each other, even though it cannot furnish proof of their link in many relevant situations. Take some of the work of Whyte (1943). One of the most interesting discoveries of his research was that the social structure, the hierarchy, of the gang dictated how gang members would perform in the context of gang activities. A striking example occurred in group bowling. On one occasion, Long

John, a gang member, actually outperformed Doc, the gang leader. For some days thereafter, Long John suffered severe headaches and sleeplessness, two uncommon occurrences for him. Whyte interpreted this to mean that because Long John had violated the hierarchical ordering of the gang by outperforming his leader, he thereby suffered some sense of guilt, which was manifested in his physical symptoms. To be able to claim that gang hierarchy and gang performance are somehow causally related to each other, a researcher would have to do more such case research covering similar situations. But, here it is evident that the detail and depth of Whyte's research enabled him to propose a highly suggestive theory of group life, one that could point the way for further work by other students (also on this sort of issue, see Blalock 1970, 41–46).

Sometimes the study of a single case, which is construed to be a deviant case, may help to illuminate how the more general social process under discussion works. One of the classic pieces of sociological research was a case study of this type. Seymour Martin Lipset and his colleagues Martin Trow and James S. Coleman (1956) noted that virtually all labor unions in America were dominated by a single ruling clique or oligarchy. Only one union, they observed, the International Typographical Union (ITU), proved the exception. By studying this exception in depth, they hoped to better understand both why democracy prevailed in the ITU and why it was absent elsewhere. What they discovered, among other things, was that the employees of the ITU were somewhat better educated than employees of most other unions and participated much more actively in union activities than members of other unions. Both elements, Lipset and his colleagues suggested, gave the ITU a much more democratic climate and reduced the chances for any oligarchy to emerge.

One strategy to buttress assessing the results of one case study is to use several case studies in a comparative framework, an approach well articulated in Glaser and Strauss's The Discovery of Grounded Theory (1967). In her report in this volume, Williams used two deviant case studies, one of women Marines and the other of male nurses, in developing her comparative insights about variation across gender roles. In another example, a person interested in the study of social revolutions over the past two centuries may conclude, as did Theda Skocpol (1979), that there exists but a handful of such revolutions and thus the intensive study of that handful exhausts the full population to be examined. Erving Goffman was particularly expert at this strategy of using several case studies to develop a myriad of new theoretical ideas. In his well-known study of mental institutions (1961), Goffman relied in part on an array of different studies of individual mental institutions to furnish the empirical grounds for his generalizations. Rosabeth Moss Kanter (1972), in a very important examination of utopian communities, drew on others' research into individual communities to develop some intriguing ideas about why people join such groups and why the groups often disintegrate.

The Debate over Reliability and Validity

Quantitative procedures seek to unearth the uniformities of social life and to render such uniformities into precise, numeric forms that easily can lend themselves to formulations, refinements, and testing of hypotheses. Qualitative procedures, which are the type most often used in case study research, seek to understand social action at a greater richness and depth and, hence, seek to record such action through a more complex, nuanced, and subtle set of interpretive categories. Moreover, such interpretations often are constructed by the observer to fit the empirical data at hand, data that are apt to address a new and original set of questions as opposed to the more routine concerns raised by the quantitative analyst. Accordingly, the data collection procedures associated with case studies frequently are said by mainstream quantitative researchers to be more suspect on the issue of reliability than those associated with quantitative procedures. *Reliability* is usually interpreted as the ability to replicate the original study using the same research instrument and to get the same results. Random-sample surveys of American voting patterns, for instance, have been regularly conducted by the University of Michigan's Survey Research Center for the past thirty-five years. The questions that are used have been carefully refined and tested for their reliability among many thousands of voters over the course of many elections (for examples, see Campbell et al. 1960). Because of the simplicity of the survey questions, and the magic of numbers, many argue that quantitative research is more reliable than qualitative research. But this is not necessarily the case.

The analyst of the case study, by comparison, is often engaged in labeling actions and codifying materials that represent empirical data on original issues and questions. Consequently, it is sometimes said that the case study, like all other kinds of qualitative research, is vulnerable to the idiosyncratic biases of the investigator and can be at best descriptive because it can invoke no more general principles than those supplied by its own data. Therefore, the interpretations and claims of qualitative research are likely to be too unreliable to permit the construction of solid, scientific evidence. Hubert Blalock, a well-known methodologist in the social sciences, puts the matter this way: "One of the fundamental difficulties with participant observation is the lack of standardization usually involved. Each social scientist is like a journalist writing his own story; there is little guarantee that several such journalists will report the same story" (1970, 44). But there are ways, in fact, of guarding against just such dangers. For instance, some case study research actually uses a team of observers to do the observations. Research on students in a medical school by Howard Becker and others (1961), for example, employed several different observers, all of whom compared and cross-checked their findings with one another. Research on the homeless, reported later in this volume by Snow and Anderson, also self-consciously chose to use several different observers to examine the same empirical data precisely as a way of solving this problem. A complement of several observers, as these studies used, makes possible the intersubjective evaluation and confirmation of brute data and thereby satisfies a crucial dictum of social science research (see, for example, Singleton et al. 1988, 32–33). Moreover, most survey research studies do *not* undertake reliability checks in the form of duplicate studies. The original questions are not repeated by another researcher. Although it is often asserted that it is easier to replicate survey studies, this remains more an assertion than a proven reality.

Another strategy used by qualitative researchers is to conduct case studies of the same phenomenon over roughly the same time period. This satisfies the need to create an intersubjective and comparative basis for observations and thereby helps insure that observations will be roughly identical from one observer to the next. In the field of urban sociology there are a growing number of case histories of different cities, all covering about the same historical periods. Such works permit comparative researchers to discover what patterns are the same from one city to another, as well as how patterns may differ from place to place.

On the matter of the validity of observations, however, the case study provides a clear advantage over other methods of investigation. Although the case study must rely on a good deal of judgment, exercised by the observer, the great strength of this form of research is that it does permit the observer to assemble complementary and overlapping measures of the same phenomena. Thus, a researcher who undertakes a social history of a city usually has at her or his disposal a variety of data sources that can be called on to assess the nature of particular events as well as the motives and interests of actors. There are diaries, correspondence, newspaper reports, and even personal interviews with participants, all of which may be used to cross-check and thereby to validate observations as well as claims based on those observations. This strategy, which Norman Denzin (1989), among others, discusses, is called the triangulation of sources. By comparison, the sample survey and the census researchers often have fewer sources of data to rely on—typically, questions given as part of either a survey interview or a census questionnaire. In most cases there are no independent sources of validation of survey question responses, particularly on attitudinal questions. One set of attitudinal responses can be checked against another in the same or another survey, but most survey researchers do not check their attitudinal findings against, for example, in-depth interviews with a small sample of respondents. The survey researcher, therefore, must assume that her or his measure of attitudes, gained from a brief survey question, accurately reflects the attitudes of the respondents. The scholar who uses the case study can check such matters, both by asking several different people the same in-depth questions and by checking with alternative and independent sources of information. Of course, most good survey research studies do involve some cross-checking, as when internal checks of question validity are made and when income distributions are checked against census data, but the principle of triangulation is not as well developed.

PRESENTATION AND PROOF

Quantitative social science, it is often said, has an advantage over case study research and qualitative methods in the manner in which proof is provided. There exists an array of textbooks that furnish statistical techniques and rules of statistical inference permitting the researcher to declare with confidence—of a statistical sort—that a relationship between variables exists. But the assertion that a statistical presentation is a "better" method of proof than a qualitative presentation is only a conventional prejudice. There are ways of communicating proof other than the statistical presentation. Of course, if one is dealing with qualitative materials, there is an obligation to be as honest and as candid about one's materials as possible and to provide a clear and buttressed presentation of one's findings. But this is true for *both* qualitative and quantitative researchers.

If there is only one case, how then does one communicate results that carry a degree of verisimilitude? How does the writer convince the reader that what he or she is saying is the undistorted truth? There is no magic formula here, for it is just as easy to be dishonest and uncommunicative in presenting quantitative data as in presenting qualitative data. However, in qualitative presentations one does have the advantage of the literary or narrative style of communication. Somehow, for more than six decades in social science, the "scientific" and the "literary" have been seen as opposites. But we, like earlier generations of social scientists (see Cooley 1930, 317), need to get this idea out of our heads. The literary-narrative approach can be precise and disciplined—and at the same time graphic, readable, and imaginative. As with the novel, the narrative form permits the sociological researcher to tell a story, a story with actors, action, and a background, even one that may possess a compelling plot. Vivid description is not the less scientific because it is descriptive. (No one has accused great scientists like Charles Darwin of being less than scientific because of their naturalistic descriptive data.) Depending on the instance at hand, one could tell a story of how a community of people respond to a disaster and seek to repair their collective life (Erikson 1976); of how a particular people exhibit a theater state (Geertz 1980); or how a dam has been successfully completed, bringing to a happy conclusion seemingly endless years of efforts by many individuals and groups (Orum 1984–85). In theory, good quantitative research can also be communicated in narrative form, but such presentations are relatively rare for the simple reason that the data collected are usually not in-depth materials with information on the historical background.

For nonhistorians who try to strike a happy balance somewhere between the rich detail of the unique event and the crisp abstraction of a generalization about many events, it sometimes is hard to find a decent medium of communication; still, increasingly this form is showing up in the writings of social scientists who do case studies. In this volume, one excellent example is to be found in the work of the sociologist R. Stephen Warner. The researcher who uses the case study typically seeks to grasp the nature of social action as it has been experienced by people themselves. He or she has chosen the case study to get at the human understandings that underlie the action he or she portrays. The narrative form is precisely adapted to communicating these meanings and understandings—the "lived" experience—as experienced by people. The historian Simon Schama, the author of a vivid and enormously popular account of the French Revolution, puts the matter this way: "As artificial as written narratives might be, they often correspond to ways in which historical actors construct events" (1989, xvi). To tell a story about individuals alone, or individuals acting as part of groups or institutions, is simply to remain most authentic to the form in which people often experience their own lives. In their popular case study of the moral beliefs of contemporary Americans, Robert Bellah and his colleagues (1985) chose an interesting device to communicate the general pattern of results uncovered in a survey. They chose several of the respondents whom they had interviewed at length, gave them fictitious names, and described them at different points in the text to illustrate some general principles. In effect, Bellah and colleagues combined the standard social scientific technique, of reporting results, with a narrative one, and the latter was helpful in providing vivid illustrative material.

A Diversity of Strategies for Research

The case study and the quantitative investigations of a large sample of cases need not be seen as mutually incompatible strategies for research. The two may be fruitfully employed in conjunction with each other. The research of the sociologist Jeffrey Paige (1975) on the origins of peasant revolutions developed certain hypotheses and insights based on a large sample of cases, involving seventy separate nations, and then explored the same claims in depth using several separate case studies, including, for instance, Angola. The array of several case studies permitted Paige to delve more deeply into the history of the economic and social circumstances that promoted the rise of revolutionary and reform movements among peasants.

We believe that the case study occupies a special place in the conduct of social research and that its achievements cannot be matched by the large-scale sample of many cases. The large-scale analysis typically must work with simple indices and measures of its concepts and claims. For example, if one wishes to study work life with a large-scale study, one may deal with a host of interviews that ask workers how they feel about their work, about their employers, and about their jobs. Such information can be fruitfully employed to convey knowledge about such dimensions as alienation on the job, tensions between workers and their employers, and even the impact of work on such matters as family life. But what such information cannot convey is the full scope of work, of daily work life, of how laborers act and are treated on the job. It cannot fathom the manner in which workers do the job, nor can it possibly reveal the way in which employers manage to harness the energies of workers to their own purposes. It cannot do, in effect, what the important research on a single factory did for Michael Burawoy (1979)—namely, reveal how capital captures the sympathies of labor. Nor can aggregate studies permit the extent of insight, and the revelations into levels of meanings and actions, as did the work of Geertz, or Breuer and Freud.

But there is something else that characterizes quantitative procedures and that transcends the information they furnish. The survey, the census, and the experiment usually assume a world of causal relations and of causal laws in a vein similar to the natural science framework. Their epistemological foundations are often similar. For quantitative analysts, things can be counted; things are related to one another as natural science forces are related, as cause and effect; and the social world may be assumed to operate according to a few underlying social laws. There are important exceptions, of course. Some survey researchers have focused on the values and meanings of phenomena as socially constructed by the unique abilities of human beings, and some have focused on idiosyncratic social systems that are not repeated in the social world. Most, however, have a picture of the world different from that of most qualitative practitioners.

Indeed, qualitative methods hold to a generally different set of assumptions about the social world. As Cooley noted long ago, "The insistence on the quantitative where it is out of place is one source of that laborious futility not uncommon in certain lines of research" (1930, 314). The qualitative research exemplified in the case study usually brings us closer to real human beings and everyday life. Rather than assuming a world of simplicity and uniformity, those who adopt the qualitative approach generally picture a world of complexity and plurality. It is the richness and subtle nuances of the social world that matter and that the qualitative researcher wishes to uncover. Thus, instead of adopting a set of standardized questions and categories with which to characterize—indeed, one can even say, to construct—social action, the qualitative researcher wishes to permit as much flexibility into the judgments made about the world as possible. Thus, the qualitative investigator typically will tend to undertake different kinds of research. And it is these forms that may, alone or in tandem, be used to constitute a case study of the social world.

Charles H. Cooley may have captured the reality of methodological debates in this 1928 comment:

> I am not sure but that methodology is a little like religion. It is something we need every day, but something we are irresistibly impelled to talk and think about, but regarding which we never seem to reach a definite conclusion. Each one, if he is clever, works out something adequate for his own use, but the more general principles remain unsettled. Others help us far more by their example than by their theory. It would appear that working methodology is a residue from actual research, a tradition of laboratories and work in the field: the men who contributed to it did so unconsciously, by trying to find out something that they ardently wanted to know. (1930, 326)

The best methodologies of qualitative and quantitative research have come from those engaged in active research in which methodology has been subordinated to the ardent desire to know and communicate something significant about human social life.

References

Anderson, Nels. 1923. *The Hobo: The Sociology of the Homeless Man.* Chicago: University of Chicago Press.

Babbie, Earl R. 1975. *The Practice of Social Research.* Belmont, Calif.: Wadsworth Publishing Company.

Becker, Howard S., Blanche Geer, Everett C. Hughes, and Anselm Strauss. 1961. *Boys in White: Student Culture in Medical School.* Chicago: University of Chicago Press.

Bellah, Robert N., Richard Madsen, William M. Sullivan, Anne Swidler, and Steven M. Tipton. 1985. *Habits of the Heart: Individualism and Commitment in American Life.* Berkeley: University of California Press.

Black, James A., and Dean J. Champion. 1976. *Methods and Issues in Social Research.* New York: John Wiley and Sons.

Blalock, Hubert M., Jr. 1970. *An Introduction to Social Research.* Englewood Cliffs, N.J.: Prentice-Hall.

Blau, Peter M. 1955. *The Dynamics of Bureaucracy.* Chicago: University of Chicago Press.

Blau, Peter M., and Otis Dudley Duncan. 1967. *The American Occupational Structure.* New York: John Wiley and Sons.

Bryman, Alan. 1988. *Quantity and Quality in Social Research.* London: Unwin Hyman.

Burawoy, Michael. 1979. *Manufacturing Consent: Changes in the Labor Process under Monopoly Capitalism.* Chicago: University of Chicago Press.

Campbell, Angus, et al. 1960. *The American Voter.* New York: John Wiley and Sons.

Dahl, Robert A. 1961. *Who Governs? Democracy and Power in an American City.* New Haven: Yale University Press.

Denzin, Norman K. 1986. *The Alcoholic Self.* Beverly Hills: Sage.

———. 1989. *The Research Act.* 3d ed. Englewood Cliffs, N.J.: Prentice-Hall.

Dollard, John. 1949. *Caste and Class in a Southern Town.* 3d ed. Garden City, N.Y.: Doubleday Anchor.

Domhoff, G. William. 1978. *Who Really Rules? New Haven and Community Power Re-examined.* Santa Monica, Calif.: Goodyear.

Erikson, Kai. 1976. *Everything in Its Path: A Destruction of Community in the Buffalo Creek Flood.* New York: Simon and Schuster.

Feagin, Joe R. 1991. "The Continuing Significance of Race: Anti-Black Discrimination in Public Places." *American Sociological Review* 56 (February 1991): 101–16.

Geertz, Clifford. 1973. *The Interpretation of Cultures: Selected Essays.* New York: Basic Books.

———. 1980. *Negara: The Theatre State in Nineteenth-Century Bali.* Princeton, N.J.: Princeton University Press.

———. 1983. *Local Knowledge: Further Essays in Interpretive Anthropology.* New York: Basic Books.

Glaser, Barney G., and Anselm L. Strauss. 1967. *The Discovery of Grounded*

Theory: Strategies for Qualitative Research. Chicago: Aldine Publishing Company.

Goffman, Erving. 1961. *Asylums: Essays on the Social Situations of Mental Patients.* Garden City, N.Y.: Doubleday Anchor.

Hochschild, Arlie Russell. 1983. *The Managed Heart: Commercialization of Human Feeling.* Berkeley: University of California Press.

Hunter, Floyd. 1953. *Community Power Structure.* Chapel Hill: University of North Carolina Press.

Kanter, Rosabeth Moss. 1972. *Commitment and Community: Commons and Utopias in Sociological Perspective.* Cambridge: Harvard University Press.

———. 1977. *Men and Women of the Corporation.* New York: Basic Books.

Lazarsfeld, Paul F., and Morris Rosenberg, eds. 1955. *The Language of Social Research.* Glencoe, Ill.: Free Press.

Lipset, Seymour Martin, Martin Trow, and James S. Coleman. 1956. *Union Democracy: The Internal Politics of the International Typographical Union.* Glencoe, Ill.: Free Press.

Lynd, Robert S., and Helen Merrell Lynd. 1929. *Middletown: A Study in American Culture.* New York: Harcourt, Brace.

McCall, George J., and J. L. Simmons, eds. 1969. *Issues in Participant Observation: A Text and Reader.* Reading, Mass.: Addison-Wesley Publishing Company.

Milgram, Stanley. 1974. *Obedience to Authority.* New York: Harper and Row.

Nachmias, David, and Chava Nachmias. *Research Methods in the Social Sciences.* New York: St. Martin's Press.

Orum, Anthony M. 1984–85. "Taming the River." *Texas Monthly Press* 30 (1): 15–23.

Paige, Jeffrey. 1975. *Agrarian Revolution.* New York: Free Press.

Rollins, Judith. 1985. *Between Women.* Philadelphia: Temple University Press.

Schama, Simon. 1989. *Citizens: A Chronicle of the French Revolution.* New York: Alfred A. Knopf.

Singleton, Royce, Jr., Bruce C. Straits, Margaret M. Straits, and Ronald J. McAllister. 1988. *Approaches to Social Research.* New York: Oxford University Press.

Skocpol, Theda. 1979. *States and Social Revolutions: A Comparative Analysis of France, Russia, and China.* New York: Cambridge University Press.

Stack, Carol B. 1974. *All Our Kin: Strategies for Survival in a Black Community.* New York: Harper and Row.

Stinchcombe, Arthur L. 1978. *Theoretical Methods in Social History.* New York: Academic Press.

Thomas, W. I., and Florian Znaniecki. 1918–20. *The Polish Peasant in Europe and America: Monograph of an Immigrant Group.* Chicago: University of Chicago Press.

Tilly, Charles. 1981. *As Sociology Meets History*. New York: Academic Press.

Wallace, Anthony F. C. 1978. *Rockdale: The Growth of an American Village in the Early Industrial Revolution*. New York: Knopf.

Whyte, William Foote. 1943. *Street Corner Society: The Social Structure of an Italian Slum*. Chicago: University of Chicago Press.

Yin, Robert K. 1984. *Case Study Research: Design and Methods*. Beverly Hills: Sage.

Gideon Sjoberg, Norma Williams,

Ted R. Vaughan, and Andrée F. Sjoberg

1

The Case Study Approach
in Social Research

Basic Methodological Issues

Our primary goal is to restore the role of the case study as a major methodological tool in social science inquiry—both as a supplement to the natural science model and as a distinctive means of providing valid social knowledge. At one time the case study was a taken-for-granted mode of carrying out research. However, in recent decades it has been pushed aside, or at least sharply downgraded, in sociology (as well as in other social sciences). Thus the case study method receives only limited attention in current textbooks on social research (e.g., Babbie 1989; Bailey 1987; Phillips 1985; Dooley 1990; Denzin 1989; Schwartz and Jacobs 1979). Both qualitative and quantitative researchers tend to shun the basic issues involved in the use of the case study method in social inquiry. Yet exceptions to this generalization can be cited (cf. Yin 1984; Whyte 1984). Perhaps the major monograph addressing the case approach in recent years is that by Ragin (1987), and the subject receives attention in the edited book by Kohn (1989). Still, our approach differs from that of other social scientists who deal with this problem area.

Although our analysis is by no means inclusive, we nonetheless address the salient aspects of the use of the case study in social research. We not only delineate fundamental methodological issues but also outline the manner in which these can be resolved. Our emphasis is on the use, rather than the construction, of case studies (though the two merge in actual research practice).

Our central thesis is that the case study not only serves as a strategic supplement to the natural science model but is an essential feature of sociological inquiry in its own right. We formulate our rather complex argument in the following manner. We first set forth our basic orientation toward methodological inquiry. Here we explicate the premises underlying the natural science model as well as our alternative formulation. This sets the stage for considering the concept of the case study, a subject of much controversy. We then discuss some of the historical issues involved in the use of the case study method, in the process spelling out how the case study approach has been crucial to the growth of grand theory and the construction of classic works in the social sciences. Our reasoning leads to the query: Why has the case approach fallen into disfavor in recent decades? By answering this question, we can better examine the dominant natural science model of inquiry and detail how and why its adherents must rely, in a variety of ways, on the case study approach to supplement their quantitative research procedures. Most important still, we contend that the case study method is essential if social science is to grapple with major social issues on both the historical and the contemporary scenes. Such matters lie beyond the grasp of the natural science model. We conclude by discussing our general orientation toward those methodological issues that demand careful exploration if the case study method is to advance effectively in social science. Throughout, our analysis rests on a broad cross-cultural approach toward the use of the case study method in social scientific inquiry.

Ours is an alternative to the natural science model on the one hand and the historicist approach on the other. As we elaborate below, the natural science model, in its present form, seeks to establish "universal laws" such as those developed in certain natural sciences. The historicist approach, in its extreme form, denies that social science can establish cross-cultural generalizations, contending instead that each sociocultural order contains its own unique patterns of development. We align ourselves with scholars who are committed to the advancement of social science not by emulating natural science but by formulating a methodology for social inquiry that has an integrity of its own. In practice we reject the basic presuppositions of the natural science model but realize that particular logical procedures can be adapted for our purposes.

The Nature of Methodology

To understand the issues that have swirled about the case study approach, we must place our analysis within a larger methodological context. Nowadays methodology is frequently equated with the resolution of technical problems, especially in the quantitative arena. This is reflected in the items that appear in *Sociological Methodology*, a publication of the American Sociological Association.

Our use of methodology harks back to a somewhat earlier era. It does not focus on the refinement of particular research procedures but, rather, involves the analysis of the intersection (and interaction) between theory and research methods and data (e.g., Galtung 1967; Gibbs 1972; Sjoberg and Nett 1968). In recent years, theorists have gone their own way and have paid scant attention to research procedures and data analysis (see such texts as Turner 1986 and Wallace and Wolf 1986); on the other hand, specialists on research methods typically set theory aside in favor of refining, codifying, and standardizing the techniques of data collection and analysis. This division of labor inhibits a constructive examination of the issues involved in carrying out social research. The case study, with both its strengths and its weaknesses, must be considered within a broad rather than a narrow framework.

Adopting a more general conception of methodology, we find that mainstream sociology—with its many shifting currents—has since World War II been dominated by the natural science model (e.g., Sewell 1987; Wilner 1985). This mode of inquiry in sociology resulted from the confluence of a variety of intellectual and social conditions. Although adherents of the natural science model often differ among themselves, they nonetheless share (as we detail below) certain basic tenets.

A major intellectual influence in shaping the natural science model in sociology has been the philosophers (originally mathematicians and natural scientists) identified with the Vienna Circle (e.g., Ayer 1959; Polkinghorne 1983). This school of thought, often termed *logical positivism* or *logical empiricism*, held sway in philosophy departments in the 1950s and onward (Rorty 1982, chapter 12) and structured intellectual discourse, not just in philosophy but in the social sciences more generally.

The Vienna Circle has not been alone in fostering the natural science model. Another source of this intellectual heritage has been the British empiricist tradition. One wing can be traced to John Stuart Mill and his analysis of the experimental design. Interwoven with (but at times separate from) the experimental tradition has been the statistical approach, which had its forerunners in the likes of Pearson, Galton, Fisher, and others. (A statistical tradition also developed in continental Europe, but this has not been as influential as the British heritage.)

An important spin-off of the Vienna Circle was the proponents of the logico-deductive mode of inquiry (e.g., Hempel 1965). Their works gave rise to a widespread championing of the logico-deductive method by such sociologists as Blalock (1969), Gibbs (1972), Blau (1977), Homans (1982), and Turner (1986). Even Merton (1957, 85–101), in an early essay, identified himself with this logical mode of analysis (although it exhibits little, if any, relationship to the functionalist analysis he has championed).

That social theory is to be equated with the logico-deductive format is expressed by, for instance, Homans:

> A theory of a phenomenon is an explanation of the phenomenon. . . .
>
> An explanation consists of a set of at least three propositions. . . . To be allowed to take part in an explanation, a proposition must meet at least two conditions. It must state a relationship between at least two variables and it must begin to state what that relationship is. . . . It must say, for instance, that if x is present, y is also present, or that if x increases in numerical value, y also increases. (1982, 285)

One of the propositions in the set (usually of a low order of generality), which Homans termed an empirical proposition, is that to be explained. Of the other two propositions, one states the condition (or conditions) under which the general proposition can be applied.

Quantitative data are used to test propositions. In some instances these data are derived from surveys or other kinds of "official statistics" (e.g., data on the money supply); in other instances they are the products of social experiments.

Although many advocates of the natural science model are committed to the logico-deductive format, others utilize what can loosely be described as the inductive approach. Skinner (1982), the behavioral psychologist on whom Homans drew for his assumptions about human nature, was a proponent of this orientation. In sociology a host of experimentalists and, especially, survey researchers—with their elaborate statistical procedures such as path analysis and regression analysis—utilize inductive logic.

To enhance our understanding of this model, we counterpose it to a version of the sociology-of-knowledge approach toward methodology (cf. Sjoberg and Nett 1968).[1] This latter orientation recognizes that social research is first and foremost a social enterprise. We view theory as a social process constructed by theorists and research as a social process carried out by researchers, both processes taking place within a social context.

For us, social theory—which empirically reflects what sociologists do and not what they say—involves a process of interpreting (and constructing) social reality (see, e.g., Vaughan and Sjoberg 1986). It has three basic aspects or components: domain assumptions, logical forms, and assessment procedures.

Gouldner (1970), for all the criticisms leveled against his work *The Coming Crisis of Western Sociology*, has nonetheless made common currency of the notion of "domain assumptions"; this in turn is congruent with Alexander's (1982) concept of "presuppositions." If we examine sociological theory and the research, we find that most of the major debates revolve around the question of the proper assumptions to be adopted by researchers. Some of these are highly abstract; others can be debated with respect to their empirical plausibility (though they cannot be tested empirically in any strict sense).

Although the "idealist-materialist" controversy involves abstract notions about the nature of human nature and of social reality, other less abstract assumptions shape the course of the research process (at times in concrete ways). We phrase these in the form of questions (though still others could be added): (1) What is the proper unit of analysis (a central issue for the case study method)? (2) Is the researcher committed to the study of the unique or of the general or of some variation thereof? (3) Are human nature and social reality consistent or are they rent by inherent tensions or contradictions? (4) Are appearances to be taken as given or is there a reality underlying appearances? (5) Are human nature and social reality fixed and well ordered or are they processual—that is, in a state of becoming? (6) What is the nature of rationality? (7) What is the relationship between the social researcher and his or her subject matter? This last query gives rise to subquestions such as: Should one take a top-down or a bottom-up perspective in carrying out research?

As indicated above, the proper unit of analysis is a major issue. Debates about this matter are typically combined, in a variety of ways, with disagreements over other assumptions. Tilly (1984), after taking note of various possible units of analysis, considered the study of the unique versus the general. He then stated: "A purely individualizing comparison treats each case as unique. . . . A pure universalizing comparison . . . identifies common properties among all instances of a phenomenon" (81). Among the scholars in the former category is the sociologist Bendix. Tilly contrasts him with researchers such as Gerhard Lenski and Barrington Moore, who are concerned with universalizing comparisons. Social scientists oriented toward the natural sciences model are committed to isolating universals—and so are certain social scientists (like ourselves) who do not align themselves with that mode of inquiry. Nevertheless, we would be remiss if we did not recognize that investigating the unique is a time-honored aspect of one facet of social research.

In ideal type terms, the social scientist's approach to the unique necessarily involves discovery of the categories developed by the system in question; social scientists then use these theoretical categories to elaborate on, and thereby provide a broader understanding of, the system (e.g., the individual or larger unit) under study. This abstract argument comes into focus when we consider social scientists' efforts to understand the Soviet Union before the Gorbachev "revolution." A source of running debate was the question of whether one could apply Western concepts—for example, "political pluralism," as formulated by U.S. political scientists—to the analysis of the Soviet system (e.g., Solomon 1983). In seeking to interpret the "command economy" (that managed from above by the governmental bureaucratic apparatus), some social scientists have contended that concepts associated with the free market are inappropriate and that one must work within the framework defined by the command economy (e.g., Birman 1989, 144–45). Moreover, we strongly suspect that the facile effort to explain significant changes in Eastern Europe and the Soviet Union in 1989 in free-market terms will, in retrospect, be viewed with disfavor, for this orientation likely reflects the ethnocentrism of Western scholars and especially politicians and newspaper reporters. For one thing, disagreement exists among scholars in Western Europe and the United States over the nature of the market, especially one dominated by large-scale bureaucratic organizations. Nowadays the contemporary "market mechanism" bears little relationship to the neoclassical economists' formulation of this concept.

The unit of analysis is linked not only with relativism versus nonrelativism (i.e., the unique versus the general) but also with other domain assumptions. Whether one takes appearances as real or looks behind them for the basic reality has been a chief source of controversy in social science. Marx and Freud took the lead in stripping the "officially defined" reality of its veneer and insisted that the basic reality lies behind appearances. Freud, in his early work on the nature of human nature, thus stressed the centrality of the "unconscious."

Although we shall not explicitly examine each of these domain assumptions as they relate to the case study approach, the interplay of domain assumptions and case studies emerges in various guises in the succeeding analysis. We must recognize that the choice of assumptions can and does shape research in concrete ways. Freud, for example, having postulated that the basic psychological reality is the unconscious, then proceeded to devise methods—such as the analysis of dreams and linguistic slips—that would permit him to understand the essential nature of human nature, which he approached primarily through case studies that he investigated either directly or indirectly by drawing on secondary sources. (We indicate below how the advocates of the natural science model have forged a link between their domain assumptions and their research procedures.)

In addition to domain assumptions, another facet of social theory is the particular logical forms a researcher employs. The natural science model has been associated with the logico-deductive format and/or the use of experimental designs and statistical procedures in testing relevant propositions. But numerous other logical forms are utilized by social researchers. The most common of these involve some form of typification (or classification). Although sociologists often equate typification with

Weber's (1949) "ideal type," Weber was keenly aware of other typological constructions (cf. Sjoberg and Nett 1968). In addition, the widespread reliance on analogy in social research is often underestimated. Goffman (1959), for example, took the theater as an analog for everyday life; others have employed biological analogies. Then there is the parts-whole logic, which is related to reductionism and holism as well as to the logic of various forms of the dialectic, as relied on, for instance, by Marx onward to Sorokin. Nor should we overlook "counterfactual analysis" in historical research. Employed by Weber (1949) in his analysis of the battle of Marathon, it continues, as Elster (1978) has documented, to be widely applied in the analysis of the past. Researchers ask: What if historical events had proceeded differently? What, for instance, would the United States be like today if the issue of states' rights (and slavery) had been resolved through peaceful means rather than through a civil war?

Besides domain assumptions and logical forms, theory involves some kind of assessment procedure. Adherents of the natural science model emphasize testability and prediction. But still other assessment procedures are employed by social scientists. One of the most notable is an interpretive criterion that Sorokin (1937) termed the logico-meaningful method. Here the validity of a theory is assessed in terms of whether the research articulates with the social categories of the broader social order. Another form of validation for social research and theory has been suggested by Prewitt, the ex-president of the Social Science Research Council, and explicated in detail by Vaughan (1989). Prewitt implied that a central criterion for evaluating research is its contribution to the extension or refinement of debate in a democratic social order. Myrdal's *American Dilemma* is a model of this kind of research. If research is validated by its contribution to democratic discourse, this in effect calls on social scientists to devise alternative ways of defining (and constructing) meaning systems and social orders.

For purposes of clarity, we shall briefly recapitulate our argument. We began with a discussion of the natural science model and contrasted this with our orientation, which rests on a different set of assumptions regarding the nature of human nature and the social order. But just what are the central features of the natural science model—in light of our discussion of domain assumptions, logical forms, and assessment procedures?

Advocates of the natural science model assume that an objective world exists independently of the researcher and that one can uncover "universal laws" of human nature and social reality. Human nature and social reality display regularities that are fixed over time and space. Moreover, human nature and social reality are internally consistent; they are not rent by discontinuities or contradictions. Social scientists committed to the natural science model also take appearances as basic reality and subscribe, as we elaborate below, to "methodological individualism."[2] Thus the units of analysis are independent entities. Typically they are individuals—human beings—but they can be larger units, such as nation-states. Most important to these researchers is the establishment of rigorous and standardized procedures for collecting and analyzing data to test hypotheses and predict the course of social reality. Again, testability and prediction are the strategic means for evaluating theories, but such can be accomplished only through the standardization and, thereby, replication of the research of others. Through standardized procedures, researchers become immune to shifts in power relationships and ideologies within the nation-state and on the world scene.

We too assume the existence of an empirical reality that is somewhat independent of any particular human agent. Moreover, human nature and social reality display an order of sorts. However, the nature of human nature and of social reality is not as fixed as the proponents of the natural science model would have us believe. The social order has been constructed by human agents, and although social patterns emerge, these patterns can, within broad limits, be revised. Human nature and the social order are processual and not necessarily consistent. They may be rent by contradictions. Although we can generalize about human nature and social arrangements, universal laws as such cannot be uncovered except in those realms wherein biological factors play a central role—and these are not critical features in social investigation. In the terminology of the natural science model, it is possible to isolate "necessary but not sufficient conditions" regarding the nature of human nature and of the social order.

Our sharpest break with the natural science model concerns the relationship of social scientists to their own social order and the one that is their focus of study.[3] (The two may or may not be the same.) Researchers cannot remove themselves from their own sociocultural setting and achieve objectivity simply by claiming to do so. Although we believe some form of objectivity is possible, it cannot be attained through social experimentation or complex statistical manipulations.

Our alternative conception of the nature of social science rests on George Herbert Mead's (1934) view of human nature—notably his conception of the "social mind" that has been rehabilitated by a variety of social theorists in recent years (cf. Vaughan and Sjoberg 1984; Smith 1982). The mind is a social creation. Reflectivity, the most distinctive feature of the social mind, involves thinking about thinking. Reason is not biopsychological in nature, as implied by the utilitarians: nor is the "rational thinking process" inherent in the individual, as Kant and Popper would contend. Instead, reason is a product of the social mind, which is, in turn, a product of social interaction. How sociologists think—as well as what they think about—emerges from their relationships with others. Thus their knowledge about social patterns is affected by their own position in the social structure. Among the many considerations, the sociologist's interrelationship with a nation-state system or systems affects the manner in which research is conducted.

In a more specific sense, the researcher is a variable in the research design—not just in the statement of the problem but also in the collection and analysis of the data. Consequently, the only way some form of objectivity can be sustained is through critical reflection, through recognition that one's research results may well be shaped by one's position in the power structure and by the ideological context within which one carries out social scientific activities. Our argument comes into focus in our analysis of the role of case studies for a comparative perspective.

The Unit of Analysis: What Is a Case Study?

Having considered broad methodological issues, we are now in a position to focus attention on a major source of debate: the unit of analysis in social research. Here we are concerned with the question "What is a case study?" In general terms, a case study involves characteristics or configurations of a particular unit of analysis—be this an individual, a community, an organization, a nation-state, an empire, or a civilization. Specifying what is a "case," as is evident in our discussion below, varies with the researcher's presuppositions of the proper unit of analysis as well as other related domain assumptions.

That the unit of analysis continues to be a source of contention is stressed by Ragin (1987) in *The Comparative Method*. For him, confusion exists about whether units of analysis are "data categories" or "theoretical categories." Ragin has suggested that Barrington Moore's data categories are countries, whereas Moore's theoretical units are classes. In the case of Wallerstein (1974, 1980), the data categories are most frequently nation-states, or core countries and periphery countries, whereas the theoretical unit is the world system.

Ragin's distinction between theoretical and data categories can be useful in some instances, but more fundamental problems are involved. Thus we shall approach the unit of analysis and the case study from another vantage point.

The question of what is a case study is related to (though not synonymous with) the micro-macro distinction that surfaced as a significant theoretical controversy in sociology during the 1980s. The micro-macro issue has long haunted the field of economics (Thurow 1984). In sociology it has been addressed by Giddens (1984), Collins (1981), Mayhew (1980), and Blau (1987), among many others (e.g., Alexander et al. 1987). We can delineate four major orientations in the micro-macro debate, some aspects of which bear, directly or indirectly, on the case approach. First, Collins reasoned, in line with the neoclassical economists, that the "individual" is the basic unit of analysis. Mayhew, on the other hand, would rid sociological analysis of individuals and focus solely on macro (or structural) patterns. Blau adopted the view that the micro and macro levels both have their own integrity and that sociologists are more or less destined to work on one or the other level. Finally, Giddens—and Vaughan and Sjoberg (1984), among others—perceived a complex interaction between the micro and the macro levels of analysis.

We can set this issue in sharper perspective by examining how adherents of the natural science model typically define the unit of analysis. These persons are committed, in the language of philosophers of science, to a form of "methodological individualism." Thus Collins, Homans, and the utilitarians in general begin with individuals as their basic unit of analysis. For them, individuals are defined in narrow biopsychological (or behavioristic) terms, in keeping with the tradition extending from

John Stuart Mill up to Homans (1982). These scholars typically adopt some form of utilitarianism (cf. Opp 1985), and this articulates with the techniques and procedures associated with modern statistics. If one quantifies units and adds them together, the parts equal the whole. Thus, in probability sampling, which today underlies much sociological (especially survey) research, the units drawn must be independent of one another. And they must all be equal. Given these assumptions, one can draw random samples and then add the units to characterize the whole.

The Mayhew and Blau positions, as noted above, are in many respects variations on methodological individualism. For Mayhew, the units are structural in nature. Indeed, a number of sociologists select units such as the nation-state or subunits thereof, including metropolitan areas or states. For example, if we select metropolitan areas as units, we can add up their characteristics to capture the nature of the whole. (To be sure, the use of units such as states or metropolitan areas has given rise to an ecological fallacy: the assumption that one cannot reason from the characteristics of these aggregated units back to individuals.) Still, one can discard individuals and use structural units instead (cf. Mayhew 1980), or one can work on the micro (individual) level and then on the macro (structural) level, recognizing that the two cannot be integrated.

Problems arise if one questions the foundations of methodological individualism. For example, standing in sharp contrast to Collins's orientation is the perspective of the Meadian (or neo-Meadian) tradition, which is being rehabilitated by the likes of Habermas (1987). In Meadian terms, the human agent is truly social in nature. The self and the social mind are products of interaction with others, and the concept of an independent actor is foreign to such theoretical orientation. Under these circumstances, it is little wonder that the Meadian heritage has fallen on difficult times in sociology, for survey or experimental procedures require that individuals be conceived of as independent units. This view is sharply at odds with Mead's (1934) conception of human agents as dependent on one another, as creatures of, and agents involved in, the construction of their social lives.

As we move to the intersection of human agents and organizational structures, the situation becomes far more complex than Blau, for instance, would have us believe. We adhere to the view that human agents not only are social beings but also intersect with organizations that are relatively autonomous. One cannot add up the characteristics of human agents and fully understand the total organization. Yet, the whole, which has a reality somewhat apart from its individual members, nonetheless is dependent on human agents for its existence. If one accepts these domain assumptions about human nature and social reality, it becomes well-nigh impossible to rely on statistical analysis per se for the investigation of certain major sociological issues. As an instance, human agents have complex relationships with nation-states and with large-scale bureaucratic structures that transcend nation-states.

A commitment to methodological individualism, and the use of cases based on this presupposition, produce a range of useful data. Yet because of this assumption, serious limitations inhere in the natural science model. A case approach that is not anchored in this model permits us to examine relationships and patterns unconstrained by the model's domain assumptions. The advantage of case studies (as we perceive them) is that researchers who utilize them can deal with the reality behind appearances, with contradictions and the dialectical nature of social life, as well as with a whole that is more than the sum of its parts. The case study approach that takes into account these kinds of assumptions can, as we shall see, provide us with fundamental sociological knowledge of human agents, communities, organizations, nation-states, empires, and civilizations.

The Historical Role of the Case Study
Approach in Advancing Social Inquiry

To more fully appreciate the case study method's role in social research, we shall step back and examine the method's place in the development of social science inquiry. The application of this research tool, viewed in historical and comparative perspective, demonstrates how it has advanced empirically grounded social knowledge. Moreover, we also find how the case study approach has expanded our understanding of "others" and "ourselves"—a rationale for social inquiry that the natural science approach, with its emphasis on prediction as the criterion for valid knowledge, chooses to ignore, thereby downgrading the contributions of many social research efforts (cf. Vaughan 1989).

Modern sociology emerged in the West in full-blown form as a result of the efforts by scholars to understand a major problem: Why did the West, as a "civilization," take the lead in the establishment of "modernity"—in the development of science, the industrial revolution, and capitalism? The classical sociologists—Marx, Weber, and Durkheim, among others—perceived this, in varying ways, as their central problem.

For example, one of Weber's (1930) major works analyzed, on the basis of historical records, the relationship of Protestantism to the rise of capitalism. Viewing Weber's corpus of work in a larger sense, we find that he not only considered the relationship of religion to economic activity in the West but also examined this problem from a wide-ranging comparative perspective, looking at China, India, and elsewhere. In his analysis of the reasons that capitalism arose in the West, Weber was responding to the ghost of Marx, who had also viewed the rise of capitalism within a cross-cultural framework. Marx had, after all, already isolated patterns relating to what he termed "the Asiatic mode of production," and he contrasted the capitalistic West with this form of economic and social organization.

The classical heritage in the form of case studies thrives in the writings of some contemporary sociologists. Merton (1970), in his first major work, addressed the problem of the relationship of Puritanism to the development of science in England; Wallerstein (1974, 1980) has revisited the origins of capitalism in the West; and a number of prominent historical sociologists continue to advance our knowledge about what some term the "miracle" of the West (Baechler, Hall, and Mann 1988). As such, the West, or Europe, constitutes a case study within the context of a broader cross-cultural setting.

But we must also consider the role of case studies in the development of social science from another angle of vision. We shall critically reflect on how Western social scientists have looked outward to other societies and sought to comprehend them (and themselves) through the case approach. Such an orientation provides us with a glimpse into the need for, and the limitations of, the use of case studies in comparative analysis.

We take the work of certain anthropologists as the basis for clarifying this reasoning. In the process we focus on the case studies presented by four figures: Malinowski, Margaret Mead, Evans-Pritchard, and Embree.

Of these case studies, Malinowski's appear to be the most innovative and compelling. Leach (1983) avers that Malinowski's (1922) *Argonauts of the Western Pacific* is the single most influential ethnographic monograph in social anthropology. Although such a claim may smack of hyperbole, Malinowski's findings continue to generate research and theorizing (Leach and Leach 1983).

The core concept of *Argonauts of the Western Pacific* relates to the *kula*: a special system of social exchange wherein necklace valuables moved in a clockwise pattern and arm shells moved in a counterclockwise direction around the "ring" of islands. How and why this particular exchange pattern functioned have not yet been determined (cf. Leach 1983). But what has been settled is that the *kula* pattern challenges social science because it runs counter to the exchange theory that has emanated from the work of classical and neoclassical economists. Although some of Malinowski's observations require modification (serious criticisms of his research have resulted from his neglect of women [Weiner 1976]), his overall description of the *kula* has withstood the test of time. This contention brings us back to our main thesis: Malinowski, as a Westerner, helped us understand others—here, the Trobrianders—which in turn has enabled Western scholars to see themselves in comparative perspective.

What can we learn from the work of Margaret Mead? In the 1920s she set out to conduct research that resulted in *Coming of Age in Samoa* (1961). The book set the stage for her reputation as the best-known anthropologist in the United States. As Howard (1984) observed in her informative biography, Mead was not a seminal thinker; nevertheless, her work on Samoa, with its focus on adolescent sexuality, captured the imagination of an educated sector of U.S. society at a time when the Puritanical tradition was still rather well entrenched but was fragmenting on the edges. Mead's worldview helped to reshape the thinking about adolescence and sexuality among members of the middle class.

Soon after Mead's death, her research was sharply challenged in a book by an Australian anthropologist, Freeman (1983), who had spent many years carrying out fieldwork in Samoa. This work, which received attention in the *New York Times* and other media, raised serious questions about the quality of Mead's research efforts. Many anthropologists, including some who had done fieldwork in Samoa, came to Mead's defense (cf. Rappaport 1986). Thus, though critical of Mead, Holmes avowed, "I find the validity of her Samoan research is remarkably high" (1987, 10).

Although Freeman set out to undermine Mead's credibility, his critique seems, overall, to have solidified her scholarly reputation. Although we are not sympathetic to Freeman's line of attack on Mead, it appears that Mead was perhaps somewhat more concerned with challenging segments of the American bourgeois society of her day than with interpreting Samoan culture within a broad cross-cultural perspective. We must thus entertain the realistic possibility that she unduly imposed the categories of U.S. society on Samoans.

Nevertheless, the problems associated with Mead's research are not as serious as those associated with, for example, Evans-Pritchard's work *The Nuer* (1940). Geertz (1988) and Rosaldo (1986), in commenting on this well-known British anthropologist, have concluded that he was a committed colonialist. While studying the Nuer, a tribal group in East Africa, he maintained complex ties to the British colonial government. Rosaldo argued that because of Evans-Pritchard's official role he was never really able to enter the world of the Nuer and that the very data in his book reflect the resistance of the people to any probing of their culture at a time when it was under political attack. Although anthropologists still seem to accept some of Evans-Pritchard's observations, they are far more likely to qualify the use of his data today than in the past. It seems apparent that Evans-Pritchard not only was excluded from the inner workings of Nuer society but also interpreted many features of Nuer culture from a Western imperialist perspective.

The research of Embree (1939) on Suye Mura constitutes our fourth case. Embree was apparently the only U.S. anthropologist to carry out a major research study on a Japanese village before World War II. Unlike Malinowski, Mead, and Evans-Pritchard, who studied relatively self-contained preliterate societies, Embree investigated a village that was part of a powerful nation-state (indeed, an empire); his work is in keeping with the research on peasant villages by such eminent anthropologists as Redfield (1941) in Mexico and Fei (1946) in China.

In recent years we have come to hold a very different view of Embree's original work. We now know far more about it as a result of Smith and Wiswell's (1982) *The Women of Suye Mura*. This research suggests how accidents of history can reshape our knowledge. Embree had gone to Suye Mura with his wife (now surnamed Wiswell), who had been born in the Russian Far East and had learned to speak Japanese while growing up in Japan. After they returned to the United States from their fieldwork, Embree and their daughter were killed in an automobile accident, and Embree's wife took up her own career and became a professor of comparative literature. On a trip to Cornell University in the 1960s she asked Smith, a distinguished expert on Japan, if he would like to have her and Embree's field notes on Suye Mura. After a time Smith delved into these and, much to his surprise, discovered that Embree had not used his wife's field notes in his book. She had carried out research among the women while he had studied the men and the community's public sphere. His theoretical framework (and the traditional lack of attention to women) led him to ignore his wife's data. Smith and Wiswell (1982) then pieced together many of these field notes in their work *The Women of Suye Mura*, which presents a view of the village in the 1930s rather different from that found in Embree's book.

What have we learned from these works? Each remains a major landmark in fieldwork on "societal units," or in the case of Embree, on a community within a broader social order. As noted above, in the case of Malinowski and Mead we are able to see ourselves more sharply by taking the roles of others. This is true of Evans-Pritchard's work as well, but in a markedly different sense. Here we see how in the name of science, Western categories were imposed uncritically on the Nuer. As to the work of Malinowski and Embree, we find that they generally ignored women, a pattern that was common among anthropologists of that era. In all the foregoing instances we can observe the limitations of case materials, but we would be remiss if we underestimated how much we have learned from these monographs. They continue to be essential sources of contemporary social scientific knowledge.

That Western social scientists have imposed their own categories on the study of non-Westerners has become (as suggested above) a source of concern to many anthropologists. And the imposition of the social and cultural categories of the powerful on the nonpowerful is a matter of consequence in other realms of social inquiry as well. Said (1979), in his highly controversial work *Orientalism*, has perhaps more than any other scholar in recent years heightened our awareness of the ethnocentrism of

Western scholarship by strongly criticizing many prominent Western historians who have studied the Middle East, often via case materials. Westerners have learned from field data on other cultures, but they have imposed false stereotypes on them and on the members of these societies; as a result, Westerners entertain false stereotypes of themselves—for example, as intellectual superiors of the people they have studied. As Herzfeld (1987) has informed us, stereotypes become a weapon for sustaining social power.

The issue of the case study evinces still another twist when we turn to its use in the United States. The Chicago School of Sociology, it can safely be argued, made a significant contribution to the empirical study of modern cities. The research on sectors of Chicago life by Anderson (1923) in *The Hobo*, by Wirth (1928) in *The Ghetto*, and by Burgess (1967) in his analysis of the spatial patterns of Chicago has shaped the thinking of a host of American sociologists. However, much of this case material is culture bound. The dependence on Chicago as a basis for generalizing about urban life is challenged in Sjoberg's (1960) *The Preindustrial City*, and today the generalizations of the Chicago School have come under attack from other perspectives: for example, in Feagin's (1988) case study of Houston.

The Rise of the Natural Science Model and Marginalization of the Case Study

Immediately after World War II, the case study approach produced major contributions to the understanding of sociological issues, particularly those relating to complex organizations or bureaucracies. One source of this intellectual development was the Department of Sociology at Columbia University, whose graduate students in the late 1940s and early 1950s, building on their dissertations based on fieldwork or documentary data, wrote books that are still the source of fundamental sociological principles (e.g., Lipset 1950; Blau 1955; Gouldner 1954). But the role of case studies began to decline at Columbia and elsewhere. Although this approach, employing in-depth analysis of particular organizational units, has not disappeared, it has become increasingly marginalized.

Sewell (1987), an advocate of one version of the natural science model and the primary force behind the construction of the Department of Sociology at Wisconsin, wrote that 85 percent of the research in sociology was then quantitative in nature (the basis of this particular statistic is unclear). His generalization was buttressed by the work of Wilner (1985), who examined articles published in the *American Sociological Review* from 1936 to 1984. Wilner concluded that this "official" journal of the American Sociological Association had come to be dominated by research carried out within the survey and quantitative tradition.

The rise to dominance of the social survey approach has resulted from the convergence of several interrelated social forces on the national scene. Although we do not pretend to unravel these herein, some knowledge of the underlying organizational support for quantitative research in the natural science mode is essential.

Before World War II, Ogburn, Bernard, and Chapin pushed quantitative analysis. During and after the war, social surveys, and the statistical analysis of the data produced by them, came to be interrelated with the growing demands for quantitative data by commercial, governmental, and academic organizations.

Converse (1987) has provided a valuable history of the rise of social surveys in American society. Her detailed analysis of the emergence of the Bureau of Social Research, the National Opinion Research Center associated with the University of Chicago, and the Institute of Social Research at Michigan is required reading for anyone interested in the manner in which social surveys come to be institutionalized.

But Converse's account is incomplete, for her objective does not include an examination of the production of survey data by government agencies such as the U.S. Bureau of the Census. Not only does the bureau carry out a national census every ten years, but it conducts a variety of other surveys. The generation of these data has been associated with the creation of, for instance, Population Research Centers at several major institutions—Michigan, Wisconsin, and North Carolina, to name three—that serve to analyze (or summarize) the data collected by the Census Bureau and other agencies. We could also cite such organizational units as the Institute on Poverty at Wisconsin, units that process a host of data produced by agencies of the federal government as well as by survey research centers.

We should not overlook the fact that the data generated by social surveys are linked with the "requirements" of commercial, academic, and, especially, governmental organizations. The significance of surveys for governmental administrators and politicians is well known. For instance, public opinion researchers assist politicians in setting agendas and provide data that often serve as the basis for campaign strategies. In this kind of research, the underlying assumptions—that "units," in this instance individuals, are independent and that they are equal—articulate with the principle of one person, one vote. So too, market survey data on the purchase of new products are relatively congruent with the assumptions of the social survey method. Even the main limitations of social surveys—for example, they do not tap the views of the truly disadvantaged—are often of little concern to politicians, for the truly disadvantaged rarely vote or affect the course of public policy.

Another aspect of the emergence of the natural science model, especially as reflected in survey research, deserves mention. Members of such agencies as the National Science Foundation have stressed the similarity between the natural and the social sciences, for this has provided social scientists with a justification for appealing to Congress for funding. After World War II, advances in scientific knowledge have increasingly been viewed as a basis for U.S. military and economic strength. And surveys or experimental methods have been perceived as providing "objective" scientific data.

So powerful is this commitment to the natural science model that its proponents have been able to co-opt potential critics, such as many neo-Marxists. Thus, Attewell, in his analysis of the drift of neo-Marxist scholarship, wrote:

Researchers have become very concerned with empirical documentation and are increasingly dependent upon sophisticated quantitative methods of analysis. . . . Nonradicals may find it easy to dismiss left scholarship as mere ideology when the work in question is purely theoretical. But when radical research emphasizes empirical data, using the most up-to-date quantitative techniques, such criticisms have a hollow ring, for in the contemporary social sciences, quantification has come to be equated with scientific rigor. Many left scholars have chosen to adopt these methodologies and have thereby succeeded in gaining greater respect in the eyes of their nonradical colleagues. Thus several areas of the new political economy do battle with academic orthodoxy by using multiple regression, factor analysis, econometrics, and the like. (1984, 26)

Given these circumstances, it is little wonder that such scholars as Erik Olin Wright at Wisconsin have adopted the methodological tools of Sewell and other leading members of that department.

But what about such historical sociologists as Tilly (e.g., 1981) and Skocpol (1979)?[4] Although their connections to the natural science model are not as straightforward as those of neo-Marxists such as Wright (1985), they too have to a considerable degree been co-opted by this orientation. Some of their underlying assumptions lead them to search for invariant relationships in historical processes. In Tilly's case, he has been one of the leaders in the quantification of historical data, and in the case of Skocpol, her commitment to Mill's experimental design reflects domain assumptions that are linked to the natural science model.

At the same time, we do not place all sociologists in the natural science camp.[5] Still, the methodological hegemony in the field is far greater than the theoretical diversity, and efforts to create alternative methodologies, for example, by feminists, have as yet failed to grapple with what we regard as fundamental issues in this area.

The Case Approach As an Adjunct to the Natural Science Model

Most social scientists who use social surveys or other types of "official statistics" are frequently critical of the case study method. However, on closer inspection we find that the case study is a necessary adjunct to their mode of investigation. We advance several interrelated arguments. First, from a historical or a cross-cultural perspective, a single national survey is a case study. Second, many surveys are carried out on subunits of the United States, and there are case studies concerning the nation-state as a whole (to say nothing of other social orders). Third, a number of social scientists adhere to theoretical and empirical goals that are unattainable without recourse to the case study approach; yet these scholars seem impervious to the contributions of case materials. Fourth, one subgroup of sociologists committed to the natural science orientation recognizes the usefulness of the case study but may not necessarily acknowledge that the kinds of case studies they advocate are at odds with some of their own methodological predilections.

Our first point is that in the context of time and space, a census or a national survey is a case study. If researchers are committed to uncovering invariant laws, their studies carried out in the United States at some point in time should lead to propositions that are valid over time. Moreover, these propositions should also apply beyond the borders of the United States. National surveys focus on a special universe—a case study—within the context of societies around the world—the theoretical universe.

Nonetheless, most researchers recognize the difficulties of standardizing survey questions over time even within a single societal unit. Certain questions asked in the 1930s regarding, for example, race and ethnic relations might make little if any sense if posed in the 1990s. And such questions would be considered biased by segments of the population. Thus the principle of replication in social surveys is more difficult to adhere to in practice than in theory.

We must also recognize that many oft-cited surveys are focused on subunits (e.g., cities or states) and as such become case studies within the nation-state context. One of the most influential works in sociology falls into this category: Sewell and his associates have over many years studied the status attainment patterns of high school graduates in the state of Wisconsin (e.g., Sewell 1988). The work of Knotternus (1987) is a useful takeoff point for commentary on Sewell's research over the years.

It is striking how few sociologists have undertaken a serious methodological critique of Sewell's effort. After all, his research, which focused on mobility patterns among Wisconsin high school graduates, has been a foundation stone for helping him build the top-ranked sociology department in the United States, if we judge a department's status by its prestige among sociologists.

To be more specific: How representative is the state of Wisconsin of the United States, to say nothing of other societies? Somehow quantification and the use of sophisticated statistics (based on a well-defined data set) seem to have been sufficient to convince social scientists of the scientific validity of Sewell's findings. However, the state of Wisconsin does not include a significant body of minorities. Sewell also chose not to study women (a point made in the literature). Actually, if one looks at Wisconsin within a larger context, one can consider it as an outlier compared with states in the South, New England, or the West—to say nothing of other societies. If sociologists recognized that Sewell's research is a kind of case study, then proponents of the natural science model would be more attentive to the limitations of their own research and less prone to dismiss the case study method in general.

Moreover, Knotternus (1987) has suggested that the status attainment model came to be accepted not because of its "predictive power" but because it articulated with the value system and aspirations of the American middle class, which includes American sociologists. The growing challenge to this model in sociology seems to have resulted from the shifting nature of the U.S. value system and the changing power alignments on the national and the world scenes.

Within the context of analyzing the Wisconsin model as set forth by Sewell, we must analyze the work of Wright, especially his book *Classes* (1985), which has generated a considerable amount of controversy. Wright in effect admitted that he reshaped his Marxism—by, for example, ridding his theory of the concept of the "dialectic"—so that he could talk about variables and thus avoid the troublesome issue of emergence in a social order.

Wright's methodological techniques took precedence over fundamental theoretical and empirical considerations in other ways as well. He spoke of his Marxist survey and attempted to operationalize variables with care. But, so far as we can ascertain, Wright, along with his critics, has been inattentive to the fact that the survey method he employed led to his neglecting the very powerful and the truly disadvantaged.

We find no internal evidence in Wright's *Classes* that he secured a representative sample of the truly economically and politically powerful segments of the U.S. population. On theoretical grounds alone, it is highly unlikely that more than a handful of this rather small group would be included in his random sample. So too, the truly disadvantaged—the blacks in the ghetto, the homeless, and others—are highly underrepresented in surveys such as that carried out by Wright. This self-proclaimed Marxist therefore ignores the two groups at either pole of the class structure: the very powerful and the highly disadvantaged.

More generally, Wright, and others in this tradition, have conveniently ignored the principle enunciated by Galtung (1967) some years earlier in his methodological work. Galtung contended that social surveys are alien to the interests of both the elite and the economically disadvantaged (cf. Goyder 1987). *The truly powerful and the truly disadvantaged can be studied only through some kind of in-depth case study approach.*

In keeping with our critique of Wright, we single out an essay by Jencks (1989), a highly respected sociologist in the field of social stratification. In a survey article on the "underclass" in the United States, Jencks attempted to delineate the subgroups within this social entity by using various kinds of "official statistics." Jencks inserted no qualifying remarks concerning the staggering difficulties of gathering data through surveys (or other official statistics) on the truly disadvantaged.[6] These kinds of research may be of little, if any, value for data on significant elements of the underclass. Many segments of this population have no fixed address or telephone, and others find it in their interest to avoid providing information to any arm of the state. One of the authors of this chapter once carried out fieldwork among undocumented workers in San Antonio and can attest to the suspicion with which members of this group view any researcher, especially someone who represents a government agency intent on deporting undocumented workers from the country.

In our effort to document the need for in-depth case studies as an adjunct to the survey method, we also examine the work of the quantitative criminologists, who in recent years have commanded considerable space in leading sociological journals. Gottfredson and Hirschi's (1987) edited book *Positive Criminology* is a useful point of departure for our discussion. The contributors to the volume are committed to the natural science model.

For many years criminologists had to rely on the FBI's Uniform Crime Reports, with their well-known flaws. Today, as Laub (1987) has observed, the Uniform Crime Reports can be supplemented by data generated as a result of surveys of the general population. But these data have built-in limitations. Laub views the information obtained from victimization surveys, products of cooperation between the Bureau of Justice statistics and the U.S. Bureau of the Census, in a more positive light. However, he, unlike many members of this school, recognizes that the FBI reports and the survey data must be supplemented by in-depth studies of individual subgroups if the etiology of crime is to be uncovered. He has called for the use of such tools as "oral histories." What he does not seem to perceive is that some of the information collected through this kind of procedure cannot be translated back into questionnaires but has an autonomy of its own in generating sociological principles.

If we consider the work of the contributors to *Positive Criminology* in a more critical manner, we find that they ignored white-collar crime. The point is that their research procedures, including their reliance on social surveys, did not permit them to grapple with major issues relating to white-collar crime in the United States. For instance, Galbraith (1990) spoke of the Savings and Loan Association scandals of the 1980s as "looting" on a scale never before seen in U.S. history. Inasmuch as this looting has been underwritten by complex secrecy systems (including intricate bookkeeping procedures), this activity cannot be captured via social surveys. But more of this below.

Our argument that various kinds of in-depth case studies are a necessary adjunct to social surveys becomes even more compelling when we turn to the comparative scene. What is often not recognized is that social surveys are predicated on a certain kind of social order—one in which the universe or population is relatively well understood and in which the respondents have the ability to answer questions in a meaningful manner. In economically disadvantaged areas of the Third World—for example, in the poverty-ridden sectors of cities in Brazil, Mexico, Nigeria, or India—not only is it exceedingly difficult to locate people in any systematic manner, but also the populace itself has not been educated to respond to social surveys. The kind of social order that permits social surveys to be utilized in a relatively effective manner is often taken for granted by American social scientists. Still, our emphasis herein is that even in an advanced industrial-urban order such as the United States, social surveys must be supplemented by in-depth case studies if certain sectors of the social order (and the sociological issues relating to them) are to be investigated empirically.

Theoretical Justifications for
the Case Study Approach

At this point we advance a more compelling, albeit more controversial, argument for the case study method: namely, that numerous major theoretical and empirical issues in the modern world cannot be addressed through adherence to the natural science model, which involves the use of such methods as social surveys and social experiments. In effect, the methodological hegemony in social science has imposed serious constraints on sociologists in their efforts to contribute to an essential understanding, or interpretation, of many strategic features of ongoing activities in today's world.

We single out three aspects of social investigation for attention, touching on problem areas that would require full-scale monographs for adequate treatment. Thus, we treat the micro social order of human interaction (broadly speaking), the shifting nature of historical processes, and the salient features of complex organizational structures.

THE ANALYSIS OF HUMAN INTERACTION

It is often conceded, even by adherents of the natural science model, that in-depth investigation limits the number of units one can study. But the obstacles to understanding the micro order are more deep-seated. We still lack an understanding of many essential features of human interaction: first, because of complex combinations and permutations in social processes and, second, because many scholars have neglected those domain assumptions regarding social life (such as the existence of contradictions) that are not in keeping with the natural science model.

Again, we can illustrate only the thrust of our basic argument. Sociologists know little, for example, about the role of "honorifics" in human interaction in complex, still somewhat traditional, societies such as those in the Middle East, India, or China. Surprisingly, most sociologists fail to recognize that linguistic cues are unobtrusive means of gaining access to the multifaceted status relationships that exist within a social order. Thus the researcher does not need to probe but has only to observe carefully, always taking account of the subtleties of the situation. In the case of honorifics, status is delineated through a variety of linguistic markers—intonation, terminology, grammatical forms, and the like—and these vary with age, gender, social class, occupational grouping, and the private versus the public sectors. Thus the permutations that flow from the nexus between language and social situations would confound most researchers.

We are not arguing that sociolinguistic patterns are simply situationally specific. Rather, general principles can be discerned, but only through in-depth case materials that are placed within a cross-cultural perspective. Moreover, because of the inherent complexity of language, combined with the meanings that emerge in different interaction situations, case materials are the order of the day. Some of the most useful material is that which derives from the researcher's reliance on his or her autobiographical data as a means of highlighting the social patterns that characterize the community setting (e.g., Jain 1969).

These patterns are not limited to traditional social orders. We know little about the "multiple languages" that are employed in modern bureaucratic settings—where, for instance, the "in group" may understand what is being said, but the "out group" (who may also be present) has no grasp of the multiple levels of social reality that are being communicated. To capture these patterns through social surveys is, in our judgment, impossible. Moreover, in the study of social interaction, little attention has been given to social contradictions, even by proponents of in-depth case materials. Once the researcher admits to the possibility of, for example, contradictory expectations, even in-depth interviews may be insufficient to ferret out the required information, for people must be observed in their natural settings if we are to understand how they cope with and even use these contradictions in creative ways (Williams 1989a, 1990).

Our general contention here is that many key assumptions of the natural science model may be inappropriate for grasping the nature of human nature and of social interaction in everyday life. So committed are some survey researchers to the principle of consistency that they often assume that inconsistent responses undermine the "validity" of respondents' replies. But how can people respond consistently in a complex social order that is itself rent by contradictory expectations? Moreover, some politicians are perceived as creative because of their ability to manage their own, as well as the social order's, contradictory expectations.

HISTORICAL EVENTS AND PROCESSES

Erikson, an ex-president of the American Sociological Association, re-flecting on the discipline of sociology, observed:

> Many of the truly decisive happenings of our own time have passed with little or no comment from the sociological community because they were too large, too prominent, too special to be contained easily within a general frame. . . . Our literature is full of distinguished exceptions to the statements I am about to make. . . . But the major preoccupations of a discipline, its prevailing intellectual commitments, are usually reflected in such places as journals it circulates and the dissertations it encourages and approves; and on that score, at least, I think we can agree that the center of the field pays very little attention to passing historical events. (1984, 306)

Erikson asks us to consider what a future historian would learn about sociology if he or she looked back on our leading journals over the past thirty-five years. Such a person would learn a great deal about courtship and dating, patterns of mobility, crime and mental health, and so on.

> But our historian would learn almost nothing . . . about the pivotal events around which the flow of modern history turned; indeed, he may not even learn that they took place at all. Where would one look on the shelves of a library for sociological insight into the invasions of Hungary and Vietnam? The bombings of Hiroshima and Nagasaki? Where would one learn about Auschwitz and Lidice and My Lai? . . . About a landing on the moon? About economic upheavals and military conflicts, riots and rebellions? About inventions and movements and elections? (306)

Erikson (1989) has reinforced these comments in his review of Smelser's *Handbook of Sociology*.

Let us recast Erikson's illuminating observations in methodological terms. Our thesis is that the preoccupation with surveys and/or experimentation—which fosters inattention to the case study approach—has led to a disregard of historical processes or, more narrowly, the turning points of history. For instance, up to now nuclear devastation, as happened in Nagasaki and Hiroshima, has been a one-time event. Nevertheless the possibility of its reoccurrence has had a major impact on the way in which world leaders and the world's citizenry have conceived of the limits of modern warfare. Although we cannot engage in any elaborate counterfactual analysis and reflect on what might have happened if the atomic bomb had not been dropped on Japan, we can reasonably assume that the destruction of these two cities had a profound effect on how the leaders of major nation-states could (and would) make war. We find a general recognition that an all-out nuclear assault might not only destroy the enemy but obliterate oneself and all humankind. Still other social consequences of the bombing of these Japanese cities have come to light, not the least of which has been a gnawing awareness, in a number of intellectual quarters, of the moral limits of "scientific progress."

We could readily consider numerous other significant events that have deeply affected the course of history during the past half century. Certainly, sociologists in the United States have been ill prepared intellectually to deal with the cataclysmic changes in Eastern Europe in the late 1980s and early 1990s—to say nothing of Gorbachev's efforts toward *glasnost* and *perestroika*. Although the theoretical (including ideological) commitments of sociologists have limited social inquiry in these realms, the methodological hegemony in the field has perhaps more than any other factor placed restrictions on addressing these grand problems.

ORGANIZATIONAL PATTERNS

It is not just interactional patterns and broad historical processes that require attention; fundamental patterns relating to complex organizations (or bureaucracy) have been neglected as a result of the methodological drift in the discipline. On both theoretical and empirical grounds, a case can be made that various major organizational issues cannot be addressed until in-depth case studies come to be viewed as not just an adjunct to the natural science model but as having an independent role of their own in advancing sociological principles regarding bureaucratic structures.

A number of organizational issues are related to the intersection of human agents and organizational structures. As two of the authors of this chapter have reasoned elsewhere (Vaughan and Sjoberg 1984), we cannot reduce organizational arrangements to a mere summing up of the activities of human agents. Yet we cannot properly interpret organizations without taking account of these human agents.

Given this context, serious problems arise from the use of surveys in the study of organizations. For example, the inability of probability sampling to examine a number of organizational issues has not been critically assessed by specialists on research methods. A probability sample assumes that units are independent and equal—but we know that the members of bureaucratic structures do not possess equal knowledge about the social arrangements or about how rules are to be interpreted and applied. Although we could proceed to criticize the research that has been conducted on organizations along these lines, we have instead chosen to build on Sjoberg and Kuhn (1989) in order to examine concrete problem areas: the decision-making patterns of the elite sector of organizations, organizational secrecy, organizational deviance, and the relationship of organizations to the disadvantaged. We can thereby indicate how case studies are the only effective means for advancing theoretical principles in this area.

Decision Making within the Organizational Elite. Some of the problems associated with research on elites have recently been surveyed by the contributors to the edited volume by Moyser and Wagstaffe (1987). The tone of this work is that social scientists can advance inquiry in this realm through adopting more rigorous methods. Our argument takes a somewhat different turn. In our view, major theoretical advances in the study of decision making by bureaucratic elites must proceed through a careful reappraisal of the use of in-depth case studies that rely on personal documents and intensive interviews.

Many social researchers lament, directly or indirectly, the fact that powerful organizational elites are uncooperative, but they fail to realize that secrecy is a fundamental means of sustaining power and influence. Cooperation with researchers in any egalitarian manner would lead elites to relinquish their monopoly on certain kinds of knowledge and thus their ability to manipulate the course of events.

Moreover, many important decisions are made by powerful elites drawn from a variety of organizational settings. Any appraisal of the decision-making process requires that sociologists have access to multiple perspectives on what has occurred. Moreover, these perspectives may not be symmetrical, for basic misunderstandings and contradictions are inherent in the process. Any effort to impose consistency and linearity (the hallmarks of the natural science model) would inhibit theoretical and empirical advances in this sphere.

Reliance on case studies that make use of personal documents leads us to call for rehabilitating the use of data such as autobiographies and biographies (Sjoberg and Kuhn 1989). Autobiographies are a source much overlooked even by sociologists who stress the qualitative approach. To study the Cuban missile crisis without some reliance on Khrushchev's autobiography (1970, 1974) would be grossly inadequate. And the autobiography of a certain ex–police chief of Budapest is an essential source for studying the organizational structures relating to the Hungarian revolution (Kopacsi 1987). Moreover, we urge sociologists to read the autobiography of the Japanese scholar Takeo (1988), who worked in the research division of the South Manchurian Railway during the 1920s and 1930s. Through this we gain a firsthand point of view of how Japanese researchers, who were assigned to a subdivision of this vast railway operation, took the lead in carrying out investigations of various facets of Chinese society to advance the cause of the Japanese empire. At this juncture we might well reflect back on our earlier discussion of the research by anthropologists and ask ourselves how this book by Takeo might lead U.S. social scientists to examine how their own activities in the modern world will be viewed in the years to come. Will their research be seen as serving to make U.S. power both a necessity and a virtue (cf. Stein 1989, 3)?

Secrecy and Bureaucratic Activities. We have alluded to the centrality of secrecy for the elite, but secrecy systems permeate bureaucratic structures (cf. Williams, Sjoberg, and Sjoberg 1983). We must not confuse secrecy with informal patterns. Secrecy can be both formal and informal. To think of secrecy only as part of the informal system is to overlook the activities surrounding the FBI, the CIA, and the KGB. Even within relatively open organizations, such as corporations and universities, secrecy systems may be difficult to decode. If there ever is an instance when surveys (or laboratory experiments) are unable to grapple with a significant social issue, it is in this realm. What is so striking about secrecy is that major survey works on organizations (e.g., Perrow 1986; Morgan 1986) are silent on the matter and that textbooks and monographs on research methods have nothing to say about how to investigate secrecy in bureaucratic organizations.

In this instance, the acceptance of appearances as real (a typical assumption in the natural science model) leads one to ignore a fundamental aspect of bureaucratic life in the modern world. Thus, in a democratic society such as the United States, most works dealing with complex secrecy arrangements have been the products of journalists (and at times historians), not sociologists. The nuclear weapons experiments in the United States, Watergate, and now the major "looting" (to use Galbraith's term [1990]) of savings and loan associations are striking instances of this neglect. In carrying out research on powerful secrecy systems, sociologists have much to learn from the methods employed by investigative journalists (cf. Sjoberg and Miller 1973). However, academic researchers seem to occupy too precarious a power base to take the lead in exposing the workings of organizations on which universities depend for their "survival."

To deal with the secrecy systems of totalitarian nation-states such as South Africa is an even more formidable undertaking. Moreover, sociologists' failure to anticipate at least some of the events in Eastern Europe and the Soviet Union in 1989 must be corrected if the discipline is to advance. We see no alternative to some kind of in-depth case approach for probing the activities emanating from bureaucratic secrecy systems—an approach buttressed as always by the researcher's sociological imagination.

In this context, another methodological issue demands attention (though its full implications must await another essay). Secrecy systems often come to light as a result of major ruptures in the fabric of bureaucratic structures. Watergate, its spillover, and the Iran-Contra affair are cases in point. So too, when the hostages were taken in Iran, the failure of the U.S. Embassy to complete the shredding of strategic documents allowed data about secret U.S. activities abroad to be pieced together by the Iranians, information that would otherwise not have come to light.[7]

We also fully anticipate that the East European crisis—with the resulting ruptures in totalitarian structures, including those relating to the pervasive influence of the secret police in many of these nations—will lead to a rewriting of organizational theory, if not by U.S. sociologists then by sociologists in other societies. This rewriting of organizational theory will be constructed on in-depth case studies of the events of 1989.

Organizational Deviance. We have already alluded to the limitations of social surveys and experiments in addressing the issue of white-collar crime. Although we do not underestimate the problems associated with the latter, we view deviance in much broader terms. We are struck by the general neglect of sociologists to examine intellectual deviance. This type of activity challenges the basic presuppositions of the organizational structure and, as such, is a matter worthy of serious attention. It has been a major issue in the United States, even with this country's democratic ideals. The repression involved in dealing with intellectual dissidents such as Emma Goldman after World War I, the repression associated with the McCarthy era after World War II, and the repression associated with the protests against the Vietnam War (note the Chicago 7 trial) are historic markers that underscore the dialectical relationship between democratic ideals and perceived challenges to powerful organizational structures within the social order. Sociologists' general neglect of intellectual deviance is still another instance of the theoretical and methodological limitations of the field.

Although the hegemony of the methodological orientation in the discipline can be faulted for this, correcting the situation requires not only a reliance on in-depth case data but also a rethinking of the theoretical nature of powerful organizations in modern society. The general issue of intellectual deviance leads us to the problem of the delegitimation of bureaucratic structures. How is it that in the face of rather rigid totalitarian controls, this delegitimation occurred at such a rapid pace in many Eastern European nations during the 1980s? We expect a backlash to occur, but still the question must be answered. In principle, this problem will need to be looked at in historical perspective. We could, for instance, go back and study the implications of the work of such intellectuals as Djilas (1975)—once the trusted ally of Josip Tito, the founder of Communist Yugoslavia—who turned against his comrade-in-arms and spent years in prison as a result of his intellectual questioning of the authority structure of modern Communist regimes, as evidenced in his work *The New Class.*

And we need to know a great deal more about dissent in, say, the Soviet Union itself. In earlier decades dissidents were killed or sent to prison, but in the 1970s and afterward such dissenters as the physicist Sakharov, supported by intellectuals in the scientific community on the world scene, came to be heard. The interplay of human agents with the powerful bureaucratic structures is a problem area that we hope sociologists will ultimately address through in-depth case analysis. The results are likely to lead to a rewriting of conventional wisdom in the field.

Organizations and the Disadvantaged. The research by Wilson (1987) on the truly disadvantaged has gained national attention outside the field of sociology. Our chief quarrel with this research effort (and others of this genre) is that it does not provide an understanding of how the powerful governmental and corporate structures keep the disadvantaged in their place (cf. Sjoberg, Vaughan, and Williams 1984). For us, bureaucratic organizations, with their emphasis on hierarchy, cannot put into practice the ideal of universalism (and fairness). There is a built-in structural bias toward keeping the poor in a disadvantaged position. Official statistics, including survey data as evidenced in Wilson's study, cannot, as we intimated in our analysis of Jencks's work above, account for the powerful role of bureaucracy in keeping the poor poor.

There are numerous ramifications of this methodological issue, ramifications that we cannot explore herein. But one deserves special mention. If the truly disadvantaged are to be given a voice—if they are to be heard—it must be through the careful collection of case material by social scientists who take the worldview of the economically disadvantaged and set the latter's voices (and their pain) in relationship to the powerful organizational structures that influence their lives and over which they have so little control.

We are in agreement with Goyder (1987), in his informative analysis of social surveys, when he demonstrates that survey researchers typically adopt a behaviorist model of human action in constructing and employing their questionnaires. By definition, the behaviorist approach does not permit the disadvantaged to be heard. Instead these respondents are treated as objects. We return to this methodological and moral issue below in a somewhat different context.

Methodological Issues in the Use of
Case Studies in Social Inquiry

Up to this point we have reasoned that in-depth case study materials are an essential adjunct to the employment of the natural science model and that, more striking, they are a strategic tool in their own right for approaching certain major sociological issues. Even if one accepts our line of reasoning, problems relating to the case study approach still require clarification if case studies are to be more effectively employed in social analysis. We shall consider selected issues that call for detailed attention in future investigations.

THE USE OF NEGATIVE (OR DEVIANT) CASES

The negative case approach has been used by social scientists who are identified with the natural science model as well as by those who advocate an alternative mode of inquiry. The former category includes sociologists who have been identified with the Lazarsfeld school of social research. Thus Kendall and Wolf (1955) spoke of two purposes of deviant case analysis: increasing the predictive value of research by demonstrating the relevance of additional variables, and helping to refine the measurement of statistical variables. Although this line of inquiry has merit, it is not the focus of our attention.

Znaniecki (1934) in *The Method of Sociology* introduced the idea of analytic induction, and the use of negative cases, as a basis for furthering sociological analysis. This method was put into practice by Cressey (1955) in his study of embezzlers and by Lindesmith (1947) in his investigation of opiate addiction. Cressey formulated generalizations about embezzlers by seeking out negative cases and revising his original generalization to fit these cases. Lindesmith proceeded along similar lines. Both have been criticized for their failure to pay heed to nonembezzlers and nonaddicts or, in other words, their failure to utilize a control group within the context of some form of experimental design.

However one judges analytic induction, the negative case will continue to serve as a major tool in social inquiry, especially for cross-cultural study. For many years the assumption was that the nuclear family and the incest taboo were cultural universals. But the research by Gough (1959) on the Nayars of South India and, more recently, by Stack (1974) on economically disadvantaged blacks presents negative cases that challenge the assertion that the nuclear family is a universal. So too, the work by Middleton (1962), among others, did much to undermine the once widely held generalization that incest taboos are a universal social phenomenon. Although we cannot establish rigorous controls in social research, we can nonetheless continue to refine sociological principles regarding, say, family life.

We must also recognize that even if the nuclear family was a universal pattern in the past, human beings may be capable of constructing a viable social order that lacks this kind of family form. Keller (1986), for instance, suggested as much when she contended that family forms having no historical antecedents are in the process of evolving in advanced industrial orders. (We return to this matter below.)

NORMAL, DEVIANT, AND EXTREME CASES

We now recast the negative case approach in a somewhat different light. Deviance is always defined in relationship to what is normal; however, the natural science mode of inquiry does not capture the inherent dialectical relationship between the two. As suggested above, we must formulate sociological principles relating to intellectual deviance. And we must account for the ever shifting nature of deviance in social orders. For example, in the Soviet Union, dissidents like Sakharov were exiled and later rehabilitated as legitimate critics. The case of Nelson Mandela, the long-time political and intellectual critic of apartheid who was jailed for many years yet who exercised considerable influence on the future course of South Africa from behind bars, requires clarification. Sociologists are in a position to outline the objectively possible range of future developments but not to predict what will actually happen.

The extreme case, in our judgment, has greater theoretical import than the deviant case. Unlike the deviant case, the extreme case stands *outside the boundaries* of historically considered human experience. We can best articulate the meaning of the extreme case by reference to the Holocaust: the systematic destruction of Jews (and other minorities) by the Nazis.

The Holocaust cannot adequately be understood as a deviant case. The Jews were defined not as deviant but rather as outside the category of what it means to be human. Once this was accomplished, the next step, extermination, was readily taken. The Nazis, within their own conceptual system, were killing nonhumans. This led to the greatest moral catastrophe of the modern West.

The Holocaust has come into clearer focus in recent years as various intellectuals and politicians, inside and outside of Germany, have attempted to redefine this extreme case in deviant terms. When President Reagan visited the Bitburg cemetery that held the graves of some SS troops who had played such a crucial role in the extermination of the European Jews, we witnessed an effort on the part of various German politicians and intellectuals to normalize the Holocaust by redefining an extreme case in deviant terms.

The Bitburg visit prefigured a major debate within German intellectual circles. On the one side were conservative historians such as Ernst Nolte, who, for instance, sought to relativize the Nazi case by comparing it to the Stalinist slave-labor camps. The preeminent social theorist Habermas entered the debate by sharply criticizing Nolte and others for their stance. Maier (1988), in his *Unmasterable Past*, surveys this intellectual controversy. One theoretical conclusion emerges from reading his work: the standard that one employs in comparative study has built-in political and moral dimensions. This issue is yet to be addressed by comparative sociologists.

To normalize the Holocaust by comparing it to other atrocities is to minimize its social and moral consequences and undermine what can happen in the future if steps are not taken to guard against the reoccurrence of such an event. So too, if the Holocaust is defined as a deviant case, we cease to understand its role in the formulation of the United Nations Universal Declaration of Human Rights. But are there other extreme cases that we can point to? We believe Hiroshima and Nagasaki fall into this category, for they dramatize how scientific advances have the potentiality to destroy all of humankind. Here we recall Erikson's plea (discussed above) to come to terms with historical events, but we go a step further by contending that it is necessary, both theoretically and empirically, to distinguish between deviant and extreme cases.

HOLISM AND REDUCTIONISM

This problem area is a source of long-standing debate in sociology, and it continues to beset social inquiry in various ways. The concept of holism—that the whole is more than the sum of its parts—was raised by Durkheim in some of his writings, and the principle has been a feature of contemporary theorizing, among both non-Marxists and Marxists (cf. Jay 1984).

Many advocates of the case study method champion its value in making possible a holistic perspective. We agree. Nevertheless, some clarification of parts-whole logic is much in order. Ragin (1987), for instance, spoke of holism in social science inquiry but sidestepped the essential features of this debate in sociology. Lyng (1988), on the other hand, addressed the problem more directly. Utilizing clinical medicine as a means of unraveling some of the problems associated with this logical form, he made the persuasive case that the principle of reductionism, not holism, holds sway in clinical medicine because medical practitioners rely on natural science for legitimacy, even though holism is an integral feature of actual clinical practice.

But why is the natural science model, and the methodological individualism associated with it, at odds with holism? If one takes the view that the whole is merely the sum of its parts, then rigorous standardization is feasible. But if the whole is conceived of as more than the sum of its parts, then the researcher is obliged to piece together the parts theoretically in order to construct the whole. This theoretical leap is not subject to careful operationalization and standardization, which, in turn, leads to the inability of one scientist to replicate, in any strict sense, the findings of another.

Researchers must be attentive to the parts-whole issue not only on empirical but also on moral grounds. We need not accept Popper's (1950) relentless attack on holism, based on his methodological individualism, to recognize the moral dangers associated with an uncritical adoption of holism. Researchers who employ the case study method should be careful to recognize that the views or interests of subgroups, such as ethnic minorities, may be at odds with the dominant majority's definition of the interests of the whole.

A TOP-DOWN VERSUS A BOTTOM-UP ORIENTATION
AND THE CASE STUDY

One means for overcoming methodological problems associated with an uncritical acceptance of the holistic orientation is an explicit recognition of the tensions involved in a top-down versus a bottom-up orientation in carrying out social research, another much-neglected methodological issue in sociology.[8]

The top-down versus the bottom-up perspective has been examined on the micro level by Rollins (1985) and Williams (1989b) and in a sense in *Arab Women in the Field* (Altorki and El-Solh 1988). For the macro level, we can point to the work of the prominent historian Hobsbawm (1985), who argues for a bottom-up approach in the historical analysis of class relations in England. In a somewhat similar vein, Andrée F. Sjoberg (1990) has used Indian civilization as a case study in her reinterpretation of the origins and development of Hinduism. She does this not from the perspective of the dominant power group, the Aryans, but from the perspective of the minority peoples, mainly the Dravidians. The relevant data are in turn analyzed within a broad comparative perspective.[9]

If we look closely at the micro level of human interaction, we typically find that the perspectives of those who command social power and the orientations of those below, who are under the control of the former, are asymmetrical. Rollins found that female domestic servants had a more intimate understanding of their women employers than the latter had of them. The same asymmetry is displayed on the macro level. The perspective of leaders of Third World countries on the utilization of the environment, equity in the financing of economic development, and so on often differs from the perspective of leaders of advanced industrial nations, who command far greater economic and military power. This tension is frequently reflected in the voting in the General Assembly of the United Nations.

That the perspectives of those in positions of power may differ from, or even clash with, the orientations of those below has several implications for the use of the case approach. First and foremost, the case study, as already suggested, may well be the only tool by which social scientists can provide the truly disadvantaged with a voice. We have already discussed the fact that social surveys typically do not include the truly disadvantaged as respondents, and even when they do, such surveys involve questionnaires that typically are pretested and standardized in terms of the knowledge base of the privileged sector. Still, if researchers are to provide the disadvantaged with a voice, they must also take pains to place this within the context of organizational power. Otherwise, researchers will find themselves blaming the disadvantaged for their plight, when, from our standpoint, their situation has resulted primarily from the activities of those who control organizational power in modern society and on the world scene.

The bottom-up versus the top-down perspective poses even more serious difficulties for those who construct case studies through the use of historical records. Historical data generally have been created from the vantage point of the powerful, and the further back one goes in time, the more likely one is to be limited to information on a small segment of the elite (see, e.g., Sjoberg 1990). Even for the period after the industrial revolution and the spread of literacy, the historical record favors the worldviews of the literati, who are intertwined with and supported by the power structure. We must be cognizant of the existence of peoples (or subgroups thereof) who are without history (cf. Wolf 1982). One criticism of the research of many historical sociologists such as Tilly and Skocpol is that they fail to address the basic sociological problems relating to the nature of historical records and thus are all too ready to accept a top-down approach, and often do so unwittingly. Sociologists who utilize historical data cannot invent the past but must carefully interpret existing records. They must critically examine, from a sociology-of-knowledge perspective, how these records were constructed and why certain data were not recorded. By bringing basic sociological principles to bear on the interpretation of historical data, sociologists can greatly advance this sphere of inquiry.

CASE STUDIES AND ANTICIPATION OF THE FUTURE

We have at several points referred to events that shook the world in 1989, particularly in the Soviet Union and Eastern Europe. Surely, Sovietologists and specialists on Eastern Europe failed rather miserably in predicting, let alone anticipating, some of these occurrences. A variety of social

factors contributed to this, but two deserve comment. One is the ideological commitment to the Cold War, and the other is the commitment
to the natural science model, which assumes that the future will in many
respects replicate the past.

The question then arises: How are we to proceed with the use of case
studies in the aforementioned circumstances? We must link case study
analysis to some form of what we term countersystem analysis (Sjoberg
and Cain 1971) and then reflect on the objective possibilities that might
ensue. With the benefit of twenty-twenty hindsight, we can recognize that
social changes were afoot in Eastern Europe well before the ruptures in
1989. Apparently an impressive number of semiunderground activities
had emerged in East Germany, for instance, and members of these groups
were questioning the authority structures that outsiders assumed were so
deeply entrenched. Some case material on this substratum of the East
German populace would have been helpful for social researchers, not for
predicting particular happenings but for anticipating the range of objective possibilities that could follow.

We believe that sociologists must begin to pay heed to the possible
patterns that may arise in the United States during the 1990s and beyond.
An analysis of the range of objective possibilities is exceedingly difficult,
but intensive case studies of a variety of "strategic" groups will enable us
to see below the surface and consider the doubts and aspirations of various subgroups and, more important, the nature of the entrenched bureaucratic structures that will shape future events.

Our argument articulates with our effort to formulate a viable alternative to the natural science model in sociology. We do not believe it is
possible to predict the future when human beings can and do play a role
in reshaping that future. Yet, we remain convinced that the attempt to anticipate objective possibilities is a worthwhile social scientific endeavor.

Conclusions

Our intent in this chapter has been to delineate a set of methodological problems relating to the use of the case study approach in
social research. Although we have not fully resolved many of the issues
raised herein, we have nonetheless been able to advance certain salient

theses. We began by outlining certain methodological issues in order to clarify the basic premises underlying the natural science model that dominates sociological inquiry. We outlined how this model—which relies on quantification, using data from social surveys (or other "official statistics") or social experiments—rests upon a selected set of domain assumptions, logical forms, and assessment procedures (i.e., the criteria for evaluating valid knowledge).

Our justification for the use of the case study method in sociology has been two-pronged in nature. First, we sought to demonstrate that if one works within the natural science model, one must still employ the case study in several ways. One's "working universe" (e.g., a sample drawn from the U.S. population) is typically a case study vis-à-vis the larger historical and cross-cultural universe. Moreover, if the champions of this model are to address the empirical problems to which they are committed, they must supplement their research with data collected via the case study approach.

Second, we go a step further and contend that the case study approach, based on in-depth fieldwork or documentary data, has an integrity of its own. By employing this method, we can entertain those assumptions or presuppositions about the nature of human nature and of social reality that are inadmissible within the framework of natural science inquiry. We can thus examine a major set of problem areas relating to social interaction, historical processes, and organizational structures, doing much to advance our knowledge about significant social issues in the modern world. For example, we must recognize that in the bureaucratic setting, appearances are not the only reality: bureaucratic secrecy is a central aspect of this organizational form. This secrecy system cannot be studied through surveys or social experimentation.

We can advance our argument in another way. Early on we contended that researchers must realize that their efforts are shaped to a considerable extent by the social and cultural context in which they function. In keeping with this view, we must realize that much social inquiry has become an extension of the administrative apparatus, a point suggested by a careful reading of Alonso and Starr's (1987) edited work *The Politics of Numbers.*

We must be keenly aware that the requirements or demands of the administrative apparatus result in a particular kind of knowledge.[10]

Given the framework within which such data are collected, they perform major societal functions. But we must not confuse—as many sociologists do—valid social knowledge with the data generated by the administrative apparatus of modern industrial social orders. Other kinds of knowledge are sorely needed—for instance, those that promote, as Vaughan (1989) has documented, more reasoned public discourse on the key issues of our age. We are convinced that social science, especially sociology, has a distinct contribution to make to our knowledge of how the social world is constructed and how it can be reshaped. To this end, we believe, it is essential to increase reliance on the case study method, using it in such a way as not to merely reproduce and sustain the administrative apparatus. We must, through in-depth investigation, reach a more profound understanding of the nature of power in a global order that is increasingly dominated by bureaucratic organizations; concomitantly, we must provide a voice for vulnerable or disadvantaged people, including ethnic minorities. The case study approach—one not committed to the natural science model or to historicism—provides us with a means of addressing problem areas outside the purview of the natural science model as well as of current administrative concerns.

We do not underestimate the limitations of the case study approach, and we have outlined some of the problem areas that require special attention. Even though the disadvantages must be directly confronted, it is perhaps paradoxical that the weaknesses of this approach are more readily perceived than those of the natural science model. Sophisticated quantitative procedures, couched in claims of objectivity, serve often to gloss over serious limitations of this perspective, which, when critically examined, makes the qualitative case approach a far more essential tool in advancing social knowledge than most contemporary sociologists have been willing to acknowledge.

Notes

This chapter is a product of a complex collaborative enterprise. Gideon Sjoberg two decades ago coauthored a book on methodology. Norma Williams contributes through her fieldwork on Mexican Americans (as well as on undocumented workers) in which she used the case study approach and worked on problems relating to research on minorities. Ted R. Vaughan and Gideon Sjoberg have for over two decades been collaborating on a variety of efforts, and the substantial revisions and refinements herein of the argument in the methodology book (especially on the nature of theory and the sociology of knowledge) are a result of their joint efforts. Andrée F. Sjoberg, who is a linguist and anthropologist by training, has brought her wide-ranging cross-cultural knowledge to bear in the development of this paper.

1. We cannot examine here the criticisms of logical positivism that have surfaced in the philosophy of science. Some of this literature is relevant for sociological methodology. See, for example, Suppe 1977 and Mancias 1987.

2. According to Lukes, "Methodological individualism . . . is a prescription for explanation, asserting that no purported explanations of social (or individual) phenomena are to count as explanations . . . unless they are couched wholly in terms of facts about individuals" (1977, 180).

3. Otis Dudley Duncan's (1984) analysis of quantification and measurement underlines our differences with adherents of the natural science model. For Duncan, measurement, if looked at historically, is embedded in the social process. On this thesis we can agree. But Duncan, who has been an exemplar of the quantification movement within sociology, is unable to step back and reflect on himself as a part of the process he describes and on how his role (together with the role of others like him) has affected social research in the United States during the past few decades, as well as how, in turn, the administrative apparatus of modern society has influenced his own efforts. If Duncan had extended his analysis by this next step, he would have found that his research is less neutral and "objective" than he and others contend.

4. One of the general problems with the works of Tilly (1981, 1984) and Skocpol (1984) is their failure to deal with historical revisionism. Consider two case studies. One concerns the debate in West Germany during the 1980s over how to interpret the Holocaust (e.g., Maier 1988); the other relates to the dramatic revisions in the interpretation of Soviet history by Soviet scholars after Gorbachev's rise to power (e.g., Davies 1989). Though we must avoid lapsing into historicism, sociologists cannot, as Tilly and Skocpol are prone to do, assume that they are immune to the political and social forces that lead to a reinterpretation of historical events. A critical sociology-of-knowledge perspective is one strategic means of coping with the problems of determining what is valid historical knowledge.

5. Blumer (1969) is one of the few contemporary sociologists to formulate a "countersystem" to the natural science model as he sought to create linkages between his assumptions and his research procedures. Blumer conceived of human nature and social reality as processual, and he stressed the primacy of taking into account contexualized meanings when interpreting human action. In line with these assumptions he called for immersion in fieldwork and reliance on case

studies as the bases for studying the social world. His emphasis on "sensitizing concepts" rather than "operationally defined concepts" is congruent with his domain assumptions.

6. Rossi and his associates sought to draw a probability sample of the most economically disadvantaged sector: the homeless. But serious questions must be raised about their effort. About one facet of their design, they wrote: "The street surveys were based on stratified random samples of the 168 blocks in the fall and 245 in the winter, drawn from among the 19,409 census blocks within the Chicago city limits. . . . This stratification was accomplished with the cooperation of precinct community relations officers of the Chicago Police Department who, with the help of beat officers, rated each block in Chicago as to how many homeless persons could be expected to be on that block in the late hours of the night" (1987, 1337). They concluded that their research "provides the first *scientifically defensible estimates*" (emphasis added) of the homeless population.

Aside from the fact that Chicago is a case study with respect to the United States, other more serious problems cannot be glossed over. Are we to believe that the street wisdom of the police concerning the distribution of the homeless is a sound foundation for a scientific probability sample? We seriously doubt that. We deem the careful work of social science fieldworkers to be superior to the leaps of faith made by Rossi et al.

In addition, Rossi and his associates observed that in the street surveys, the interviewers were accompanied by off-duty Chicago policemen as they searched for the homeless in all possible places in the sampled block. The authors studiously avoided the basic ethical and human rights issues that social scientists encounter when social surveys become extensions of the police apparatus.

7. A major rupture in the social fabric of Chinese society occurred with the trial of the "Gang of Four" after Mao's death. This trial provided data—on certain aspects of organizational life in China under Mao—that had previously been hidden from the scrutiny of outsiders. See, for example, Hsü 1990.

8. Approaching the problem of the bottom-up versus the top-down perspective with respect to minorities from vastly differing vantage points, two of the authors of this paper have examined the difficulties encountered by members of dominant power groups in interpreting the roles and activities of ethnic minorities. Williams (1989b) has detailed the barriers encountered by privileged researchers who seek to take the roles of economically disadvantaged minorities in interpersonal situations, whereas Sjoberg (1990) argues that the persistent Aryan bias in Indology has led to a general failure to recognize that Hinduism is primarily the product of the Dravidians and other minority peoples in India, not of the politically dominant Aryans.

The power and ideological factors that have structured the course of Western scholarship on Indian civilization await systematic examination. A plausible thesis is that the Aryan perspective has been fostered mainly by the fact that most of the religious texts of Hinduism were composed in Sanskrit, an Indo-European language. This has made it possible for Eurocentric scholars to perceive of India as an Asian extension of their own "superior" European culture.

9. Sjoberg's (1990) analysis rests on two forms of contextualization that must be distinguished by proponents of the case study method. First, she discusses the relationship of the Dravidians to the Aryans in the context of the cultural history of the Indian subcontinent. Second, she contextualizes the data by placing both groups within a broader comparative setting, arguing that Hinduism (not to be confused with the Vedism earlier introduced by the Aryans) could not be fundamentally Aryan, as has long been assumed, because its particular constellation of central concepts, and many of its other features, have no counterparts outside India (specifically, in Central Asia, the Middle East, or Europe—areas through which the ancestors of the Aryans passed on their way to India or within which they first took shape as a distinct sociolinguistic entity).

10. A critical evaluation of the nature and use of, for instance, personal documents in the construction of case studies is sorely needed. One starting point is to markedly update the contribution of Gottschalk, Kluckhohn, and Angell (1945). A great deal of attention must be given to why particular documents come to be constructed and why other materials are never recorded. More generally, the place of documents in preindustrial civilized societies in contrast to industrial societies deserves careful scrutiny. Within the context of modern social orders, special attention needs to be given to the role played by bureaucratic structures in creating certain data and repressing others.

We must also consider the matter of why some documents survive and others are lost to the historical record. For instance, the Spaniards, in order to insure their conquest of the Maya, destroyed the latter's written records. The basic questions regarding the nature of documentary data generally remain unaddressed by sociologists or, for that matter, historians.

References

Alexander, Jeffrey C. 1982. *Theoretical Logic in Sociology: Positivism, Presuppositions, and Current Controversies*, vol. 1. Berkeley: University of California Press.

Alexander, Jeffrey C., Bernard Gresen, Richard Münch, and Neil J. Smelser, eds. 1987. *The Micro-Macro Link*. Berkeley: University of California Press.

Alonso, William, and Paul Starr, eds. 1987. *The Politics of Numbers*. New York: Russell Sage Foundation.

Altorki, Soraya, and Camillia Fawzi El-Solh, eds. 1988. *Arab Women in the Field: Studying Your Own Society*. Syracuse: Syracuse University Press.

Anderson, Nels. 1923. *The Hobo: The Sociology of the Homeless Man.* Chicago: University of Chicago Press.

Attewell, Paul A. 1984. *Radical Political Economy since the Sixties.* New Brunswick, N.J.: Rutgers University Press.

Ayer, A. J. 1959. "Editor's Introduction." Pp. 3–28 in *Logical Positivism,* edited by A. J. Ayer. New York: Free Press.

Babbie, Earl. 1989. *The Practice of Social Research.* 5th ed. Belmont, Calif.: Wadsworth Publishing Company.

Baechler, Jean, John A. Hall, and Michael Mann, eds. 1988. *Europe and the Rise of Capitalism.* Oxford: Basil Blackwell.

Bailey, Kenneth D. 1987. *Methods of Social Research.* 3d ed. New York: Free Press.

Birman, Igor. 1989. "Rosefielde and My Cumulative Disequilibrium Hypothesis: A Comment." *Soviet Studies* 41:144–48.

Blalock, Hubert M. 1969. *Theory Construction from Verbal to Mathematical Formulations.* Englewood Cliffs, N.J.: Prentice-Hall.

Blau, Peter M. 1955. *The Dynamics of Bureaucracy.* Chicago: University of Chicago Press.

———. 1977. *Inequality and Heterogeneity.* New York: Free Press.

———. 1987. "Microprocess and Macrostructure." Pp. 83–100 in *Social Exchange Theory,* edited by Karen Cook. Newbury Park: Sage.

Blumer, Herbert. 1969. *Symbolic Interactionism.* Berkeley: University of California Press.

Burgess, Ernest. 1967. "The Growth of the City." Pp. 47–62 in *The City,* by Robert E. Park, Ernest Burgess, and Roderick D. McKenzie. Chicago: University of Chicago Press.

Collins, Randall. 1981. "On the Micro-Foundations of Macro-Sociology." *American Journal of Sociology* 86:984–1014.

Converse, Jean M. 1987. *Survey Research in the United States.* Berkeley: University of California Press.

Cressey, Donald R. 1955. *Other People's Money.* New York: Free Press.

Davies, R. W. 1989. *Soviet History in the Gorbachev Revolution.* Bloomington: Indiana University Press.

Denzin, Norman K. 1989. *The Research Act.* 3d ed. Englewood Cliffs, N.J.: Prentice-Hall.

Djilas, Milovan. 1975. *Parts of a Lifetime.* Edited by Michael Milenkvitch and Deborah Milenkvitch. New York: Harcourt Brace Jovanovich.

Dooley, David. 1990. *Social Research Methods.* 2d ed. Englewood Cliffs, N.J.: Prentice-Hall.

Duncan, Otis Dudley. 1984. *Notes on Social Measurement: Historical and Critical.* New York: Russell Sage Foundation.

Elster, Jon. 1978. *Logic and Society: Contradictions and Possible Worlds.* New York: John Wiley and Sons.

Embree, John. 1939. *Suye Mura: A Japanese Village*. Chicago: University of Chicago Press.

Erikson, Kai. 1984. "Sociology and Contemporary Events." Pp. 303–10 in *Conflict and Consensus: A Festschrift in Honor of Lewis A. Coser*, edited by Walter W. Powell and Richard Robbins. New York: Free Press.

———. 1989. "Drawing Boundaries." Review of *Handbook of Sociology*, edited by Neil J. Smelser. *Contemporary Sociology* 18:511–13.

Evans-Pritchard, E. E. 1940. *The Nuer*. Oxford: Clarendon Press.

Feagin, Joe R. 1988. *Free Enterprise City*. New Brunswick, N.J.: Rutgers University Press.

Fei, Hsiao-T'ung. 1946. *Peasant Life in China*. New York: Oxford University Press.

Freeman, Derek. 1983. *Margaret Mead and Samoa: The Making and Unmaking of an Anthropological Myth*. Cambridge: Harvard University Press.

Galbraith, John Kenneth. 1990. "The Ultimate Scandal." *New York Review* 36:15–16.

Galtung, Johan. 1967. *Theory and Methods of Social Research*. New York: Columbia University Press.

Geertz, Clifford. 1988. *Works and Lives: The Anthropologist As Author*. Stanford: Stanford University Press.

Gibbs, Jack P. 1972. *Sociological Theory Construction*. Hinsdale, Ill.: Dryden Press.

Giddens, Anthony. 1984. *The Constitution of Society*. Berkeley: University of California Press.

Goffman, Erving. 1959. *The Presentation of Self in Everyday Life*. Garden City, N.Y.: Doubleday.

Gottfredson, Michael, and Travis Hirschi, eds. 1987. *Positive Criminology*. Newbury Park: Sage.

Gottschalk, Louis, Clyde Kluckhohn, and Robert Angell. 1945. *The Use of Personal Documents in History, Anthropology, and Sociology*. New York: Social Science Research Council.

Gough, Kathleen. 1959. "The Nayars and the Definition of Marriage." *Journal of the Royal Anthropological Institute of Great Britain and Ireland* 89:23–34.

Gouldner, Alvin W. 1954. *Patterns of Industrial Democracy*. New York: Free Press.

———. 1959. "Reciprocity and Autonomy in Functional Theory." Pp. 241–70 in *Symposium on Sociological Theory*, edited by Llewellyn Gross. New York: Harper and Row.

———. 1970. *The Coming Crisis of Western Sociology*. New York: Basic Books.

Goyder, John. 1987. *The Silent Majority: Nonresponders on Sample Surveys*. Boulder: Westview Press.

Habermas, Jürgen. 1987. *A Theory of Communicative Action—Lifeworld and System: A Critique of Functionalist Reason*, vol. 2. Boston: Beacon Press.

Hempel, Carl G. 1965. *Aspects of Scientific Explanation*. New York: Free Press.

Herzfeld, Michael. 1987. *Anthropology through the Looking-Glass: Critical Ethnography in the Margins of Europe*. Cambridge: Cambridge University Press.

Hobsbawm, Eric. 1985. "History from Below—Some Reflections." Pp. 75–93 in *History from Below: Studies in Popular Protest and Popular Ideology in Honour of George Rudé*, edited by Frederick Krantz. Montreal: Concordia University.

Holmes, Lowell D. 1987. *Quest for the Real Samoa: The Mead/Freeman Controversy and Beyond*. South Hadley, Mass.: Bergin and Garney.

Homans, George. 1982. "The Present State of Sociological Theory." *Sociological Quarterly* 23:285–99.

Howard, Jane. 1984. *Margaret Mead: A Life*. New York: Simon and Schuster.

Hsü, Immanuel C. U. 1990. *China without Mao*. 2d ed. New York: Oxford University Press.

Jain, Dhanesh K. 1969. "The Verbalization of Respect in Hindi." *Anthropological Linguistics* 11:79–97.

Jay, Martin. 1984. *Marxism and Totality*. Berkeley: University of California Press.

Jencks, Christopher. 1989. "What Is the Underclass—And Is It Growing?" *Focus* 12 (Spring and Summer): 14–26.

Keller, Suzanne. 1986. "Does the Family Have a Future?" Pp. 520–32 in *Family in Transition*, edited by Arlene Skolnick and Jerome Skolnick. 5th ed. Boston: Little, Brown.

Kendall, Patricia L., and Katherine M. Wolf. 1955. "The Two Purposes of Deviant Case Analysis." Pp. 167–70 in *The Language of Social Research*, edited by Paul F. Lazarsfeld and Morris Rosenberg. New York: Free Press.

Khrushchev, Nikita S. 1970. *Khrushchev Remembers*. Edited by S. Talbott. New York: Little, Brown.

———. 1974. *Khrushchev Remembers: The Last Testament*. Edited by S. Talbott. New York: Little, Brown.

Knotternus, J. David. 1987. "Status Attainment Research and Its Image of Society." *American Sociological Review* 52:113–21.

Kohn, Melvin L., ed. 1989. *Cross-National Research in Sociology*. Newbury Park: Sage.

Kopacsi, Sandor. 1987. *In the Name of the Working Class: The Inside Story of the Hungarian Revolution*. New York: Grove Press.

Laub, John H. 1987. "Data for Positive Criminology." Pp. 56–70 in *Positive Criminology*, edited by Michael Gottfredson and Travis Hirschi. Newbury Park: Sage.

Leach, Jerry W. 1983. "Introduction." Pp. 1–26 in *Kula: New Perspectives on*

Massim Exchange, edited by Jerry W. Leach and Edmund Leach. Cambridge: Cambridge University Press.

Leach, Jerry W., and Edmund Leach, eds. 1983. *Kula: New Perspectives on Massim Exchange*. Cambridge: Cambridge University Press.

Lindesmith, Alfred R. 1947. *Opiate Addiction*. Bloomington, Ind.: Principia Press.

Lipset, Seymour Martin. 1950. *Agrarian Socialism*. Berkeley: University of California Press.

Lukes, Steven. 1977. *Essays in Social Theory*. London: Macmillan.

Lyng, Stephen. 1988. "Holism and Reductionism within Applied Behavioral Science: The Problem of Clinical Medicine." *Journal of Applied Behavioral Science* 24:101–18.

Maier, Charles. 1988. *The Unmasterable Past: History, Holocaust, and German National Identity*. Cambridge: Harvard University Press.

Malinowski, Bronislaw. 1922. *Argonauts of the Western Pacific*. New York: E. P. Dutton.

Mancias, Peter T. 1987. *A History and Philosophy of the Social Sciences*. New York: Basil Blackwell.

Mayhew, Bruce. 1980. "Structuralism vs. Individualism." *Social Forces* 59:335–75.

Mead, George Herbert. 1934. *Mind, Self, and Society*. Chicago: University of Chicago Press.

Mead, Margaret. [1928] 1961. *Coming of Age in Samoa: A Psychological Study of Primitive Youth for Western Civilization*. New York: William Morrow.

Merton, Robert K. 1957. *Social Theory and Social Structure*. Rev. and enl. ed. New York: Free Press.

———. [1938] 1970. *Science, Technology, and Society in Seventeenth Century England*. New York: Howard Fertig.

Middleton, Russell. 1962. "Brother-Sister and Father-Daughter Marriage in Ancient Egypt." *American Sociological Review* 27:603–11.

Morgan, Gareth. 1986. *Images of Organization*. Newbury Park: Sage.

Moyser, George, and Margaret Wagstaffe, eds. 1987. *Research Methods for Elite Studies*. London: Allen and Unwin.

Opp, Karl-Dieter. 1985. "Sociology and Economic Man." *Journal of Institutional and Theoretical Economics* 141:213–43.

Perrow, Charles. 1986. *Complex Organizations: A Critical Essay*. 3d ed. New York: Random House.

Phillips, Bernard. 1985. *Sociological Research Methods*. Homewood, Ill.: Dorsey Press.

Polkinghorne, Donald. 1983. *Methodology for the Human Sciences*. Albany: State University of New York Press.

Popper, Karl R. 1950. *The Open Society and Its Enemies.* Rev. ed. Princeton, N.J.: Princeton University Press.

Ragin, Charles C. 1987. *The Comparative Method.* Berkeley: University of California Press.

Rappaport, Roy A. 1986. "Desecrating the Holy Woman: Derek Freeman's Attack on Margaret Mead." *American Scholar* 55:313–47.

Redfield, Robert. 1941. *Tepoztlan: A Mexican Village.* Chicago: University of Chicago Press.

Rollins, Judith. 1985. *Between Women.* Philadelphia: Temple University Press.

Rorty, Richard. 1982. *Consequences of Pragmatism.* Minneapolis: University of Minnesota Press.

Rosaldo, Renato. 1986. "From the Door of His Tent: The Fieldworker and the Inquisition." Pp. 77–97 in *Writing Culture,* edited by James Clifford and George Marcus. Berkeley: University of California Press.

Rossi, Peter H., James D. Wright, Gene A. Fisher, and Georgianna Willis. 1987. "The Urban Homeless: Estimating Composition and Size." *Science* 235 (March 13): 1336–41.

Said, Edward W. 1979. *Orientalism.* New York: Vintage Books.

Schwartz, Howard, and Jerry Jacobs. 1979. *Qualitative Sociology.* New York: Free Press.

Sewell, William H. 1987. "Getting On-Line." P. 15 in *The Meaning of Sociology,* 2d ed., edited by Joel M. Charon. Englewood Cliffs, N.J.: Prentice-Hall. (Originally published in the *New York Times,* April 28, 1985, section 4, p. 7.)

———. 1988. "The Changing Institutional Structure of Sociology and My Career." Pp. 119–43 in *Sociological Lines: Social Change and the Life Course,* vol. 2, edited by Matilda White Riley. Newbury Park: Sage.

Sjoberg, Andrée F. 1990. "The Dravidian Contribution to the Development of Indian Civilization: A Call for a Reassessment." *Comparative Civilizations Review.* No. 23: 40–74.

Sjoberg, Gideon. 1960. *The Preindustrial City.* New York: Free Press.

Sjoberg, Gideon, and Leonard D. Cain. 1971. "Negative Values, Counter System Models, and the Analysis of Social Systems." Pp. 212–29 in *Institutions and Social Exchange: The Sociologies of Talcott Parsons and George C. Homans,* edited by Herman Turk and Richard Simpson. Indianapolis: Bobbs-Merrill.

Sjoberg, Gideon, and Kathryn Kuhn. 1989. "Autobiography and Organizations: Theoretical and Methodological Issues." *Journal of Applied Behavioral Science* 25:309–26.

Sjoberg, Gideon, and Paula Jean Miller. 1973. "Social Research on Bureaucracy: Limitations and Opportunities." *Social Problems* 21:129–43.

Sjoberg, Gideon, and Roger Nett. 1968. *A Methodology for Social Research.* New York: Harper and Row.

Sjoberg, Gideon, Ted R. Vaughan, and Norma Williams. 1984. "Bureaucracy As a Moral Issue." *Journal of Applied Behavioral Science* 20:441–53.

Skinner, B. F. 1982. *Skinner for the Classroom: Selected Papers*. Edited by Robert Epstein. Champaign, Ill.: Research Press.

Skocpol, Theda. 1979. *States and Social Revolutions: A Comparative Analysis of France, Russia, and China*. New York: Cambridge University Press.

———, ed. 1984. *Vision and Method in Historical Sociology*. New York: Cambridge University Press.

Smith, Charles W. 1982. "On the Sociology of Mind." Pp. 211–28 in *Explaining Human Behavior*, edited by Paul F. Secord. Beverly Hills: Sage.

Smith, Robert J., and Ella Lury Wiswell. 1982. *The Women of Suye Mura*. Chicago: University of Chicago Press.

Solomon, Susan Gross. 1983. "Pluralism in Political Science: The Odyssey of a Concept." Pp. 4–59 in *Pluralism in the Soviet Union*, edited by Susan Gross Solomon. London: Macmillan.

Sorokin, Pitirim A. 1937. *Social and Cultural Dynamics*, vol. 1. New York: American Books.

Stack, Carol. 1974. *All Our Kin*. New York: Harper and Row.

Stein, Burton. 1989. *A New Cambridge History of India: Vijayanagara*. Cambridge: Cambridge University Press.

Suppe, Frederick, ed. 1977. *The Structure of Scientific Theories*. 2d ed. Urbana: University of Illinois Press.

Takeo, Ito. 1988. *Life along the South Manchurian Railway*. Armonk, N.Y.: M. E. Sharpe.

Thurow, Lester. 1984. *Dangerous Currents*. New York. Vintage Books.

Tilly, Charles. 1981. *As Sociology Meets History*. New York: Academic Press.

———. 1984. *Big Structures, Large Processes, Huge Comparisons*. New York: Russell Sage Foundation.

Turner, Jonathan H. 1986. *The Structure of Sociological Theory*. 4th ed. Belmont, Calif.: Wadsworth Publishing Company.

Vaughan, Ted R. 1989. "Validity and Applied Social Science Research: A Theoretical Reassessment." *Journal of Applied Behavioral Science* 25:291–305.

Vaughan, Ted R., and Gideon Sjoberg. 1984. "The Individual and Bureaucracy: An Alternative Meadian Interpretation." *Journal of Applied Behavioral Science* 20:57–69.

———. 1986. "Human Rights Theory and the Classical Sociological Tradition." Pp. 127–41 in *Sociological Theory in Transition*, edited by Mark Wardell and Stephen P. Turner. Boston: Allen and Unwin.

Wallace, Ruth A., and Allison Wolf. 1986. *Contemporary Sociological Theory*. 2d ed. Englewood Cliffs, N.J.: Prentice-Hall.

Wallerstein, Immanuel. 1974. *The Modern World System: Capitalist*

Agriculture and the Origins of the European World-Economy in the Sixteenth Century. New York: Academic Press.

———. 1980. *The Modern World System II: Mercantilism and the Consolidation of the European World-Economy.* New York: Academic Press.

Weber, Max. 1930. *The Protestant Ethic and the Spirit of Capitalism.* London: Allen and Unwin.

———. 1949. *The Methodology of the Social Sciences.* New York: Free Press.

Weiner, Annette. 1976. *Women of Value, Men of Renown.* Austin: University of Texas Press.

Whyte, William Foote. 1984. *Learning from the Field.* Newbury Park: Sage.

Williams, Norma. 1989a. "Theoretical and Methodological Issues in the Study of Role Making." Pp. 167–84 in *Studies in Symbolic Interaction,* vol. 10, edited by Norman Denzin. Greenwich, Conn.: JAI Press.

———. 1989b. "Role Taking and the Study of Majority/Minority Relationships." *Journal of Applied Behavioral Science* 25:175–86.

———. 1990. *The Mexican American Family: Tradition and Change.* Dix Hills, N.Y.: General Hall.

Williams, Norma, Gideon Sjoberg, and Andrée F. Sjoberg. 1983. "The Bureaucratic Personality: A Second Look." Pp. 173–89 in *Bureaucracy As a Social Problem,* edited by W. Boyd Littrell, Gideon Sjoberg, and Louis A. Zurcher. Greenwich, Conn.: JAI Press.

Wilner, Patricia. 1985. "The Main Drift of Sociology between 1936 and 1984." *History of Sociology* 5:1–20.

Wilson, William Julius. 1987. *The Truly Disadvantaged.* Chicago: University of Chicago Press.

Wirth, Louis. 1928. *The Ghetto.* Chicago: University of Chicago Press.

Wolf, Eric R. 1982. *Europe and the People without History.* Berkeley: University of California Press.

Wright, Erik Olin. 1985. *Classes.* London: Verso.

Yin, Robert K. 1984. *Case Study Research: Design and Methods.* Beverly Hills: Sage.

Znaniecki, Florian. 1934. *The Method of Sociology.* New York: Farrar and Rinehart.

Howard M. Bahr and

Theodore Caplow

---

2 Middletown As an Urban Case Study

It is now six decades since the publication of *Middletown* pro-
pelled Muncie, Indiana, to national prominence as archetypical middle
America. Acclaimed by the critics, Robert and Helen Lynd's *Middletown*
became the first sociological best-seller of the century. Among its distinguished reviewers was H. L. Mencken, who commended the "highly diligent and intelligent snooping" that had produced this full-length portrait
of a normal American town, a portrait that was "one of the richest and
most valuable documents ever concocted by American sociologists."
Mencken was as impressed by the Lynds' methods as by their findings
and called for further applications: "My hope is that it [*Middletown*] will
be followed by other volumes of the same sort, for despite its scale it
leaves certain fields unexplored. . . . There is room . . . for many others,
general and regional. The American village deserves far more serious
study than it has ever got. The Southern cotton-mill town has never been
investigated adequately. The anthropology of Kansas waits for an
explorer."[1]

Middletown instantly became a kind of benchmark from which to
measure changes in the collective behavior of Americans. The Lynds
themselves made notable use of the benchmark, contrasting Middletown
during the Great Depression with the city they had observed a decade
earlier. On publication of their *Middletown in Transition* in 1937, *Life*

noted that numerous others had been busy studying Middletown as a specimen of American life: "For 12 years it has been surveyed, studied and talked about more than any other city in the world. Sociologists use it as a specimen, advertisers as a test tube."[2]

Middletowners continued to be consulted by journalists, graduate students, and market researchers, but there was no attempt to systematically replicate the Lynds' study of the entire city until 1976, when our Middletown III research team initiated an encounter with the city. Lasting for fourteen years, what began as a fairly straightforward replication has turned into an experience in long-term urban case history. Endurance, as the poet said, has fostered embrace. In writing the present essay, we have tried to understand that embrace a little better, clarifying for ourselves and our readers the reasons for expending so much time and thought on the study of one atypical, undistinguished Indiana city.

We approach the task in four stages. First, we reconsider two of Middletown's characteristics relevant to its utility as a case study of community change. Then we review the urban case study method, both ideally and with reference to Middletown. Third, we discuss some of the challenges and opportunities involved in this kind of research. Finally, we discuss our experience in Middletown and what we learned there.

Middletown As Urban and Atypical

We begin with two characteristics of Middletown that were obvious to the Lynds but sometimes overlooked by later commentators. First, Middletown is a *city*, not a town. Second, it is not typical of American cities.

MIDDLETOWN AS A CITY

Middletown was the first attempt to apply holistic ethnographic research to an American city,[3] and it is still the best-known ethnography of an American community. But the genre it inspired was largely concerned with small towns, and the *town* in the pseudonym *Middletown* made it easy to forget that this most famous of community studies was also one of the most ambitious. It tackled the complexity of an entire city, not a small town. That fact is submerged when Middletown is described as "the social world of the small town," "the town of Muncie," or "a normal American town of the third rate."[4] Middletown is an *urban* case study. It had a population of 39,000 when the Lynds did their original fieldwork in 1924–25. A decade later, when Robert Lynd returned to collect data for *Middletown in Transition*, it had grown to 47,000.[5] By 1941 it would qualify as a metropolitan area.

Yankee City, site of the second most famous American community study, was only one-third the size of Middletown in the mid-thirties when that study was under way and W. Lloyd Warner's staff did their fieldwork.[6] The sites of other well-known community studies were even smaller. Old City, the southern trade center of *Deep South*, had a population of 10,000,[7] and Jonesville (also known as Elmtown) had 6,200.[8] John Dollard's Southerntown, at about 2,500, was "just large enough to qualify under the census as an urban area,"[9] and Plainville had only about 1,000 inhabitants ("an estimated 275 nuclear families, plus many older people [living] alone").[10]

Later community studies continued the small-town tradition. Springdale's population included 1,000 in the village proper and 2,000 in the rest of the township.[11] Coal Town had a population of 2,300, and Appleton, the midwestern town "somewhere between Peoria and Dubuque," had 3,160.[12] The well-known studies of suburbia also treated smaller, simpler settings than Middletown. Park Forest's population in the mid-1950s was about 25,000; Crestwood Heights had 15,000 residents when it was studied, and Levittown about 12,000.[13]

Almost no one has followed the Lynds' lead in attempting to describe a modern city and chart its changes.[14] And even the study of small towns cannot be called thriving. Sociologists have yielded the field to historians and anthropologists.[15] The historian Richard Jensen concluded that the type of study exemplified by *Middletown* had virtually died out, and he urged historians to fill the void: "Intellectual styles in sociology changed, and Robert Lynd was overshadowed at Columbia by more theoretical and more quantitative sociologists who lost sight of the community midway between microscopic technical studies and grand macroscopic theories. . . . it is a task more suited for the historian to examine other cities—and yes, Muncie again—in the late nineteenth and early twentieth century to discover exactly how the process of modernization affected life in America." [16]

Middletown changed the way Americans viewed themselves. Whether the place was truly typical was beside the point; readers saw enough of themselves and their neighbors in the book to accept it as a mirror, despite the many ways that Middletown was *unlike* the rest of America. Norman Cousins, reviewing *Middletown in Transition*, described the city as "the least common denominator of contemporary American culture" and added, "It is America, and not Middletown alone, that is here revealed." [17] Earlier, Mencken had said that *Middletown* got "closer to the truth about the normal American than any other [account] I have ever heard of." [18]

The Lynds intended Middletown to be "as representative as possible of contemporary American life," but their criteria of representativeness were fairly arbitrary. They listed a temperate climate, a prairie location, a fairly rapid growth rate, and the absence of "outstanding peculiarities." They specified the city not be a college town or a satellite city, not be dominated by a single industry, and not have too many immigrants or blacks. This last criterion alone made Middletown stand apart from most other American industrial cities, but the Lynds did not want to deal with ethnic complexities while examining social and cultural change. They emphasized that Middletown was *not* typical but could be considered in some sense representative: "A typical city, strictly speaking, does not exist, but the city studied was selected as having many features common to a wide group of communities." [19]

Middletown was, and still is, quite extraordinary in some ways. The impetus for its early industrial growth was a sudden and spectacular gas boom. During the 1920s it was a hotbed of Ku Klux Klan activity. It had a "ruling family" of unusual wealth and influence.[20] It was a "demographic curiosity" in industrial America in having a labor force almost exclusively composed of native-born Protestant whites.[21] During the mid-1930s, it proved atypical in other ways: it weathered the depression better than most other American cities because one of its dominant industries was the production of glass jars for home canning, and it changed into a college town as its normal school grew to be a college and then a state university.

Sociology is a generalizing science, and the purpose of the Middletown III Project was to learn about processes common to many American cities by studying them in Middletown, where more exact measurement is possible. But we have had continually to remind ourselves that these processes always occur in particular contexts. Mencken might announce with Olympian oversight that most of the 143 American cities of Middletown's size were "as alike as peas in a pod,"[22] but no one who has systematically studied change in a living city would take his hyperbole seriously.

Three decades ago Maurice Stein concluded that there are *no* representative communities. Not only is every community study confined to a specific time and place, but the national or regional processes experienced in local settings are invariably modified by local conditions.[23] That is why local history is an essential part of the urban case study.

Unfortunately, the production of local history is expensive and time-consuming. Only under very favorable circumstances can Stein's advice that "every community study . . . start with a description of the social structure as this has changed over a period of time"[24] be given more than lip service. Among the major assets of Middletown as a research site are the extensive local history studies carried out by historians at Ball State University.[25]

The general paucity of urban case histories heightens the value of the Lynds' work and the importance of Middletown as a research site. Urban historians have to make do with surviving records and relics. They cannot return to the past and make direct observations. But for Middletown, we have two sets of direct observations taken fifty-five and sixty-five years ago. As far as we can tell, no other American city offers an equivalent foundation for the long-term study of social change.

The Urban Case Study Method

Before talking about the virtues and defects of the research strategy used in the Middletown studies, we will describe it in more detail. The strategy includes, but is not dominated by, participant observation in the tradition of Malinowski, "intensive field study extending over at least a year and preferably over several."[26] It also embodies the collection of both qualitative and quantitative data by any appropriate methods.

The resulting data are analyzed both diachronically and synchronically, for the city *is* change,[27] and it can be understood only in a comparative perspective. In the very first sentence of *Middletown*, the Lynds stated their intention "to study synchronously the interwoven trends that are the life of a small American city." Three pages later they spoke of viewing Middletown "in the light of the trends of changing behavior observable in it during the last thirty-five years."[28]

Another aspect of the Lynds' method—lightly developed in *Middletown*, more apparent in *Middletown in Transition*, and emphasized in Robert Lynd's *Knowledge for What?*—is the recognition of multiple contexts and levels of organization. The researcher pays attention to the city as a component of regional, national, or international systems; to both "internal" and "external" forces; to people's attitudes and beliefs; to the larger intellectual climate of the time; to the microcosm of family interaction and the macrocosm of international economics and international conflicts. Related to the alternation among levels is interdisciplinary work that combines the efforts of historians, anthropologists, sociologists, political scientists, geographers, city planners, and others.

In short, the urban case study seeks to grasp the characteristics of all major institutions in a city, the interconnections among these institutions, and their links to other systems and seeks to illuminate changes in all these characteristics over time. It emphasizes the reality of the city at the level of individual experience as well as at the level of collective representations. The ideal urban case study is necessarily replicative (of long duration, allowing for follow-up studies and the checking and rechecking of previous findings as well as extension into new areas), triangulative (or multi-operational, allowing the application of different research methods to common problems), and cumulative (thereby easing the confrontation with complexity by making it possible to draw on the resources of several cohorts of researchers).

Much as we cherish the case study as a method of procedure, we do not for a moment suppose that it can supersede the principal alternative method of social research, the analysis of statistical distributions and time series obtained from official statistics, sample surveys, administrative records, and other sources of quantitative data. Nor, for that matter, would we decry the use of rarer methods like experimentation, controlled observation, ethnomethodology, network mapping, or content analysis. The construction of social reality produces structures too intricate and multifaceted to be adequately described from any single perspective.

In the long run, social science, like most other science, requires the quantitative representation of phenomena, but to interpret the numbers in a table of occupational prestige or educational inequality, we need to reattach these abstract characteristics to living people and to interpret what they mean in context. In emphasizing that social characteristics or institutions cannot be properly understood without reference to the people who exhibit the characteristics and enact the institutional structures, we echo Robert Lynd's plea for a more realistic and responsible social science. In *Knowledge for What?*, a book based on lectures delivered just one year after the publication of *Middletown in Transition*, Lynd warned that overspecialization and excessive concern with statistical quantification prevented American social scientists from understanding the realities of their own culture.

He argued that much social research was irrelevant to the real problems of society. It was too removed from the lives of real individuals in real communities and too focused on isolated intellectual problems. In language that echoed his justification of in-depth, "vertical" case analysis in the preface to *Middletown in Transition*, Lynd called for holistic analysis, with attention to historical context as well as cultural patterns. In the earlier work, he had said that "social research seems . . . to make larger gains by digging vertically rather than by raking together the topsoil horizontally" and had described the Middletown study "as integrating scattered vertical research borings."[29]

In *Knowledge for What?*, Lynd defined culture as "all the things that a group of people inhabiting a common geographical area do, the ways they do things and the ways they think and feel about things, their material tools and their values and symbols." The social scientist's proper task was to understand American life in all its variety: "Here our science and technology are caught and held in focus with our economic and political institutions, our educational and familial systems, our values and desires, our symbols, and our illiteracies. And if such a concept is inclusive horizontally throughout every area of living, it is no less inclusive vertically in the historical sense, since it forces attention to the fact that we live by habits of thought and action generated in and shaped by many different eras."[30]

In addition to the broad array of contemporary institutions and culture and the historical processes that had produced them, Lynd returned again and again to the individuals whose lives were the enactment of the culture. Defining specific institutional problems in their total cultural context was not enough. Social scientists must also "take the further step of viewing culture as living in and operating as the learned habits and impulses of persons." Lynd continued:

> The emphasis upon persons as the active carriers, perpetuators, and movers of culture performs for us the indispensable service of resolving the dualism of "culture *and* the person," and of placing the primary emphasis where it basically belongs, upon people.
>
> ... culture *is* the patterned habits of behavior of individuals, who in their teaching and research *are* current social science theory in action.
>
> We watch culture change and say that "it changes." But culture does not "work," "move," "change," but is worked, is moved, is changed. It is *people* who do things, and when their habits and impulses cease to carry an institutional folkway, that bit of the culture disappears.
>
> The culture does not enamel its fingernails, or vote, or believe in capitalism, but people do, and some do and some do not.
>
> When culture changes—a new law is passed, a custom falls into disuse, women wear shorts, anti-Semitism becomes a problem, or automatic machinery replaces human labor—it is the behavior of people that provides the dynamics of change. Neither a "culture" nor a "society" learns, but individual people do.[31]

Lynd's emphasis on the individual was intended to enlarge, not to replace, the older type of study that abstracted cultural patterns from their day-to-day basis in individual activities and beliefs:

The explicit use of the concept "culture" compels overt recognition of the fact that all the jumbled details of living in these United States . . . are interacting parts in a single whole. . . . And our focus is further unified and sharpened by viewing the place where this patterned culture *is* and *lives* and *changes* as in the habits of thought, sentiment, and action of individuals, who in turn tend to impart their rhythms, growth processes, and motivations to each other, and thereby to the culture. Without disparaging the continuing utility of the older type of studies which view institutions *qua* institutions, these studies are now seen to be but *one* level of analysis. The approaches are complementary and each is therefore indispensable. The newer one will utilize the older for the sense of orientation and direction which analysis of large masses of data at the institutional level yields; and the older approach will draw new hypotheses for its theories of "value," "prices," "sovereignty," "social classes," "community," and "social change" from the effort to understand these abstractions in action in the cultural microcosms, living individuals.[32]

Our own view, which owes a heavy debt to the Lynds, is that the urban case study involves three concurrent research roles: (1) the field ethnographer, in the tradition of Malinowski or Franz Boas;[33] (2) the urban survey specialist, in the tradition of Charles Booth; and (3) the master of archival and document analysis, in the tradition of Emile Durkheim and Max Weber.

It may be that the method we have defined is rarely practiced because it demands too much of its practitioners. The city, as opposed to the small town, may be too complex for holistic description. In any case, long-term urban research must be team research, and those who attempt it must recognize that "mastering" their subject is in practice impossible. For example, part of the challenge is to consider the city as an entity functioning in a hinterland, a region, a nation, and a world social system. Some ethnographers of small communities have set out to explore the effects of extracommunity linkages, and one of the trends applauded by recent reviewers is "a movement away from the notion of community as a bounded, isolated, and self-sufficient place toward a concept of community as a dependent part of a larger system."[34] But every effort to take the larger system into account imposes additional burdens on research-ers, with the unsurprising result that

> while they are keenly aware of the penetrations of the larger systems
> into their subjects' lives as formative of culture itself, [they] do
> not challenge the convention of restricting ethnographic description
> to a delimited field site, or locale, and set of subjects. They still
> very much frame their research and writing in terms of knowable
> communities, to use Raymond Williams's phrase, the kind of setting
> in which, by definition, ethnographers have always worked. Yet
> the traditional holistic ambition of ethnography ... has pushed
> it in the direction of an equal concern with representing the large-
> scale historic processes of political economy themselves. At the cur-
> rent moment in this domain of experimentation, the reach of the
> interpretive/political-economy ethnography has exceeded its grasp,
> so to speak. That is, there are kinds of texts imagined that are not
> yet fully achieved.[35]

Cities are made more knowable by theories that specify what should and should not be taken into account. Middletown in the mid-1920s was made to seem more knowable by the Lynds' decision not to study the city's blacks; by their identification of two social classes rather than six or a dozen; by their decision to interview housewives rather than husbands; and by their heavy reliance on certain key informants and documents.

Such choices are unavoidable in social research. We mention them here to make the point that different observers—the other thirty-odd observ-ers necessary to capture Middletown according to the current ethno-graphic standards—would have made other choices, applied alternative concepts, chosen different informants, and relied on other written mate-rials. Muncie then was far more diverse than the Middletown the Lynds described. It is still more diverse today. It may not be objectively know-able at all. Still, we lament the neglect of these suggestions offered over thirty years ago by John Gillin:

> The great bulk of human behavior these days takes place in complex
> urbanized communities or in definite relationship to them. The civi-
> lizations of modern nation-societies and world areas, although ap-

parently conforming to the general laws of culture, are vastly more complicated than the cultures traditionally studied by field ethnologists. . . . Yet no one at present can claim, on the basis of scientific study at least, to understand and grasp these modern cultures in any way approaching the certainty and inclusiveness with which we know many a so-called simpler way of life. To be sure, there is on record a vast amount of data concerning the United States. . . . But this information is departmentalized and uncoordinated.[36]

Gillin called for less compartmentalization and more interdisciplinary work where diverse specialists combined their skills in common effort. He remarked that most researchers "need the better part of a life-time to acquire a specialized, detailed knowledge of only a small part of our or any other modern system of culture," and he concluded that "the understanding of modern complex cultures . . . can be achieved only as a cooperative venture involving all scientists and humanists concerned with human cultural behavior and its products."[37] A 1980 critique of contemporary anthropological and sociological research echoed Gillin's comments:

The rate of change has been so rapid and the new elements so many that the received paradigms of both fields have been seriously strained or have collapsed under unanticipated pressures . . . [and] more specific and frequently internal problems have limited resources and generated confusion in the attack on macro-issues of unprecedented size and complexity; professionals tend to perceive prior failures as evidence of the insoluble character of human group problems in the modern world. Not uncommon are retreats into ever-narrower specialization and preoccupation with the minutiae of technique.[38]

The urban case study method forces the investigator to confront rather than to retreat from complexity; it fosters multidisciplinary work, team effort, replication, and triangulation. It necessarily attends to history and ecology and to connections between local events and wider events. The genius of Charles Dickens, said Raymond Williams, was that his work "forced into consciousness" much about the experience of the city "that was important, and even decisive, [that] could not be simply known or simply communicated." The serious effort to master a city, via long-term case study, is likewise an experience in forced consciousness. Consider John Bennett and Seena Kohl's reflection on the personal consequences of their thirteen-year study of Jasper, Saskatchewan, and its environs: "We did what the subject matter required; hence we adopted and adapted a variety of analytical and theoretical tools from a variety of fields. . . . Perhaps, in the final analysis, this was the most anthropological aspect of all: our willingness to be eclectic and to learn everything there was to learn and to acquire the skills or knowledge necessary to learn it." [39]

Selected Problems in the Urban Case Study

Most of the problems encountered in an urban case study are those of social research in general. However, there are some unique problems of scale and duration associated with treating an entire city as a research subject. This is not the place for a full account of the problems in the Middletown III Project, but we do want to comment on several methodological issues: (1) case selection and generalization; (2) the conduct of "insider research"; (3) identifying cultural continuities via discontinuous fieldwork; (4) the question of whose viewpoint prevails; and (5) the problem of cost.

CASE SELECTION AND GENERALIZATION

A principal weakness of the case study method is the possibility that the case selected is, after all, less typical than the researcher assumes. In the social science case study, the investigator selects a particular social system and sequence of activities that presumably exemplify larger categories of systems and events. That is what distinguishes the work of the sociologist or anthropologist doing a case study from the conventional historian or biographer. The perpetual trap that hides behind that presumption is the possibility that the given case may be atypical in ways that matter and the investigator may not detect the deviation from the norm.

Although the scientific justification for case analysis is that a particular case represents some larger family of cases, the choice of cases is often fortuitous. Thus, most of the accounts in a collection of essays on long-term ethnographic research attribute the selection of the research site to a chance visit or encounter, an assignment to an area already being studied, or a funding opportunity.[40] The investigators's career and marital situation, ties to members of a local elite, and personal predilections have much to do with case selection, as do such events as the reaction of a village to an initial visit.[41]

The chosen case must be judged suitable for the work in question but *suitable* is a far cry from *ideal*. The question of how well the chosen case represents the designated family of cases is usually answered by assertion rather than evidence. Some researchers claim the question cannot be answered at all. Thus Herve Varenne said, "There is no way I can ascertain from my data alone the extension in time and space of the culture I have outlined." But he nevertheless asserted that his Appleton was "as good an example as any of American democratic life" and that he "saw there the best and truest America." Elvin Hatch simply declared that his California hamlet was typical: "Starkey is representative of other towns throughout America."[42]

Such forthright affirmation is in line with the Warner tradition of community study, as may be seen in Warner's foreword to *Democracy in Jonesville*:

> The city we call Jonesville was chosen because it satisfied the exacting requirements we had established. Jonesville, the City of the Common Man, is an actual place which we have come to know well. . . . Although we chose it above all other places for its particular qualifications for our study, we know that most other places, for purposes of evidence, might have done equally well. The Jonesvilles, Smithtowns, Greenfields, and *all the other -villes, -towns, and -fields of America are essentially alike.* Sometimes the road signs at their entrances say Dallas, Seattle, or maybe Indianapolis or Buffalo, or they might spell out Atlanta, Springfield, or Walla Walla, but *no matter what the signs say or how the alphabetical letters are arranged they still spell Jonesville.* No two American habitations are identical, but all of them, big or little, bear the strong family resemblance of the same parentage.
>
> Jonesville has been our laboratory for studying Americans. . . .

Borrowing from the Gospel of John, we can say that *Jonesville is in all Americans and all Americans are in Jonesville, for he that dwelleth in America dwelleth in Jonesville, and Jonesville in him. . . .*

To study Jonesville is to study America; it is a laboratory, a clinic, a field study for finding out what we are as a people and for learning why we think and feel and do the things we do.[43]

In the end, whether Jonesville or Appleton or Middletown is America or is only itself is a question that cannot be definitively answered. Moreover, the question may not matter much. The history of the first Middletown project is instructive in this regard.

John D. Rockefeller's Institute of Social and Religious Research had been planning a "small city study" for some time when they hired Robert Lynd as study director. He replaced the study's first director, the sociologist William Louis Bailey, who was terminated without notice "on the grounds that while he was a diligent soul he did not have the makings of a personable, insightful participant observer." Lynd was appointed in May 1923 and chose South Bend, Indiana—one of five cities Bailey had been considering—as the research site. In November, concerned about the complexities facing him, Lynd sought permission to limit the study to nonimmigrant whites in South Bend. "The interaction of the material and cultural trends in the city with our native psychology," he argued, was problem enough without having to deal with "the complicating factor of a psychology molded by a foreign environment." The committee accepted his reasoning but recommended that he find a smaller "white-American" city he could study in its entirety. In December, Lynd visited Decatur, Illinois, and Kokomo and Muncie, Indiana, and chose Muncie. A month later, he was on site.[44] Muncie had a sizable black population, but the Lynds maintained their focus on "white Americans" by excluding blacks from their data collection and analysis.

Questions of case selection and generalizability of findings are less compelling in a replication. For the Middletown III research team, the overriding consideration was simply that the Lynds had studied Middletown half a century before, a fact that perhaps made the place more atypical. We argued in the proposal to the National Science Foundation that there was a "priceless opportunity to advance our understanding of social and cultural change in the United States" because the baselines for studying social change in Middletown were unequaled anywhere else. For the purpose of replication, Middletown was more than suitable, it was the best site we could find. We confronted the issue of representativeness in an addendum to the proposal:

> Why does it seem so important to go back to Muncie and not to some other community? Precisely because it is so difficult to replicate a study of change in a socio-cultural system, it is highly desirable to preserve as many stable elements as possible. I do not feel challenged to prove that Muncie is as typical of American culture in 1975 as it was in 1925. It was not that typical then, if by typical we mean approximating national averages in the characteristics of its population and local institutions. It *was* typical in the sense of not being extreme on any salient characteristic. . . . In this sense, Muncie is still typical. . . . it continues to be unextraordinary in most respects and therefore a suitable specimen for the study of the American community. *And its participation in the larger society is so extensive that whatever we do find there is certain to have wider applicability.*[45]

Our faith that patterns observed in Middletown would have wider applicability was not unlimited. We were well aware of the danger of generalizing beyond the case; the proposal and most of the reports emanating from the project talked about Middletown, not America. Even so, in at least one respect—in overstating the persistence and solidarity of conventional family patterns—we seem to have yielded to the temptation to overgeneralize.

It is undeniable that the disintegration of conventional family patterns in the United States has been greatly exaggerated and mythologized. Nevertheless, we have concluded, on the basis of studies conducted since the publication of our *Middletown Families*, that the family structure of Middletown has been unusually resistant to the forces of change generated by the mass entry of married women with children into the labor market, the extension of individual control over conception, and the partial deregulation of sexual relationships.

Our present position, explicit in much of our work, is that Middletown is valuable *in and of itself* as a study of urban social change. Many of the trends observed there can be seen elsewhere. Whether a particular local trend is generalizable is an empirical question that can be answered only with data from elsewhere.

ON "INSIDER RESEARCH"

Despite a long line of ethnographic studies of modern America, the discussion of the advantages and drawbacks of doing ethnography in one's own society still goes on.[46] In one view, the results of such efforts are akin to "an ethnography of witchcraft as written by a witch."[47] Alternative positions are that anthropologists who bring their tools of discovery and analysis to bear on contemporary society are reacting responsibly to the "crisis" of our time,[48] or else are finally facing an overdue encounter with the self.[49]

Among sociologists, the study of one's own culture has always been considered legitimate, and disparities between the perspectives of the observer and those of the observed are regarded as data for analysis. Our experience as "insiders" observing Middletown revealed how misleading it can be to think of social research in an urban setting as involving observers and subjects, enthnographers and informants.

The following edited journal entry, combining aspects of our joint experience in Middletown, illustrates the essential ambiguity of labels like *observer* and *observed, insider* and *outsider*, or *citizen* and *transient* in this type of research.

It may be different in small towns, preliterate societies, or ethnic enclaves. But here, already, I belong. A city has oldtimers and newcomers, fixtures and transients. I have gradually moved into the solid middle between those extremes, part of the normal distribution of this normal city. Many people whom the Census Bureau would count as city residents moved here after I did. Shopping in the mall, standing in line for a movie, bidding at estate auctions, answering the market research questionnaire that came in the mail, visiting a sick neighbor, struggling to keep the lawn mowed, attending a church picnic, I am part of Middletown.

I am more permanent than many of the college students. We have purchased a home, and so will show up in the "permanent" structure of the city recorded in the Polk Directory. I have a local lawyer and physician, hold a library card, am locked into a mortgage, have a credit rating, belong to a credit union, and am a card-carrying member of the university community. My participation in religious activities serves the objectives of the local congregation as well as my own, and in that setting, and in matters of family, health, and household economics, I am participant first or entirely, observer occasionally and superficially.

I attend the junior high football game because my son is playing. The teacher I confront at PTA doesn't know or care about my occupation; to her, I represent "local parent," linked to her by a child disgorged from the bus each morning like all the other children she serves. My family's encounter with Middletown is real and permanent. The city is no specimen to my daughter, who will always write "Muncie, Indiana" as her birthplace. Once, I argued that "permanent" residents of the city were ill-equipped to do an ethnography of it. Now, hooked into gas lines and a water-softener contract, I too am a "member," my independence of judgment questionable.[50]

The ambiguity about whether participant observers in Middletown were studying their own or a different culture applied to the Lynds as well as to our replication of their work. Robert Lynd was born 140 miles south of Muncie in New Albany, Indiana. In 1935 he responded to criticism of his "East Coast sophisticate" point of view by emphasizing to a local reporter his Indiana roots and the culture he shared with Middletown: "No one is more conscious than I of the impossibility of avoiding some errors, at least of emphasis, in the difficult task of catching the complicated life of a city as dynamic as Muncie between the covers of a book. As a Hoosier born and bred, I was in a very real sense writing in *Middletown* about my own culture, and I am accordingly eager to get suggestions and criticisms."[51]

Looking back at their sojourn in Middletown, Helen Lynd remarked much later that her husband had been "completely at home there"; he had once told her that "he could have happily spent the rest of his life there."[52] The detached ethnographic tone that made *Middletown* such compelling reading was largely a literary device. On the basis of his reading of the project documents in the Rockefeller archives, Richard Fox gave the following account:

What the institute staff discovered as the Lynds' chapters rapidly accumulated in the spring of 1926 was that the "spiritual" focus of the study had been completely supplanted by what Robert Lynd now terms a "cultural" approach to Muncie. . . . Now Lynd was in effect building criticism and even satire right into the framework of his book, much as Veblen had done in *The Theory of the Leisure Class*. He was now posing as a "naive observer" who had happened upon Muncie the way Margaret Mead had just come upon Samoa. He had made his personal detachment from Muncie the cornerstone of his perspective. He had suddenly relativized, and therefore challenged, Muncie's entire mode of life even while refraining from outright fault-finding.[53]

Like any ethnographer, Lynd played a multiple role, sometimes true participant, sometimes participant for the sake of observation, sometimes observer more than participant. In the analysis and writing that followed the fieldwork, it was easier to take a detached view. Fox suggested that the biting cultural critique in *Middletown in Transition* had more to do with what had happened to Lynd in the interim since *Middletown* than with what happened to Muncie.[54]

IDENTIFYING CULTURAL CONTINUITIES
VIA DISCONTINUOUS FIELDWORK

Sometimes the ethnographer's problem is too much participation; sometimes it is too little. It can be very difficult for the temporary resident of a community to recognize unusual events. That is one reason ethnographers tend to underestimate the impact of outside influences on "their" community. Warner, for example, never took any account of how the depression affected social relations in Yankee City.

The Lynds and ourselves were partly immunized against this error by our obsession with social change, but we did not escape it entirely. As Ben Wattenberg pointed out in a documentary film on the Middletown III Project, much of what we found about industrial employment in 1976–78, when Middletown's industrial sector was relatively prosperous, was no longer applicable in 1982, when the local unemployment rate approached 20 percent and several of the largest local enterprises went bankrupt.[55]

There is a related tendency for the field-worker to identify those patterns observed during a first extended visit as more stable and fixed than the patterns that emerge later. Elizabeth Colson's critique of contemporary ethnography highlights this problem well:

> . . . a single field trip, even extending over several years, encourages a description that emphasizes homogeneity and the coercive influence of customary ways. And perhaps because we have not watched while members of the community grow dissatisfied with what they have and have not seen how they exert themselves to change their condition, we also overvalue the momentary state of affairs existent during our stay. We see ideal solutions in what the actors see as an unsatisfactory compromise or believe that there is a single formal solution which they are trying to achieve. Even though we focus upon change, we are likely to extrapolate trends from the fact that people behave differently at different points in time while overlooking the subtle forces that make for major shifts.[56]

It is hard not to assume that the things we first observed in a community were normal and customary in a way that later developments are not. Lengthy and repeated observations are a partial corrective to this kind of error, and Colson pointed to several long-term community studies that have yielded insights about the uneasy balance of continuity and change:

> We have learned that we cannot understand [these societies] unless we pay a great deal of attention to political and economic decisions that take place at the national and international level and that we flounder when we define our population in terms of a local area. We have had to break with the idea that social or cultural systems are homeostatic systems, but we do not yet have any idea of what kind of systems we are dealing with. . . . But we have also learned that peoples and cultures are tougher than we thought and able to cope with change. The people we work with value customary ways only in so far as these help them to attain their ends and so their culture is continually at test. As is our own.[57]

WHOSE VIEWPOINT PREVAILS? THE RESEARCHER'S INABILITY TO TRANSCEND TIME, LOCATION, AND SOCIETY

The question of observer bias in community studies hardly requires further documentation, having been endlessly discussed by ethnographers who recognize that the selection of any point of observation necessarily distorts one's view of a culture and that the mental furniture of both observers and subjects determines what is seen and how it is interpreted. Let us briefly consider each of these points.

Occupying Any Social Position Obscures the View from Other Positions. The investigators move into the community and acquire a friendship network that immediately limits their access to people who are socially distant from their friends and that endows them with the prejudices of their friends. What is worse, the friends are never selected at random. To assure entrée, investigators entering a local society seek out persons of high status, and when entrée has been gained, they find themselves to be courtesy members of the local elite and constrained to share the interests and prejudices of their hosts.

The Lynds, for all their efforts to achieve a comprehensive view, were dramatically trapped by this kind of involvement. Among their main sources were three members of the local business class—a physician, a banker, and a realtor—who met weekly with Robert Lynd for "dinner and discussion." Three other key informants were the Lynds' "loquacious landlord," a "radical schoolteacher," and "one of the three socialists in town, who went so far as to steal unidentified documents from his employer for the Lynds' use." Fox called these people "ordinary Middletowners,"[58] but the schoolteacher and the socialist hardly represent the city's mainstream. In addition, Lynd had a close and continuing conversation with a member of the leading Y family and perhaps for that reason stayed aloof from the rival X family, so much so that many years afterward members of the X family complained to us that Lynd had written a book about their grandfathers without ever interviewing them.

Finally, Robert Lynd made extensive use in his second Middletown study of a paper by Lynn Perrigo, a long-term resident of Muncie then doing graduate work in history at the University of Colorado. Perrigo had critiqued *Middletown* and had done some research of his own on what he thought were the Lynds' omissions. His residence in Muncie during the 1920s and early 1930s made him familiar with some of the "backstage" aspects of the town. Having learned Lynd was returning for a follow-up study, Perrigo sent him a copy of the paper and gave him permission to use it. A comparison of Perrigo's paper with the text of *Middletown in Transition* shows Perrigo's work to have had a considerable influence on the book and a particularly strong influence on the famous chapter about the X family.[59]

Our own experience in Middletown was similarly influenced by a network of friends and associates whose viewpoints are overrepresented in our work. Unlike the Lynds, we were from the outset associated with Ball State University, where we held courtesy appointments. We also recruited much of our staff from the students of that institution. We were closely associated with several faculty members. In particular, we drew heavily on Dwight W. Hoover's encyclopedic knowledge of Muncie's history and on his network of local friends and associates (Hoover later helped to create the Center for Middletown Studies at Ball State and became its director). We were also influenced by other members of the university faculty, several of whom collaborated with us in research proposals, cooperated in data collection and analysis, and generously critiqued our work. We came to be especially indebted to Whitney Gordon, then the chairman of the Sociology Department and himself the author of an interesting book about Middletown,[60] and to John D. Hewitt, whose friendship with Bahr and Chadwick antedated the project by several years and who became a full member of the research team, in addition to his continuing responsibilities at the university.

Like the Lynds, the Middletown III researchers also had their share of ties to atypical Middletowners outside the university community. Bahr and Chadwick became personally involved in the local Mormon congregation, and Caplow in the Episcopal; neither of these denominations looms large in Middletown. Caplow had a pilot's license, and his comings and goings generated a set of acquaintances among flyers who used Middletown's airport. Bahr and Chadwick purchased a home in a nearby suburb, thereby acquiring the commuter's perspective.

The Emic-Etic Issue. This dilemma, so much discussed by anthropologists, becomes a personal problem for the investigator who is a participant observer.[61] The issue is whether one describes the world of the subjects as they interpret it (emics) or according to the conceptions of the observer (etics): "The question of whether a construct is emic or etic depends on whether it describes events, entities, or relationships whose physical locus is in the heads of the social actors or in the stream of behavior. In turn, the question of whether or not an entity is inside or outside some social actor's head depends on the operations employed to get at it."[62]

The investigator has not only the problem of deciding whether to substitute his or her own interpretation of local events for interpretations by natives but the additional problem of not being able to distinguish very clearly between the two. Indeed, the investigator is likely to hold concurrently to interpretations acquired by virtue of his or her local roles and to other interpretations that arise from the theoretical framework with which he or she came equipped.

There is likely to be some incongruity between the customary ways that observers perceive social change and the orientations of their subjects. Cultures order external events in accustomed patterns, and so people see "progress," "decline," "growth," or "cycles" as their myths and metaphors suggest.[63] Observers and subjects alike are influenced by the prevailing myths. For instance, the cultural myth of the declining family affects the way Middletown people evaluate their own experiences as family members,[64] and it also influences the way investigators interpret reports of those experiences.

The problem is compounded by the fact that the researcher must rely on informants for accounts of events, and sometimes those accounts are "translated" *by the informant* into the researcher's (perceived) framework or into some (perceived) mutually shared framework. In other words, "informants may provide either etic or emic descriptions of the events they have observed or participated in,"[65] and both informants and observers may confound or combine points of view as they interact. The longer and more intense the interaction, the more difficult it becomes to separate the perspectives of observer and informant.

To the sociologist, all of these processes take place in a context where

(1) everyone has a unique experience and a more or less unique point of view; (2) no point of view is a priori more real, accurate, or worthy of study than any other; (3) everyone misses much of what is "actually" going on; and (4) each observation or communication process—between observer and informant, between researcher and colleague, between writer and reader—carries an appreciable probability of distortion.

THE HIGH COST OF THE URBAN CASE STUDY

Studies of this kind are expensive, involving as they do the simultaneous utilization of a variety of time-consuming procedures. There is an intrinsic disparity between the complexity of the city as an object of study and the limited resources ordinarily available for urban research.

The multiplicity of urban processes is mirrored in the research program. It is necessarily multi-method, multi-investigator, and multi-disciplinary and must cope with multiple levels of organization and multiple eras.

The multi-disciplinary approach is essential. The perils of amateur scholarship in someone else's specialty are well illustrated by the collapse of the superficial and erroneous histories of Yankee City[66] and Middletown[67] sketched by Warner and the Lynds, respectively. But the benefits of interdisciplinary collaboration do not come cheaply. Someone has to pay the historians, the statisticians, the archivists, the educators, and the economists whose efforts are essential to an urban case study.

The Lynds selected Middletown in the belief that it was "compact and homogeneous enough to be manageable in . . . a total-situation study." They emphasized that they were studying a city, not a town, and had picked one in the 25,000–50,000 class so that it "would be large enough to have put on long trousers and to take itself seriously, and yet small enough to be studied from many aspects as a unit."[68]

The Lynds used virtually every data collection method known to social scientists at the time, including participant observation, the examination of documentary materials, the compilation of statistics, content analysis, the analysis of census reports, interviewing, and questionnaire surveys. They compiled demographic projections, traced banking trends, analyzed employment statistics, ransacked federal reports, read student research papers, studied hospital records, and counted library books. In fact, what distinguishes the first two Middletown studies from much of the subsequent community research was the lesser reliance of the later studies on hard data. Compare, for example, the statistical underpinnings apparent in the footnotes, tables, and statistical appendixes of *Middletown* and *Middletown in Transition* with the virtual absence of such material in *Democracy in Jonesville, Small Town in Mass Society*, or *Americans Together*.[69]

The small scale of recent community studies reflects a growing realization of just how unmanageable as object of study a city can become. Later investigators were much less ambitious than the Lynds. Among the criteria leading Herman Lantz and his associates to select Coal Town for study was that the population was "sufficiently small [population 2,300] so that the community could be studied intensively." Appleton was appropriate for Varenne's year of fieldwork because, among other things, its population of 3,160 made it "of a size that could be encompassed by one investigator." Elliot Liebow originally intended to produce several ethnographies of one-block urban enclaves during his year of fieldwork but found the social worlds of street-corner men on a single urban intersection interesting enough to occupy his entire time.[70] A review of case studies of American culture lists scores of such small-scale studies: neighborhoods, small towns, local ethnic communities.[71] One looks in vain for efforts to capture a larger community, as the Lynds tried to do.

Another weakness of the urban case study method is the necessity of collecting a huge mass of data to be analyzed, analysis that funding agencies are reluctant to pay for. In thirty months of continuous fieldwork in Middletown, we gathered enough data for perhaps a decade of analysis. In twelve years of sporadically funded effort since that time, we have accumulated much more.

Middletown III: Methods, Findings, Lessons

Our principal interest is in social change in the United States. Like our predecessors, we had no direct interest in Muncie. Caplow had been there only once, for an afternoon, before we did the study; none of us had relatives there or any close ties to that part of the world. But for the study of social change, Muncie had the incomparable advantage of the earlier benchmarks provided by the Lynds' work and a number of later studies.

DOING MIDDLETOWN: REFLECTIONS ON METHOD

While a student at Columbia University, Caplow was converted from historical to sociological studies by a chance encounter with Robert Lynd. Lynd encouraged him to leave Columbia University for Chicago, then the leading center for training in sociological research, and Caplow took his advice. By coincidence, Caplow joined the Columbia faculty in 1960, when Lynd retired, and was assigned Lynd's old office. Some time after that, when a graduate student proposed to do a small-scale follow-up of the Middletown studies, Caplow asked Lynd for his blessing and was surprised to hear that Lynd, then in his late seventies and in poor health, still planned to do such a study himself. From then on, the project was never completely forgotten.

Lynd died in 1970 without having returned to Middletown. Meanwhile, Caplow and Bahr had begun a period of active research collaboration, which has now lasted for twenty-five years. When the last of a series of projects on homelessness came to an end around 1974, Caplow and Bahr discovered that the long-discussed Middletown research was next on their list. Another long-term collaborative effort had begun in 1968, when Bahr and Chadwick had begun working together. The three jointly designed the Middletown III Project in 1974. Since that time, we have worked together on half a dozen other research assignments. Although the funding for our combined Middletown effort ended in 1982, our commitment to Middletown research continues. No end is in sight.

The execution of the project involved elaborate moves by all three principals, each of whom temporarily deserted his home and colleagues to live for a while in Muncie. We were accompanied by our families and by student assistants and their families. Among us, we enrolled nine children in Muncie's public schools. The total site time was calculated to match that of the Lynds, and a local staff of associate investigators, assistants, and clerks was recruited. The project office occupied a small building at the edge of the business district.

One of the most agreeable features of the project was that it attracted collaborators from Muncie's university, from our home universities, and from half a dozen other institutions. Altogether twenty-four postdoctoral scholars, and about the same number of students, contributed to the project at one time or another. More than fifty scholarly publications based on Middletown III data have appeared, and new ones are still being added.

The excitement and interest of this replication was enhanced for us by the fact that we were just in time to establish relationships with people who had participated as informants or advisers in the original 1924–25 study.

In accord with that study, which we tried to replicate faithfully, we used an extremely wide range of research methods, including interview surveys, mail surveys, network interviewing, participant observation, ecological mapping, the collection of documents, the recording of public events, the gathering of life histories and oral histories, the content analysis of newspapers, the extraction of statistical series from local records, the examination of school curricula and administrative practices, the review of federal programs, and the examination of nineteenth-century census records and of twentieth-century census tract data. If we had it to do over again, we would probably extend rather than restrict this array of methods. For example, we might have done more with the counting of artifacts, services, and facilities; the mapping of mobility patterns; and the tracing of organizational change. We have not yet analyzed all of the material we did collect, but all things considered, we are not dissatisfied with the procedure of casting as wide a data-collection net as possible.

It is, so to speak, a serendipitous benefit that in the process we, like the Lynds, developed a moderately full ethnography of Middletown as a local community. That ethnography has proved useful to Middletown, and it accounts for the enormously favorable reception our work had in the community itself. Middletown III enjoyed much better press than had Middletown I five decades earlier. Community reaction ranged from mildly favorable to enthusiastic, and before the project ended, a locally funded Center for Middletown Studies had come into existence to encourage further social science interest in the community.

After only a few months of fieldwork we realized that we were likely to collect more data than we could analyze. However, from the outset we had had the secondary objective of accumulating baseline material for future studies of social change in Middletown. During the full-time fieldwork we thought, "If we don't collect the data now, it may be lost for-ever." That sense of urgency drove us to pay more attention to accumu-lation than to analysis and writing. The rule of thumb for the scheduling of social research—that equal time be allotted to data gathering, to analysis, and to writing up the results—was more honored in the breach than in the observance.

Caplow gave warning at a 1977 staff meeting. The warning proved prophetic:

> It's expensive and difficult and time consuming to have to include what you *know* you're going to need. To include anything you *think* you might need is just frivolous, because there's no end. We could get data from now until doomsday, but we have to make them con-tribute to finished products. And the way you do that is to analyze the data you have and see where it leads you and what new questions are given priority by the analysis. In a sense, any kind of research operation, any intellectual operation, consists to a large extent in correcting your own excesses as you go along, and there's no other way to do it. If you find you spend too much time on the theories, you say "All right, that's enough, let's stop; let's get some empirical data." Here we find that we've been spending too much time on data gathering, not because we did it wrong, but because we've suddenly arrived at the point where you begin to weigh the pile of data we already have provided for and the man-hours necessary to get it ana-lyzed and down in some useful form. You begin to see that right now we ought to shut [down] as much as we can—it seems to me we can do that in some things—that we ought to shut the data door and start the mill turning, to grind into findings. Otherwise, you have big heaps of data sitting out there spoiling in the rain.[72]

The creation of the Center for Middletown Studies has meant that there is a repository where unanalyzed or semianalyzed data can be pre-served and made available to other scholars. As a result, the unanalyzed data have not entirely spoiled in the rain; some have aged quite nicely. We are still concerned about seeing that the center keep data that may be useful to future scholars, even though we ourselves will never be able to analyze these data. We now realize that an urban case study, on the scale we conceived, requires far more resources than were ever available to our team. It is not, however, beyond the capability of the community of researchers using the facilities of the Center for Middletown Studies. The creation of that center provided a partial solution to two of the perennial problems in long-term research, namely who shall preserve the accumulation of data when the original researchers have passed on, and how shall "new blood" be recruited to carry on the work.[73]

ILLUSTRATIVE FINDINGS, SUBSTANTIVE AND THEORETICAL

Theoretical Issues. Historically, single cases have been used far more often than have statistical series to illuminate basic theoretical issues in sociology. But one is not likely to extract theoretically interesting results from a study that lacks clear theoretical intentions. Initially, the Middletown III study was rather tightly focused on the key concepts of modernization, stratification, and alienation and on their interrelationships.

We derived these concepts from the original Middletown study, although they had perhaps more salience for us than for our predecessors. For various reasons, we did not pursue certain theoretical lines that were of special interest to the Lynds, such as the nonsynchronous impact of cultural change on subgroups of the population or the use of ideology to secure business-class domination. Some of these issues had lost their relevance during the long interval between the studies. We learned a great deal about the theoretical issues on which we did focus, and some of what we learned was new and interesting. For example, we were able to show that the convergence of social classes with respect to life-styles and the lowering of the barriers between the community's two major classes did not imply any net reduction in economic or social inequality. This finding provides useful hypotheses for the study of social inequality in the United States as a whole.

Perhaps the most important contribution of Middletown III to sociological theory was to improve our understanding of social change in modern industrial societies. The model of social change we developed has been set forth in detail elsewhere,[74] but three features of it deserve particular notice. First, institutional change turns out to be more discontinuous than is generally imagined, with abrupt and rapid changes followed by long periods of apparent stability. Second, rapid change in one institutional sector does not imply or require rapid change in other institutional sectors; the former is more likely to inhibit the latter. And third, there appears to be no invisible hand or functional imperative that requires social and cultural changes to be consistent, cumulative, or interdependent. The effects of a given innovation or of an environmental shift or of a change in market conditions must be discovered empirically. They cannot be inferred a priori. This means, among other things, that statements of general cultural tendencies (e.g., increased permissiveness, attitudinal volatility, the weakening of traditions, the disappearance of inequalities, or the acceleration of social change) are not likely to stand the test of empirical evidence either in a local community or in the larger society.

Substantive Findings. We have mentioned above some of the theoretical insights developed by the Middletown III study. On a somewhat lower level of abstraction, we have been able to develop a reasonably complete picture of social and cultural change in Middletown between 1890 (the Lynds selected that year as the retrospective baseline for the original study) and the 1980s (our most recent Middletown survey was completed in 1988). Moreover, with the help of the historian Alexander Bracken, we are able to go back beyond the Lynds' 1890 baseline, as far as 1850, for information on demography, family composition, occupational distribution, and some aspects of inequality.[75] Because the Lynds were among the earliest sociologists to use sample surveys to elicit the attitudes and practices of a population, we are in some cases able to compare the responses to identical questions presented to similar samples in similar contexts more than sixty years apart.

The results are too extensive to be easily summarized, but there are scores of individually interesting findings. To take a few examples almost at random, we discovered that the movement of married women into the labor force between the 1920s and the 1980s was a phenomenon essentially limited to business-class women. Their labor force participation rose from virtually nothing to almost 60 percent, whereas the labor force participation of working-class women rose only fractionally to achieve the same level. We were also able to show for Middletown that the enormous increase in television viewing in the postwar period was accompanied with an increase in the time adults devoted to reading and in the proportion of that time given to serious books.

Among other counterintuitive findings were the discoveries that both the form and the content of religious experience have remained virtually unchanged among Middletown Protestants from 1890 to the present; that the generation gap between parents and adolescent children has not been widening and may indeed have narrowed; and that kinship networks, rather than class or occupational affiliation, now provide the essential ligaments of community solidarity. Along with the persistence of many traditional attitudes, there has been a remarkable decline in ethnic hostility and religious bigotry.

Perhaps the most interesting aspect of our work, which goes beyond the consideration of the community as a specimen of the larger society, is our investigation of the entire matrix of interaction between the local community and the larger society. We gave particular and prolonged attention to "the federal presence," which in sixty years increased from a few postal employees and the occasional visit of a U.S. marshal to scores of federal agencies and programs impinging on nearly every aspect of local life. Today the federal presence engages nearly every household in a complex web of financial transactions. The mass media, especially television, are another form of outside influence to which Middletown residents are exposed for the larger part of their discretionary time. The effects of these intrusions have not yet been charted in equal detail for any other American community so far as we know and cannot be adequately treated in any other methodological mode.

Reflections on Long-Term Urban Research. We have learned that you cannot *know* a city of 77,000 people, or for that matter of 39,000, by living in it for a year or two and speaking the language well. Our observations, guided though they were by the observations of our talented predecessors, were necessarily superficial. We did not have the resources to learn as much about any corner of Middletown as William Whyte learned about street-corner society or Liebow about Tally's corner.[76] We would like to see a series of ethnographies of subcultures and subcommunities *within* Middletown. Some day, perhaps . . .

The list of important undone studies is depressingly long. Among the unwritten volumes that we consider essential to a proper sociological-anthropological-historical understanding of Middletown are the following:

— A Social History of Middletown (Dwight Hoover has proposed this but has yet to find funding)
— The College and the Community: The Reciprocal Influence of Middletown and Its State University in the Twentieth Century
— Middletown in Context: A Functional Analysis of Middletown in Relation to Other Indiana Cities and Towns
— Education in Middletown: Local Control in the Midst of State and Federal Influence
— Minorities in Middletown: Ethnic Relations in the Context of the Civil Rights Movement and Its Aftermath
— The Federal Presence and Its Consequences for Middletown
— The Changing Balance of Leisure and Work in Middletown
— Sin and Ignorance: Middletown Responds to Its Social Problems

The list could be extended almost indefinitely. Each additional study increases the utility of Middletown as a specimen of American society to be examined under high magnification.

One model of long-term research is the lifelong effort of a lone scholar; another is the team approach, in which a handful of committed professionals recruit the specialized collaborators needed for present and future work. Still another model is the permanent research site, where the resources and opportunities are sufficient to attract a diversity of talented and energetic people to pursue their own interests within the framework of an accumulated body of work.

When we began the Middletown III Project, efforts to study Middletown represented a combination of the lone scholar and the team approach. By now, the accumulation of previous work and usable data about the city seems to have reached the appropriate point for the permanent research site model. There is already an abundance of specialized studies of Middletown: a recent bibliography on "Muncie as Middletown"—that is, studies that refer to the Lynds' work in one way or another or to subsequent efforts that treat the city as a specimen—contains almost eight hundred entries.[77] In addition, there is an extensive literature on Muncie (*not* Middletown) that does not appear in the bibliography;

there are scores of relevant theses and dissertations, hundreds of government documents, shelves of educational records, and numerous biographies, autobiographies, and organizational histories. Already the *literature*, not merely the accumulated data, on Muncie is becoming too extensive to master.

Let us repeat a plea made not long ago to students of another "Middleplace," Mesoamerica, that they not multiply disconnected studies but rather tie some of the existing work together. "Perhaps the greatest need," wrote Erve Chambers and Philip Young after reviewing more than fifty book-length community studies published in the previous decade, "is for comprehensive, analytic studies of the available literature. . . . We need analytic studies of the genre of community study and of the results of community study research. . . . These analyses should include study of the available literature and an assessment of the methods and traditions of scholarship employed."[78]

The plea for contemplation and consolidation fits Middletown as well as Mesoamerica. It is still true, as Robert Lynd said, that digging vertically is generally more profitable than horizontal raking. Thanks to the past efforts of hundreds of researchers, good vertical work is easier to do in today's Middletown and promises more valuable results than ever before.

Notes

1. Mencken, "A City in Moronia," 379, 381.
2. Bourke-White, "Muncie Ind.," 15.
3. We must note the priority of W. E. B. DuBois's *The Philadelphia Negro* (1899), an exhaustive account of the characteristics and living conditions of the 8,900 black Philadelphians living in the city's Seventh Ward in 1896–97. DuBois combined survey data from house-to-house canvassing with "such official statistics and historical matter as seemed reliable," supplemented by interviews with informed persons and by personal observation. He "attended their meetings, their churches, their business, social and political gatherings, visiting their schools and institutions, and, most important of all, conducting a house-to-house visitation in their families, through which he came in personal contact with over ten thousand Negro inhabitants of the city" (vii–viii, 1–2, 58). DuBois's work was patterned after Charles Booth's *Life and Labour of the People in London* (1889–1903) and surveys of Chicago neighborhoods associated with Jane Ad-

dams's Hull House. It reflected the research procedures of reform-minded sociologists rather than the anthropological tradition.

4. Szacki, *History of Sociological Thought*, 454; Bell and Newby, *Community Studies*, 82; Mencken, "A City in Moronia," 379.

5. Lynd and Lynd, *Middletown in Transition*, 517.

6. Warner and Lunt, *Social Life*. Unlike Middletown and the country as a whole, Yankee City did not grow. It lost population between 1920 and 1940, dropping from 15,618 to 13,916. Its 1980 population of 15,900 barely surpassed the 1920 figure. Over the same period, Middletown's population more than doubled, rising to 77,216 in 1980.

7. Davis, Gardner, and Gardner, *Deep South*, 3.

8. Warner et al., *Democracy in Jonesville*, ix; Hollingshead, *Elmtown's Youth*, 59.

9. Dollard, *Caste and Class*, 2.

10. Gallaher, *Plainville Fifteen Years Later*, 13–14; West, *Plainville, U.S.A.*

11. Vidich and Bensman, *Small Town in Mass Society*, 15.

12. Lantz, *People of Coal Town*, 3; Varenne, *Americans Together*, 1, 19.

13. Whyte, *Organization Man*, 313; Seeley, Sim, and Loosley, *Crestwood Heights*, 437; Gans, *Levittowners*, 22.

14. The most notable exception to this generalization is Drake and Cayton's (1945) *Black Metropolis*. It drew on two decades of urban research by sociologists at the University of Chicago, supplemented by extensive ethnographic fieldwork under W. Lloyd Warner's direction and WPA funding. Chicago's black community was chosen for study because Warner wished to compare the situation of blacks in a rapidly changing, complex metropolitan area with black-white relations as observed in Davis, Gardner, and Gardner's *Deep South*. *Black Metropolis* is a monumental example of the urban case study method, "the classic study of urban Negro life." It represents the combination of the best sociology and anthropology of its time, portraying, in the words of Richard Wright's introduction, the most intensely scrutinized community of the most "known" city in the world. It is a model of long-term, well-financed, cumulative research. "Its like may not be produced again," said Everett Hughes, in part because "it took a New Deal to mobilize the small army of able young social scientists who did the footwork that made the book possible" (Drake and Cayton, *Black Metropolis*, xviii–xix, xxxvii, xl, 776–77). The entire "Chicago as urban laboratory" effort of Robert Park and his associates at the University of Chicago might also be cited as an exception. Consider, for example, Peter Hall's characterization of their work as a joining of the techniques of mass social observation developed by Charles Booth and his collaborators with the theoretical traditions of German sociology "to work towards a total understanding—based on theory, tested by observation—of the social structure of a great city" (*Cities of Tomorrow*, 366). Of course, the Chicago School did not follow the Lynds' lead but was rather a parallel and much more massive development.

15. In the past three decades, American anthropologists have shown increased interest in American culture. There are scores of case studies of small communities, ethnographic examinations of specific institutions and cultural settings, or particularistic analyses of single contexts (see, for example, Spindler and Spindler, "Anthropologists View American Culture"). Contemporary urban anthropology is heavily ethnographic and largely focused on small-scale settings rather than holistic urban analysis in the tradition of the Lynds.

16. Jensen, "The Lynds Revisited," 318–19.

17. Cousins, "The World in Books," 2.

18. Mencken, "A City in Moronia," 379.

19. Lynd and Lynd, *Middletown*, 3, 7–8.

20. The Lynds describe the family at length in the most famous chapter of *Middletown in Transition*, but they knew of the family's influence shortly after moving to Middletown in 1925. Robert Lynd said that if he had known about the "X" family before moving his research team to Middletown, he would have chosen some other city because he recognized that they made Middletown atypical. However, "by the time he had grasped their commanding role in town, he claimed, the research team was already in place" (Fox, "Epitaph for Middletown," 135). Robert Lynd's choice of an atypical city was purposive and in contrast to the approach of the Chicago School, "with various members of which he conferred several times in December [1923] and January [1924]. The Chicago sociologists studied the ethnically mixed city because it was typical of modern society. Lynd agreed that it was typical and self-consciously selected the atypical, traditional, vanishing Protestant town—for him the locus of inherited virtue and 'spiritual energy'"(ibid., 119).

21. Jensen, "The Lynds Revisited," 306.

22. Mencken, "A City in Moronia," 379.

23. Stein, *The Eclipse of Community*, 94, 98–99.

24. Ibid., 103.

25. See, for example, Frank, "Politics in Middletown"; Bracken, "Middletown As a Pioneer Community"; Holmes, "A History of Professional Nursing Education"; Hoover, Hewitt, and Kirchner, "Crime and Mental Illness"; Hoover, "To Be a Jew"; and Szopa, "Images of Women."

26. Colson, "Culture and Progress," 269.

27. We like Rodney Stark's emphasis of this point in his excellent introductory text: "A city is not an enduring physical structure, despite its permanent appearance. Instead, *a city is as much a process as a structure: It is constantly changing*" (*Sociology*, 576).

28. Lynd and Lynd, *Middletown*, 3, 6.

29. Lynd and Lynd, *Middletown in Transition*, ix.

30. Lynd, *Knowledge for What?*, 20.

31. Ibid., 25, 37, 38, 39, 46.

32. Ibid., 50–51.

33. The anthropological paradigm is memorably portrayed by Anthony F. C. Wallace: "Whether accurately or not, one thinks of Franz Boas stepping off the boat in an Eskimo village with his suitcase in hand, preparing for a long stay in residence. This image *is* the paradigm: the subsequent development of field techniques, standards of ethnographic description, ethnological theory, and training requirements for the Ph.D. stem from, and are implied by, the symbol of Boas as lone fieldworker taking up prolonged residence in a small community" (*Rockdale*, 479).

34. Spindler and Spindler, "Anthropologists View American Culture," 49.

35. Marcus and Fischer, *Anthropology As Cultural Critique*, 90.

36. Gillin, "Application of Anthropological Knowledge," 24.

37. Ibid., 28–29.

38. Record, "Anthropology and Sociology," 29.

39. Williams, *The Country and the City*, 165; Bennett and Kohl, "Longitudinal Research," 105.

40. Foster et al., *Long-Term Field Research*.

41. Relevant to the issue of "insider research" in community study, which we take up later, is Wolcott's statement that a major difference between doing ethnography "at home" and doing research in more exotic settings is that at home, "time, place, and focus have always been relatively subject to my control." In contrast were his more traditional ethnographic efforts: "There, serendipity played a bigger role—I have set out for places at periods of time largely determined by others (personal contacts influenced the choice of region, institutional calendars determined when I should depart and return) and with my research purposes defined in the broadest of terms" ("Home and Away," 256).

42. Varenne, *Americans Together*, xii, 229; Hatch, *Biography of a Small Town*, 10.

43. Warner et al., *Democracy in Jonesville*, ix (emphasis added).

44. Fox, "Epitaph for Middletown," 112–13, 117–19.

45. Caplow, letter to Donald Ploch (emphasis added).

46. See, for example, Chock, "Irony and Ethnography," and Aguilar, "Insider Research."

47. Geertz, *Local Knowledge*, 57.

48. Goldschmidt, "Anthropology and the Coming Crisis," 300.

49. Messerschmidt, *Anthropologists at Home*, 14.

50. Bahr, personal journal, 1976.

51. Fox, "Epitaph for Middletown," 129–30; Lynd's statement was originally published in the *Muncie Evening Press*.

52. Ibid., 119–20.

53. Ibid.

54. Ibid. Anthropologists have lately become self-conscious about writing as an essential part of the ethnographic process. Some contemporary analysts would

see Lynd's adoption of naive outsider status as a literary device, to be considered along with his observations, and perhaps as more important than the observations, as a component of the "reality" of Middletown. Consider, for example, Van Maanen's point that "a culture or a cultural practice is as much created by the writing (i.e., it is intangible and can only be put into words) as it determines the writing itself" (*Tales of the Field*, 6). See also Clifford and Marcus (*Writing Culture*) and Geertz (*Works and Lives*), who concluded, "Once ethnographic texts begin to be looked *at* as well as through, once they are seen to be made, and made to persuade, those who make them have rather more to answer for" (138). At bottom, Geertz said, the idea that ethnographic description accurately represents social reality is pretension, "an attempt to get round the un-get-roundable fact that all ethnographical descriptions are homemade, that they are the describer's descriptions, not those of the described" (145).

55. Wattenberg, "Middletown Revisited."

56. Colson, "Culture and Progress," 269–70.

57. Ibid., 270.

58. Fox, "Epitaph for Middletown," 120.

59. Bahr, "The Perrigo Paper."

60. Gordon, *A Community in Stress*.

61. See, for example, Harris, "History and Significance," and Feleppa, "Emics, Etics, and Social Objectivity."

62. Harris, "History and Significance," 335.

63. See Nisbet's analysis of the influence of metaphor on Western history in his *Social Change and History*.

64. Caplow et al., *Middletown Families*, 322–30.

65. Harris, "History and Significance," 341.

66. Thernstrom, *Poverty and Progress*.

67. Bracken, "Middletown As a Pioneer Community"; Bahr and Bracken, "The Middletown of Yore."

68. Lynd and Lynd, *Middletown*, 7–8.

69. Warner et al., *Democracy in Jonesville*; Vidich and Bensman, *Small Town in Mass Society*; Varenne, *Americans Together*.

70. Lantz, *People of Coal Town*, 3; Varenne, *Americans Together*, 19; Liebow, *Tally's Corner*, 235–38.

71. Spindler and Spindler, "Anthropologists View American Culture."

72. Caplow, Middletown III Project staff seminar.

73. Foster et al., *Long-Term Field Research*.

74. See, for example, Bahr, Caplow, and Leigh, "The Slowing of Modernization"; Caplow et al., *Middletown Families*; and Caplow, "Paretian Theory."

75. Bracken, "Middletown As a Pioneer Community."

76. Whyte, *Street Corner Society*; Liebow, *Tally's Corner*.

77. Tambo, Hoover, and Hewitt, *Middletown*. Some of these are simply re-

views or newspaper articles about the various Middletown researchers and their doings or about the reactions of locals to the books, articles, television coverage, etc., but the number of legitimate scientific books and articles is impressive.

78. Chambers and Young, "Mesoamerican Community Studies," 64–65.

References

Aguilar, John L. 1981. "Insider Research: An Ethnography of a Debate." Pp. 15–26 in *Anthropologists at Home in North America: Methods and Issues in the Study of One's Own Society*, edited by Donald A. Messerschmidt. Cambridge: Cambridge University Press.

Bahr, Howard M. 1982. "The Perrigo Paper: A Local Influence upon *Middletown in Transition*." *Indiana Magazine of History* 78:1–25.

Bahr, Howard M., and Alexander E. Bracken. 1983. "The Middletown of Yore: Population Persistence, Migration, and Stratification." *Rural Sociology* 48:120–32.

Bahr, Howard M., Theodore Caplow, and Geoffrey K. Leigh. 1980. "The Slowing of Modernization in Middletown." Pp. 219–32 in *Research in Social Movements, Conflicts, and Change*, vol. 3, edited by Louis Kriesberg. Greenwich, Conn.: JAI Press.

Bell, Colin, and Howard Newby. 1972. *Community Studies: An Introduction to the Sociology of the Local Community*. New York: Praeger.

Bennett, John W., and Seena Kohl. 1981. "Longitudinal Research in Rural North America: The Saskatchewan Cultural Ecology Research Program, 1960–1973." Pp. 91–105 in *Anthropologists at Home in North America: Methods and Issues in the Study of One's Own Society*, edited by Donald A. Messerschmidt. Cambridge: Cambridge University Press.

Booth, Charles et al. 1889–91. *Life and Labour of the People in London*. 2 vols. London: Williams and Norgate.

Bourke-White, Margaret. 1937. "Muncie Ind. is the Great 'U.S. Middletown.'" *Life*, May 10, 15–25.

Bracken, Alexander E. 1978. "Middletown As a Pioneer Community." Ph.D. diss., Ball State University.

Caplow, Theodore. 1975. Letter of August 21 to Donald R. Ploch, Program Director for Sociology, National Science Foundation.

———. 1977. Middletown III Project staff seminar, April 18, manuscript in authors' possession.

———. 1987. "Paretian Theory Applied to the Findings of the Middletown III Research." *Revue Européenne des Sciences Sociales* 25 (76):55–78.

Caplow, Theodore, Howard M. Bahr, Bruce A. Chadwick, Reuben Hill, and

Margaret Holmes Williamson. 1982. *Middletown Families: Fifty Years of Change and Continuity.* Minneapolis: University of Minnesota Press.

Caplow, Theodore, Howard M. Bahr, Bruce A. Chadwick, Dwight W. Hoover, Laurence A. Martin, Joseph B. Tamney, and Margaret Holmes Williamson. 1983. *All Faithful People: Change and Continuity in Middletown's Religion.* Minneapolis: University of Minnesota Press.

Chambers, Erve J., and Philip D. Young. 1979. "Mesoamerican Community Studies: The Past Decade." *Annual Review of Anthropology* 8:45–69.

Chock, Phyllis Pease. 1986. "Irony and Ethnography: On Cultural Analysis of One's Own Culture." *Anthropological Quarterly* 59 (April): 87–96.

Clifford, James, and George E. Marcus. 1986. *Writing Culture: The Poetics and Politics of Ethnography.* Berkeley: University of California Press.

Colson, Elizabeth. 1976. "Culture and Progress." *American Anthropologist* 78 (June): 261–71.

Cousins, Norman B. 1937. "The World in Books." *Current History* 46 (April): 2–5.

Davis, Allison, Burleigh B. Gardner, and Mary R. Gardner. 1941. *Deep South: A Social Anthropological Study of Caste and Class.* Chicago: University of Chicago Press.

Dollard, John. 1949. *Caste and Class in a Southern Town.* 3d ed. Garden City, N.Y.: Doubleday Anchor.

Drake, St. Clair, and Horace R. Cayton. [1945] 1962. *Black Metropolis: A Study of Negro Life in a Northern City.* Rev. ed. New York: Harper and Row.

DuBois, W. E. Burghardt. [1899] 1967. *The Philadelphia Negro: A Social Study.* New York: Benjamin Blom.

Feleppa, Robert. 1986. "Emics, Etics, and Social Objectivity." *Current Anthropology* 27 (June): 243–55.

Foster, George M., Thayer Scudder, Elizabeth Colson, and Robert V. Kemper. 1979. *Long-Term Field Research in Social Anthropology.* New York: Academic Press.

Fox, Richard Wrightman. 1983. "Epitaph for Middletown: Robert S. Lynd and the Analysis of Consumer Culture." Pp. 102–41 in *The Culture of Consumption: Critical Essays in American History, 1880–1980,* edited by Richard Wrightman Fox and T. J. Jackson Lears. New York: Pantheon.

Frank, Carrolyle M. 1974. "Politics in Middletown: A Reconsideration of Municipal Government and Community Power in Muncie, Indiana, 1925–1935." Ph.D. diss., Ball State University.

Gallaher, Art, Jr. 1961. *Plainville Fifteen Years Later.* New York: Columbia University Press.

Gans, Herbert J. 1967. *The Levittowners: Ways of Life and Politics in a New Suburban Community.* New York: Pantheon.

Geertz, Clifford. 1983. *Local Knowledge: Further Essays in Interpretive Anthropology*. New York: Basic Books.

———. 1988. *Works and Lives: The Anthropologist As Author*. Stanford: Stanford University Press.

Gillin, John. 1957. "The Application of Anthropological Knowledge to Modern Mass Society: An Anthropologist's View." *Human Organization* 15 (Winter): 24–29.

Goldschmidt, Walter. 1977. "Anthropology and the Coming Crisis: An Autoethnographic Appraisal." *American Anthropologist* 79 (June): 293–308.

Gordon, Whitney M. 1964. *A Community in Stress*. New York: Living Books.

Hall, Peter. 1988. *Cities of Tomorrow: An Intellectual History of Urban Planning and Design in the Twentieth Century*. Oxford: Basil Blackwell.

Harris, Marvin. 1976. "History and Significance of the Emic/Etic Distinction." *Annual Review of Anthropology* 5: 329–50.

Hatch, Elvin. 1979. *Biography of a Small Town*. New York: Columbia University Press.

Hollingshead, August B. 1949. *Elmtown's Youth*. New York: John Wiley and Sons.

Holmes, Marilou Judy. 1983. "A History of Professional Nursing Education in Middletown, 1906–1968." Ed.D. thesis, Ball State University.

Hoover, Dwight W. 1985. "To Be a Jew in Middletown: A Muncie Oral History Project." *Indiana Magazine of History* 51 (June): 131–58.

Hoover, Dwight W., John D. Hewitt, and Jack Kirchner. 1983–84. "Crime and Mental Illness in Middletown, 1870–1910: A Study in Social Control." *Indiana Social Studies Quarterly* 36 (Winter): 33–44.

Jensen, Richard. 1979. "The Lynds Revisited." *Indiana Magazine of History* 75 (December): 302–91.

Lantz, Herman R. 1958. *People of Coal Town*. New York: Columbia University Press.

Liebow, Elliot. 1967. *Tally's Corner: A Study of Negro Streetcorner Men*. Boston: Little, Brown.

Lynd, Robert S. 1939. *Knowledge for What? The Place of Social Science in American Culture*. Princeton, N.J.: Princeton University Press.

Lynd, Robert S., and Helen Merrell Lynd. 1929. *Middletown: A Study in American Culture*. New York: Harcourt, Brace.

———. 1937. *Middletown in Transition: A Study in Cultural Conflicts*. New York: Harcourt, Brace.

Marcus, George E., and Michael M. J. Fischer. 1986. *Anthropology As Cultural Critique: An Experimental Moment in the Human Sciences*. Chicago: University of Chicago Press.

Mencken, H. L. 1929. "A City in Moronia." *American Mercury* 16 (March): 379–81.

Messerschmidt, Donald A., ed. 1981. *Anthropologists at Home in North America: Methods and Issues in the Study of One's Own Society*. Cambridge: Cambridge University Press.

Nisbet, Robert A. 1969. *Social Change and History: Aspects of the Western Theory of Development*. New York: Oxford University Press.

Record, Wilson. 1980. "Anthropology and Sociology: Three Common Problems." *Anthropological Quarterly* 54 (January): 28–35.

Seeley, John R., R. Alexander Sim, and Elizabeth W. Loosley. 1956. *Crestwood Heights: A Study of the Culture of Suburban Life*. Toronto: University of Toronto Press.

Spindler, George D., and Louise Spindler. 1983. "Anthropologists View American Culture." *Annual Review of Anthropology* 12:49–78.

Stark, Rodney. 1989. *Sociology*. 3d ed. Belmont, Calif.: Wadsworth Publishing Company.

Stein, Maurice R. 1960. *The Eclipse of Community: An Interpretation of American Studies*. Princeton, N.J.: Princeton University Press.

Szacki, Jerzy. 1979. *History of Sociological Thought*. Westport, Conn.: Greenwood Press.

Szopa, Anne. 1987. "Images of Women in Muncie Newspapers, 1895–1915." Ph.D. diss., Ball State University.

Tambo, David C., Dwight W. Hoover, and John D. Hewitt. 1988. *Middletown: An Annotated Bibliography*. New York: Garland.

Thernstrom, Stephen. 1964. *Poverty and Progress: Social Mobility in a Nineteenth-Century City*. Cambridge: Harvard University Press.

Van Maanen, John. 1988. *Tales of the Field: On Writing Ethnography*. Chicago: University of Chicago Press.

Varenne, Herve. 1977. *Americans Together: Structured Diversity in a Midwestern Town*. New York: Teachers College Press, Columbia University.

Vidich, Arthur J., and Joseph Bensman. 1968. *Small Town in Mass Society: Class, Power, and Religion in a Rural Community*. Rev. ed. Princeton, N.J.: Princeton University Press.

Wallace, Anthony F. C. 1980. *Rockdale: The Growth of a American Village in the Early Industrial Revolution*. New York: Alfred A. Knopf.

Warner, W. Lloyd, with the collaboration of Wilfrid C. Bailey, Arch Cooper, Walter Eaton, A. B. Hollingshead, Carson McGuire, Marchia Meeker, Bernice Neugarten, Joseph Rosenstein, Evon Z. Vogt, Jr., and Donald Wray. [1949] 1964. *Democracy in Jonesville: A Study in Quality and Inequality*. New York: Harper and Row.

Warner, W. Lloyd, and Paul S. Lunt. 1941. *The Social Life of a Modern Community*. New Haven: Yale University Press.

———. 1942. *The Status System of a Modern Community*. New Haven: Yale University Press.

Wattenberg, Ben. 1982. "Middletown Revisited: With Ben Wattenberg."

Muncie, Ind.: WIPB/PBS-TV. Sixty-minute segment, first aired April 28.

West, James. 1945. *Plainville, U.S.A.* New York: Columbia University Press.

Whyte, William Foote. 1943. *Street Corner Society: The Social Structure of an Italian Slum.* Chicago: University of Chicago Press.

Whyte, William H., Jr. 1957. *The Organization Man.* Garden City, N.Y.: Doubleday Anchor.

Williams, Raymond. 1973. *The Country and the City.* London: Chatto and Windus.

Wolcott, Harry F. 1981. "Home and Away: Personal Contrasts in Ethnographic Style." Pp. 255–65 in *Anthropologists at Home in North America*, edited by Donald A. Messerschmidt. Cambridge: Cambridge University Press.

Anthony M. Orum and

Joe R. Feagin

3 A Tale of Two Cases

Introduction

A case study is a method that relies on the examination of a
single instance of a phenomenon to explore, often in rich detail, the
hows and whys of a problem. Some of the most famous case studies in
the annals of social science have been done on cities and communities.
Long before it was technically feasible for social scientists to examine a
multitude of cities, using an array of statistics and equipped by sophisticated statistical techniques, scholars like Robert and Helen Lynd (1929),
W. Lloyd Warner (1963), Floyd Hunter (1953), and Robert Dahl (1961)
were studying cities and communities to probe particular questions. The
Lynds were the pioneers. Using both historical data and extensive interviews, the Lynds studied the development and nature of Muncie, Indiana,
in two classic works, *Middletown* and *Middletown in Transition*. These
books showed how industry came to Muncie, how the working class
developed, and how rule was exercised over the city by a dominant
family. As so often happens, these case studies became the rich and fertile
source of empirical inferences, inferences that would later be examined
as well as criticized in other empirical works.

There are remarkable gaps in the literature on American cities. Particularly striking is the small number of theoretically informed, relatively

comprehensive, in-depth analyses of major U.S. cities. Over the last decade or two we have seen some excellent additions to the city literature. There are book-length analyses of limited aspects of a particular city's development, such as histories of key politicians and urban renewal (Stone 1976); general histories with more attention to data than to theory (Hoffecker 1983); specialized books on small towns (Olien and Olien 1982); and important edited collections on particular cities (Bernard and Rice 1983). Only recently, a few in-depth case studies of Austin, Houston, Washington, Detroit, and Chicago have been published. Sunbelt cities in particular have suffered neglect. The two of us embarked on studies of cities using the method of the case study. We each had somewhat different questions in mind, and we employed somewhat different techniques of collecting data. Over time we compared our cases, looking for overlaps in our empirical results as well as talking over questions of theory and method. Our investigations became the stimulus for thinking about how social scientists conduct studies of cities and about the advantages and drawbacks to the method of using a single case to explore sociological questions.

In this chapter, we shall tell separately our stories of how we went about studying our specific cities—Orum discussing Austin, Texas, and Feagin commenting on Houston, Texas. We shall talk about the analytic thinking that went into our work, the inferences we were able to draw, and the limitations to what we accomplished. In the conclusion, we move beyond our single cases to discuss common issues and problems that face anyone who chooses to study a single city as an instance of a more general phenomenon.

The Case of Austin (Orum)

The study of Austin began for me in a casual and informal way. I had been living in the city for about eight years, teaching at the University of Texas. My interests, at the time, lay in the study of politics and in social theory. Gradually, however, I came to be interested in some concrete questions of urban growth and politics. My interest was sparked by changes taking place around me. Wide-open spaces, outside Austin in the hills just west of the city, were, it seemed, being turned overnight into jungles of residential and commercial development. Hordes of new immigrants, it also seemed, were swarming into Austin by day. What had once appeared a happy and peaceful hamlet was becoming transformed, in front of my very eyes, into a small, booming, and at rush hours, often jam-packed highwayed metropolis.

As a sociologist with more than a dozen years of work under my belt, I was well prepared both to be curious and to undertake some research about these changes in the city. My interests and knowledge of politics shaped my first questions. Who was behind all this growth? How was growth going to change the political complexion of the city? What sorts of conflicts were at stake—what sorts of interests were about to clash?

DILEMMAS OF GROWTH

At first I thought I would write an article, or two, examining the connection between population growth and politics. I intended to use Austin as an empirical instance of a city that was undergoing very rapid population growth. At the height of its expansion, for example, in 1983, the city added 32,000 jobs to its labor force. From 1970 to the early 1980s, it had increased in size by 50 percent; and, for a while, it was leading the United States in the rate of its overall population expansion. But, as I became more deeply involved in studying the city, my questions and my curiosity took me far afield. Eventually my articles turned into a book on the order of four hundred pages, and it was no longer just sociology that I was writing, but rather the history of how and why a city grew over the course of the twentieth century.

The study of Austin thus turned into the study of the development of an American city. Urban growth, or more precisely, rapid and explosive urban growth, had become very much a hot topic in the 1970s. For one thing, many of the newer Sunbelt cities, in states such as Florida, Arizona, Colorado, and Texas, were home to small towns that, like Austin, had mushroomed into minor metropolises within the space of a few short years. For another thing, students of cities had begun to turn their analytic attention to these matters. New ideas were flourishing—new concerns about the political economy of growth, about the power and wealth that lay behind the new urban growth. Sociologists like Harvey Molotch (1976) had begun to write perceptively about these matters. And, living in one such urban hot spot, I found what they wrote to be very compelling and persuasive. I also came to share with them a view that ran counter to the prevailing wisdom in sociology about the nature of urban growth. The dominant view of growth—of the increase in numbers of people as well as of the ever enhanced value of land and industry in cities—had argued that the spur to larger numbers was the development of new industries and that the conflicts between different groups were the "natural" result of competition over land and space in the city. Like Molotch, I found myself uncomfortable with this point of view. It seemed to me that politics and wealth lay behind the changes taking place much more than did simply the battles between aggregates of the population, as was argued by the dominant school of human ecology. In other words, human actors, as Feagin and I would soon agree, were very much behind urban development.

In brief, then, I entered this arena of urban study armed with some informed and perceptive views on the new urban growth in America, and also with a point of view much shaped by my years of studying politics and conflict in American society. But, instead of taking the normal sociological route of seeking to test empirical generalizations, or even theoretical generalizations, by using Austin as a strong instance of a particular kind of city, I embarked on something far more fluid and ambitious. I set about to uncover the explanation of the growing numbers of people and of the greater economic might in the city by immersing myself in the study of Austin's history. The deeper and more profound explanations of growth in the 1980s, I came to assume, lay not merely in the moves made by a handful of real estate developers in the 1980s. It lay in a more complex, and also more hidden, reality. It lay somewhere, somehow, back in the past.

METHODS AND THE LOGIC OF INFERENCE

In order then to undertake this reframed project on the city of Austin, I had to employ a new methodology for myself as a sociologist, and I had to also employ a certain way of what at best may be called "making sense" of my empirical data. Trained as a sociologist, I was primarily accustomed to dealing with survey data, or census data, drawn from large numbers of instances and cases, whether people or institutions. To pursue my questions now, I had to turn to various other kinds of data, those with which historians clearly are more accustomed. These were newspapers, of which I went through hundreds, if not thousands, of full days or of scraps; diaries; city records; letters and correspondence involving key personalities, such as Lyndon Baines Johnson; and a host of other materials.

I also had to invent certain methodological devices as I went along. The most important one was that of oral histories. During the 1980s, oral histories had come into vogue, especially among people interested in local history. There were no standard devices to guide one in conducting such histories. Since I had had long experience in using survey materials, and since I had conducted some interviews myself, I elected to rely on this experience as a guide for conducting the oral histories. Ultimately, my students and I completed almost two hundred such histories. They provided information invaluable in confirming specific historical events and the specific actions of people involved in the events. They also helped occasionally in identifying the social context within which events occurred. In undertaking this manner of data collection on the city, I also had to decide how to draw inferences from the empirical materials I had assembled. In this regard I acted very much more like a sociologist than a historian. I defined Austin as an empirical instance of a larger set of rapidly growing cities in America. Thus, I sought to identify events and happenings that were associated with the growth of the city and that also, as a class of events, could be associated with the growth of any such American city. In my mind's eye, I also tried to imagine whether an event, happening, institution, or even actors could promote growth, or not. In effect, I always asked myself the question: Could the city have grown, in terms of population, physical size, or industry, in the absence of this particular thing, whether it be an event, an institution, or an actor?

This method, of *imaginary analytic induction*, is something that students of case studies are compelled to employ, particularly if they are trying to draw inferences about causality. Lacking comparative material, the student must do the comparison to some extent on an imaginary basis. Unlike the historian, who seeks to describe the unique configuration of events and people, the sociologist seeks to draw inferences of a more general sort, of a sort that will enable other observers to make comparisons with their cases, to prove or to disprove assertions. Thus, even though it appeared that I was explaining the history of urban growth only in Austin, in my mind I always was trying to develop conclusions that would lend themselves eventually to future comparative work, either by myself or by other researchers. If my conclusions were wrong, I assumed, other students, of Austin or of other rapidly growing cities, would eventually be able to say so. I later came to frame these more general sorts of conclusions in another paper (Orum 1991).

EXPLAINING AUSTIN'S GROWTH

Over the course of its 150-year history, Austin, Texas, has grown from a tiny hamlet to a city that today encompasses about 750,000 people in its broader metropolitan environs. There appear to be at least three major stages to this growth. The first stage lasted until about 1930. During this period Austin reached a maximum size of only a little over 50,000 people, clearly a small town by any standard. The second stage ran from about 1930 to 1970, during which time Austin more and more came under the influence of a variety of forces both within the state and nationwide. And the third stage, which runs from 1970 to the present time, is the stage during which the economy crept out from under its parochial nature and began to reflect the significant trends and events of the national economy.

The causes, or explanations, for Austin's growth vary from stage to stage. Those causes that most occupied my work were the ones that could account for change during the first and second stages of the city's growth. I sought to examine them in terms of the sheer weight of empirical evidence and to make inferences about those forces that promoted growth during these first two stages. Here, I confess, I was guided principally by certain empirical recurrent themes and happenings, and I deliberately refrained from drawing on the esoteric debate and discussion within urban intellectual circles about which particular theoretical perspective may, or may not, have been correct.

As a result of my immersion in the empirical data, it was clear that several different forces could account for the basic expansion of Austin through 1970: key actors, or what I came to call *urban entrepreneurs*; the solution to fundamental environmental hardships, in particular the creation of dams along the Colorado River; the action of the federal gov-

ernment, particularly during the 1930s when the New Deal poured millions and millions of dollars into central Texas to lay the foundations for
its later urban takeoff; and various local organizations, particularly the
chamber of commerce, that acted to merge and to marry conflicting interests in Austin, and acted also to press for resources vital to the livelihood of the city. Let me consider each of these elements separately.

Take the matter of the urban entrepreneurs first. Trained as a sociologist, of course, I had come to believe that individual actors counted for
very little in the long run of cities or societies. My case study of Austin
convinced me otherwise. Over the course of a period of time, running
from roughly the end of the nineteenth century through the 1950s, there
was a group of individuals who lobbied continuously on behalf of the
growth of Austin. These individuals included Tom Miller, who served as
the mayor of the city from 1933 through 1949; Alexander Wooldridge,
who served as a key city spokesman in the late nineteenth and early twentieth centuries; Edgar Perry, who was one of Austin's wealthiest businessmen in the 1920s, 1930s, and 1940s and who would become Lyndon
Baines Johnson's major sponsor in Johnson's first run for Congress in
1937; and Walter K. Long, the longtime manager of the Austin Chamber
of Commerce. Each of these men individually seemed to possess an uncommon commitment to the growth of the city, a commitment that
stretched far beyond the limits of mere self-interest. Each spent enormous
amounts of his time on projects that would redound principally to the
benefit of the city rather than himself. And each man took risks on behalf
of the city, urging action when inaction would have been the safer course.

Hence, I came to call them urban entrepreneurs because they took risks
on behalf of the city and because they worked over long periods of time
to make the small town into a substantial city. I assembled much of the
evidence in the first parts of my book on Austin in order to flesh out these
people and to reveal how devoted they became to the city. In identifying
them as such, naturally I had to confront the question I raised above:
Would the city have grown, both in numbers of residents and in the
strength of its economy, in the absence of these men, or others like them?
My answer, after careful reflection, came out in the negative. Even if a
Tom Miller had not existed, or an Edgar Perry, clearly, for a small town
to get a place on the map, individual actors had to play a decisive role.
These men did. They drummed up money from private companies to

come to Austin; they also drummed up monies from the federal government to help out on Austin projects. In other words, they provided the energy and the personal links that brought Austin into the broader national economy. Eventually too there were others who followed in their footsteps. Some came in the 1950s, including C. B. Smith, Jr., who gave evidence of a similar style of devotion to the city. Later, as I shall discuss shortly, the urban entrepreneurs came to be replaced by a different sort of human actor in the expansion of the city.

Next, there is the question of the heavy challenges posed to the growth of the city, and of central Texas generally, by the handicaps of the environment and, by implication, the handicaps of limited access to the state and national marketplaces. Unlike Houston, which lay on the Gulf, or other cities that possessed such natural advantages, Austin and many other small towns in central Texas had no such edge. Although Austin had been the state capital since 1872, and although its life was filled with the machinations of state and local politicians as well as with the cerebrations of people at the University of Texas, few people, aside from the urban entrepreneurs, had given much attention to what would be required to make Austin more than just another small southwestern town. Eventually, owing to the efforts of Alexander Wooldridge and a handful of other men at the end of the nineteenth century, an effort was made to try to develop a system of dams on the Colorado River.

Wooldridge was particularly keen on the issue, and in a famous declaration in the pages of the *Austin Statesman* of January 1, 1888, he urged his fellow Austinites to support the construction of a dam in Austin. What would such an enterprise—which to many outsiders sounded horribly mundane—do? In fact, as Wooldridge noted, it would help to control the waters of the Colorado, preventing the periodic floods that devastated Austin and much of central Texas below the city, as well as providing residents much-needed electricity. That dam, and a later series of dams, became an obsession and a symbol for the life of the city. Over the course of almost forty years, the citizens of Austin struggled to build dams, only to have one after another destroyed by the periodic floods. With such destruction came illness, poor crops, and especially, little hope of industry.

Finally, after a number of unsuccessful efforts, dams were completed above Austin, creating Lake Travis among other things, and dams were built below the city as well. Not only did these projects provide needed jobs for citizens during the terrible years of the Great Depression, but shortly after the dams were completed in the late 1930s, the city began to expand. And to expand. This was just the beginning of the second stage of its growth. And it was clear that the dams had provided the mechanism to overcome the handicaps of the natural environment and thereby enable the citizens to develop an economy and a government that would flourish.

Alongside the notion of urban entrepreneurs and the concept of the successful resolution of environmental handicaps comes a third factor, that of the federal government, or the state, as many today prefer to call it. The impact of the federal government on the expansion of the city came as a major surprise to me. In large part, I was surprised because most of the classic studies of cities, such as those of the Lynds (1929) and Dahl (1961), simply failed to mention the degree to which the federal government intervened to affect local events in cities. My attention was drawn to the federal government's influence on one major event in the life of Austin—the dams. Every effort on the part of free enterprise had failed to make any substantial inroads in the construction of dams. In the late 1920s, just when it had seemed that private enterprise would bring the dams to fruition, the venture collapsed.

In stepped the federal government. Or rather, in stepped our urban entrepreneurs and a number of state officials and Texas congressmen in Washington. They prevailed on and convinced both Franklin Roosevelt and his advisors that many benefits would result from a loan by the federal government to the state of Texas. The combination of factors here, I realized, was important. The federal government did not simply take over and build the dams, although its money secured them and therefore its efforts ultimately contributed to the expansion of the city. What happened, in fact, was a serious effort of lobbying at both state and national levels to get that federal money to Texas instead of some other state, or some other city. Once again, individual actors, the urban entrepreneurs and others such as Lyndon Baines Johnson, served as the personal vehicles whose efforts made an impact on this issue—that of why the city of Austin was able to expand.

Feagin too came to observe how important the role of the federal government proved to the growth of Houston; and in recent years, more and more studies have revealed the connection between actions at the national level and the success of building and expansion among cities (see, for example, Mollenkopf 1983). The advantage of the case study of Austin is that it permitted me to observe in great detail just how the federal government became important to the city. I learned that the federal government was able to solve a problem critical to the livelihood of the city, a problem that had lasted for many decades. And once that problem was solved, the city was able to expand in degree and directions previously unknown.

Lastly, at a somewhat different level of analysis, there was the important part played by the Austin Chamber of Commerce, and its officers, in the growth of the city. The chamber and its manager, Walter Long, were among the first people to actively lobby on behalf of the expansion of central Texas and, in particular, of the construction of dams on the Colorado. Later it would be the chamber that would aggressively seek out new industry for the city of Austin. Here, in other words, was a collective force and agent in the city whose exclusive purpose was to act as a voice on behalf of city expansion and whose way of doing so was to act as the one assemblage of different political and business interests in town. Sometime after I completed my analysis and report on Austin, I learned, from a number of other studies (see, for example, Judd 1984), how important the chamber of commerce everywhere has been to urban interests and to growth.

In brief, then, the story of the growth of Austin, during its first two stages of expansion, became a story of dams and a story of how forces, at different levels of analysis—individuals, collective agents, and even the state—acted on and about dams.

The third, and most recent, stage of Austin expansion, dating from about 1970, involves a different set of actors and a different set of problems. Here, as I learned, one could no longer speak properly of urban entrepreneurs—with the aging of C. B. Smith and the death of people like Tom Miller, there no longer seemed to be such figures in Austin. Rather, those who emerged to take the leadership in the expansion of the city essentially were businessmen and real estate developers, people who I came to call *market entrepreneurs* to distinguish them from *urban entrepreneurs*. During the wildly ecstatic and money-flowing days of the 1970s and early 1980s, there were a number of such figures in Austin.

Most were people who made money by buying and developing land. They were people who profited from the growing numbers of individuals and new enterprises that were lured to Austin during its time in the national limelight. These market entrepreneurs were exclusively interested in their own profits and thus stood in strong contrast to the urban entrepreneurs, who had devoted so much of their time to the development of the city. Indeed, in locating and identifying the differences between these two types of entrepreneurs, I found a story not only of the changing causes of growth but also of the changing orientations to the community. Those who built the city in its early years seemed to have built it out of love for a place they envisioned, whereas those responsible for the city's development in the most recent years exploited the city for their own interests. Nonetheless, the outcome was the same—the expansion of Austin.

There is in this third stage no single human monument that stands as a testament to the life and times of the city, as the dams did during the first two stages. In fact, the problems today are ones of sustaining the expansion of the late 1970s and early 1980s. And they are problems that, once again, do not lie easily in the grasp of Austin residents so much as they lie outside their grasp—to wit, the declining economy of the state, as of the Southwest generally. The blows suffered by the oil industry and, consequently, the great travails endured by Texas and Austin banks have had ramifications throughout the region and in Austin especially. What they point up is the extent to which the fate of Austin today has become inextricably linked with the fate of the state and of the region. In its first two stages, the Austin marketplace was to a great degree invulnerable to these forces. Today, as a result of all the factors that have contributed to the city's historical growth, its life depends vitally on the life of agencies and institutions beyond it. To solve the new problems may effectively require another New Deal or, perhaps, quite simply a more vigorous local economy.

The Case of Houston (Feagin)

When I began the study of Houston, I was not a resident of the city. I had lived in the city for most of my first two decades as a Texan but had, apart from occasional visits, been away for some time. When I first started exploring Houston in the early 1980s, I again began regular trips to the city for the purpose of data gathering; and like Orum, I did not initially envision a full-blown case study. The study of Houston began for me in a specific attempt to gather information on major urban developers for a book on real estate development in the United States. Since World War II, developers have become perhaps the most significant new actors in the urban real estate game. Because there was remarkably little empirical material available on developers, my initial interest was in gathering concrete examples of how real estate developers operate in a major city. Since Houston was nearby, and reputed to be the developer's free enterprise city par excellence, I chose it as the place to explore a few examples of development. The more I explored the role of the developers, the more I learned of the remarkable developmental history of the city. Perhaps even more than Austin, Houston was a proverbial boomtown, having grown from a population of just 79,000 in 1910 to more than 1.7 million in the late 1980s, with most of that growth in the period since 1950. In 1880 Houston held only 1 percent of the Texas population, but by the 1980s the Houston metropolitan area was the residence of more than a fifth of the Texas population. The average population growth per decade in the period between 1850 and 1980 was striking—an increase of 66 percent for the city and nearly 50 percent for the metropolitan area. These rates of population growth, over so many decades, are probably the most sustained for any city in North America.

As I began gathering materials from diverse sources, the city began to change under my feet. The sustained prosperity of the 1850–1980 period came to an abrupt end in the mid-1980s. The city's economy went into a major tailspin, and unemployment, bankruptcies, mortgage foreclosures, and despair hit an all-time high for the city that had missed most previous economic difficulties. During the U.S. recession of 1981–82, a number of people had migrated to Texas cities from other parts of the country in a quest for a decent job. But by 1983 it had become clear to many of these "Snowbirds" that such a decision was a mistake. In 1982 there had been a net immigration of 417,000 people entering Texas; by 1986 this had dropped to fewer than 5,000 people. Although these population losses have not been documented by an official census, some experts have estimated the net loss at a few thousand in the 1983–87 period. By 1987 the out-migration had slowed to the point that the city's population had stabilized. While I had been studying the city, it had gone from boom to bust, and then recovered a little.

Like Orum, I was fascinated by this growth-decline pattern and began to ask myself a series of questions about the what, when, and where of these developments, as well as the who behind the developments. At the same time, in connection with writing the aforementioned book *The Urban Real Estate Game*, I was reading some of the growth coalition literature of Harvey Molotch and John Mollenkopf and the new political-economic, neo-Marxist-influenced writings of scholars like Michael Peter Smith, Mark Gottdiener, and Manuel Castells, whose work stimulated my thinking in regard to concepts and ideas relevant to the Houston case. Thus I began to look closely at the relationship of Houston's growth to the surrounding political-economic structure of modern urban capitalism. In my earliest work on cities in the 1960s, I had learned the prevailing ecological perspective on urban development but had increasingly found that approach unsatisfactory because of its grounding in the assumptions of neoclassical economics and thus its neglect of both state issues and the structure-agency distinction. Thus my embarkation on a detailed urban history of Houston coincided with a close reading of the exciting new critical sociology literature. This literature suggested numerous analytic ideas that sharpened my eyes as I explored a variety of materials on the Houston case. In the case study I did not see myself as testing statistical propositions or seeking to make statistical generalizations about cities in general, but rather as exploring the utility of some of the ideas, concepts, and theories in the new critical approach to urban sociology. These existing theoretical analyses suggested the dimensions that I should pay heed to. In this way there was a constant interplay of ideas and data.

My reading of Houston's history and the clarification and development of the theoretical themes developed in tandem with or on the heels of the oil exploration and production effort. Different subsectors in the oil sector have distinctive trajectories, with oil production and marketing dating back to the early 1900s. Oil-related manufacturing had joined this primary production by the 1920s, when prominent oil-refining facilities and oil tools complexes were established in the greater Houston area. I used several methodologies, including a review of all the issues of the major business magazine (*Houston*) since the 1920s, a careful searching of most issues of the *Houston Post* since the 1970s, and a selective reading of the *Houston Press, Post*, and *Chronicle* for the last several decades. Newspapers are a neglected source of data for urban research; they are particularly useful for historical research on city political and economic development because the major issues and events in this regard are normally recorded. I also made use of letters and papers of various key actors, papers that are in the Library of Congress, the Rice Library in Houston, and the LBJ Library in Austin. Much of this work in the libraries was unrewarding, however, because the papers often appeared to be "sanitized"; critical debates and controversies rarely appear in the materials. A variety of other sources filled out my methodological tool kit, including two dozen interviews with knowledgeable local researchers and political, real estate, and other business-elite decision makers, out-of-print books, developers' brochures and pamphlets, local governmental publications, census materials, and a survey of other business-elite magazines and journals such as the *Port of Houston* magazine and the *Houston Business Journal*. In this fashion, I was able to build portraits of key dimensions by using several sources, a pyramiding process.

As I read and moved into ever deeper levels of new critical urban theory and also deeper levels of Houston's history, I came to emphasize in my own thinking three general dimensions: (1) an understanding of the growth and economic layering of Houston requires a serious consideration of the global context; (2) the development and structuring of this "free-enterprise" city has often been dependent on the decisions of state officials operating at various levels; and (3) without substantial public planning in the public interest, Houston's local residents have paid a heavy price for the free-market approach of the city's business leadership.

ECONOMIC GROWTH: LAYERING AND THE GLOBAL CONTEXT

Growth Coalitions. As Orum suggests, the study of growth is a study of growth coalitions. The growth coalition literature suggests that a major activity of coalitions is boosting one's own city. Town entrepreneurs have been important in the history of the location and early development of U.S. cities. Houston began with the activities of two brothers, the Allen brothers, who, as town entrepreneurs, formed its first growth coalition.

In 1836 J. K. and A. C. Allen bought six thousand acres of land in southeast Texas for a little over a dollar an acre and talked General Sam Houston, a Texas military hero, into giving his name to their development scheme.

An 1836 newspaper advertisement placed by the Allens proclaimed: "The town of Houston is located at the point on the river which must ever command the trade of the largest and richest portion of Texas. . . . [It] will warrant the employment of at least One Million Dollars in capital, and when the rich lands of this country shall be settled, a trade will flow to it, making it, beyond all doubt, the great interior commercial emporium of Texas" (McComb 1981). These entrepreneurs solicited outside capital and offered the land to investors, merchants, and settlers, with the expressed view that Houston would become the regional center of commercial capitalism and the government of the new Texas Republic. Note the vision of growth and the growth ideology.

The Layering of Urban History. Looking at the city's economic and political history from the foundation years in the 1830s to the turbulent boom and bust years of the 1970s and 1980s, I studied the evolution of Houston from an agricultural marketing and primary extraction economy to a more complex economy with agricultural marketing, primary resource extraction, refining, petrochemicals, and other oil-related manufacturing as principal features. Much writing about the Houston metropolitan area has portrayed its economy as a petroleum monoculture. Such a view is exaggerated, for the metropolitan economic structure is in reality a palimpsest with a number of layers built up over a century and half, each with its distinctive characteristics. Historically viewed, Houston's economic structure can be dissected into six major sectors. The first and oldest dimension of the Houston economy is agricultural production, marketing, and processing, particularly sugar, cotton, and grain operations. This agricultural sector became important during Houston's first decade, and it has remained so to the present. Certain products, such as cotton, had become less significant by the 1960s, but other agricultural products, such as grains, took up the slack. Food processing had become consequential by 1900. The agricultural boom stimulated the development of a number of business service firms, including banks and law firms. The agricultural economy also provided the demand that led to the

construction of port facilities and of numerous railroads, the latter bringing the first large industrial workshops to the city. The next major sector
in the palimpsest economy of the greater Houston area is that of "primary commodity" production—not only oil and gas but also sulphur,
water, lumber, lime, and salt. Oil was not the first extracted resource.

After 1901, oil and gas gradually became the dominant extraction
commodities. Over the next three decades the oil and gas business up-
staged the other extraction industries, but the former have remained important to the present day. The petroleum sector is complex, encompassing as it does oil exploration, refining, and tools and services industries,
as well as the petrochemical industry. The manufacturing and service
sectors developed in tandem with or on the heels of the oil sector have
distinctive trajectories, with oil production and marketing dating back
to the early 1900s. Petrochemical production became a major subsector
in the 1940s. The refining and petrochemical industries have been among
the most technologically advanced of U.S. industries. The most recently
developed sectors of the Houston economy are the medical sector and
the space sector, large parts of which have also been labeled high-tech.
The medical and space sectors are the most significant of the new types
of economic activity and growth that have come to the city since the
1960s.

One idea that developed as I examined the transition from one period
to another was that an understanding of the cumulative aspects of capitalistic development can help with the answer to the question of why and
how a city such as Houston becomes the dominant center for a particular
industry. The economic situation in one historical period of a city often
lays the foundation for the development in the next period, as can clearly
be seen in the role of agricultural marketing in Houston in the nineteenth
century. As we trace the translocal linkages of a particular city through
historical periods, we may well discover that the urban economic
rhythms become as closely tied to events in the global market as to those
in the national economic system. International cotton marketing brought
service companies in the form of railroads, law firms, and banks, and this
business support system enabled the city to compete with other Gulf
Coast cities to draw the oil industry to Houston. Moreover, once the
internationally oriented oil business came to town, that laid yet another
foundation for the worldwide expansion of the petrochemical industry in

a later period, for the Port of Houston had developed extensively in response to the oil-exporting trade. The palimpsest of economic layers in the Houston case is impressive, and each layer builds on the previous layer.

The Global Dimension. Another idea that became clearer to me as I got into the historical materials on the Houston economy was the importance of the global context. I discovered that from the cotton and trade of the nineteenth century to the oil exploration, oil tools, and oil services of the twentieth century, Houston has long been a global city, one integrated into the world market system. Whereas an argument can be made for Houston as a culturally provincial city before the 1960s, one can also argue with considerable evidence for the city's essential openness to international trade and influence from the middle of the nineteenth century. Houston had to be assessed within the relevant international context and not, as the mainstream ecologists would have it, primarily as part of some national filtering-down process. There has been a tendency for social science analysis in the United States to analyze social phenomena, including metropolitan development, within a regional or nation-state context. Although it is probably the case that ignoring the global context of cities limits one's understanding of urban development in any historical period, neglecting the world context seems an egregious error in assessing a modern city. Most larger cities around the world have become more and more integrated into the global market of capitalism since the world wars. In the case of the Houston metropolitan area, the relevant context for analysis is definitely this capitalistic world market. The growth and development of Houston has involved the flow of domestic and foreign capital, primary resources and construction materials, and migrant labor to the city and the export of oil-related products, agricultural products, and money capital out of the city. Some of these factors have U.S. origins and destinations, whereas others have international sources and destinations. The actual entrance of Houston into the global market system began in the nineteenth century with the cotton trade between Houston and British cities. By the mid-1980s Houston was so well integrated into the world market that its severe economic recession was rooted in economic decisions of the international oil cartel and in the export problems caused by the high American dollar. The 1980s crash in oil prices brought substantial cutbacks in production and employee layoffs in the greater Houston area. Moreover, when the price of oil increased in 1987, selected sectors of the Houston economy rebounded to some extent.

THE STATE IN THE FREE-ENTERPRISE CITY

I had come to the study of Houston with an awareness of its symbolic status as a laissez-faire, free-enterprise city in the United States. But as I got into the project, the worldwide character of this symbolism became even clearer. By the late 1970s, Houston had achieved the status of a widely cited model of the positive consequences of a free-enterprise, laissez-faire approach to economic development. Conservative think tanks such as the Adam Smith Institute in Great Britain utilized the Houston case as a primary example of the economic prosperity that comes from an unrestrained free-enterprise approach to economic investment and development. Thus in an Adam Smith Institute book titled *Town and Country Chaos* (1982) Robert Jones extols the virtues of Houston's lack of governmental planning and public sector intervention in the local economy and uses the Houston case to argue against the strict city-planning controls in British cities. From the mid-1970s to the mid-1980s, leading political figures in the United States and in Europe cited the unplanned free-enterprise economy and philosophy of Houston as the reason for the city's remarkable record of material progress.

The Reality Is Not Laissez-Faire. As I did the basic research on Houston, it became apparent to me that Houston's political-economic history, from the earliest point in time, involved the recurrent intervention of the local and federal government in the Houston economy, usually at the behest of local business elites. Governmental action has been such a constant thread throughout the city's history that prevailing theories of the local state might be illuminated by a consideration of the theoretical hints in these Houston materials. Not only are such cities disproportionately shaped by decisions made by executives in a few large corporations in the relevant industries, but they are also substantially fashioned and formed by state intervention, often at the behest of business leaders. From Houston's earliest days, government funds have been used to facilitate private profit making. The Allen brothers called on the local and Texas government to subsidize their profit making in land speculation. Their success in getting the new Republic of Texas capital located in Houston guaranteed that their new town would become visible. Moreover, their immediate successors in the local business elite used local government funds and bonds to pay for the road and utility projects they required. We see here the central importance of governmental infrastructure aid for early projects desired by the local business community. Later there would be large sums of federal money for highways and bridges, as well as substantial military-industrial aid for the burgeoning Houston petrochemical industry during World War II and later for the business-elite-generated NASA Johnson Space Center built in south Houston in the 1960s. This aid was aggressively sought by the business elites that have long controlled Houston's economy and government. We can also see here the example of local government aid for transport facilities, in the form of special bonds to expand local port facilities, and the example of government officials working in coordination with the local business leadership to maintain a weak set of regulatory mechanisms for the city.

Houston has become famous as the city with weak planning and no zoning. Although Houston is often advertised as the premier free-enterprise city, in reality the city's business leadership has regularly taken major governmental "handouts" for projects that support or create profit making in the city. Government action has in fact been opposed only for such activities as the provision of certain types of infrastructure for neighborhoods, the regulation of development with zoning or planning, the increase in taxation for many public services, and the assistance of poorer residents in the form of social welfare programs.

SOCIAL COSTS OF UNPLANNED GROWTH

A third theme that became obvious as I dug deeply into the past and present of this free-enterprise city is the unplanned character of Houston's remarkable growth and subsequent decline. Houston is indeed the unplanned city that many scholarly and popular writers have written about, but that relatively unplanned character, coupled with a relative starvation of the public infrastructure and a relatively low level of taxation, has brought particularly massive social costs to the city's residents, with the heaviest burden often being borne by the poorest Houstonians.

Houston has been celebrated by free-market advocates the world over as the city where private enterprise has brought to the citizenry the unadulterated benefits of private development and private markets, without much in the way of social problems. Free-enterprise Houston has a huge "laundry list" of urban problems, all of which have been either generated by or aggravated by the creation of low-tax, business-oriented government and an emphasis on the "good business climate." Among these are significant subsidence, flooding, water pollution, toxic waste, sewage, and street maintenance problems. Whereas the residents in most U.S. cities have faced some of these difficulties, albeit to a variable degree, Houstonians have faced all of them, and more; indeed, most of these urban dilemmas have gotten worse over the last few decades.

ACTORS AND INSTITUTIONS

The three themes just discussed can be analyzed at two levels—that of actors and that of structures and institutions. Some critical scholars emphasize that the actors within the economic and political structures should become a major focus for researchers concerned with understanding the realities of urban growth and decline. Particular urban actors make the concrete, everyday decisions that in effect create or shape economic and political institutions.

Houston has been ruled by a strong business elite from its first decade. The character of that establishment has changed over time, but in every decade since the 1830s, the local power structure has been dominated by business leaders such as merchants, cotton "factors," bankers, oil entrepreneurs, developers, lawyers, and corporate executives in multinational firms. In some cities, politicians have emerged out of urban machines or union backgrounds to compete with business leaders, but not in Houston. The top politicians of the city, with rare exceptions, have been members of, or heavily dependent on, the business elites. There is a correspondence between the character of the actors dominant in the power structure in a particular period and the economic organizations characteristic of, or emerging in, that period. The first group to dominate the city was composed of the founding entrepreneurs, the Allen brothers, and a few other merchants. General and cotton merchants would be very influential over the next few decades. They made the initial economic and political decisions that created the city of Houston, but they made those decisions within the context of, and limited by the logic of, the precapitalist plantation economy and the commercial capitalistic economy. In the 1880s and 1890s the merchant aggregation was supplemented with a group of bankers, lawyers, and railroad entrepreneurs. They too made decisions that shaped the economic structure and spatial layout of the city, but within more of a national political-economic framework than their predecessors. This framework allowed a broader range of decisions because of the greater resources available. But it also, depending on the issue, provided more institutional restrictions, as we will discover in examining the ties of the municipal bond structure to the troubled national banking system. By the late 1920s, a few oil entrepreneurs had become part of the city's power structure.

It was in the 1930s that the most cohesive clique emerged, one with a distinctive name (later called the "Suite 8F crowd"). This elite appears to have been the most powerful in the city's history, in large part because of its cohesion and its distinctive personalities as well as its corporate networks and national and international resources. Operating in an expanding world economy, this group presided over several decades of Houston's formative growth and development. When Suite 8F power waned in the 1970s, a larger and less cohesive power structure emerged; the Houston Chamber of Commerce moved to the center of the business leadership. Although this organization is headed by an assortment of principal corporate executives, its influence has been limited by the larger contextual factors associated with a major disinvestment and declining rate-of-profit cycle in the sectors of the capitalistic economy so vital to the city of Houston.

This series of elite actors illustrates the importance of conscious human actions in creating and maintaining social structures and social frameworks. In cities such as Houston, economic and political structures do not develop according to inevitable general laws or inexorable necessity. They develop in coordination with the conscious actions of human agents. But the decisions of the agents are not made randomly or whimsically. The array of possible decisions is often limited or shaped by the economic and political frameworks inherited from the past. There are the business decisions, particularly investments made in consonance with the logic of capital accumulation, that created (or did not create) jobs for workers in selected industries and that created corporations. And then there are the business elite's decisions to create the type of local government that can meet both business requirements and pressures for services from the general citizenry. In the struggle for control over government, however, the contest has been extremely one-sided. The business elite has done much of the goal setting and the planning for Houston; that elite has provided government officials. Although all cities seem to have elite power structures, Houston's extraordinarily powerful capitalists, generally unrestrained by labor unions or local government officials, would seem to be distinctive even among U.S. cities. These influential urban actors and their consequential decisions illustrate the point that it is individuals who provide the concrete connections between the abstract institutional structures of local and national economies and local and national states. Economic and political structures are very important to an analysis of metropolitan development. Yet the evolution of a specific city often entails a complex tapestry of relationships held together by individuals, with the most powerful individuals playing the greater role in binding together, formally and informally, the structural realities of state and economy.

Conclusion

Cities mean different things to different people. The tourist looks at the city and sees excitement. But the same city is barely noticeable to the person who goes through life's daily routines. He or she "envisages neither its extent or form nor its links with past and future" (Abu-Lughod 1971, v). A historian may ignore its modernity for its past. We have been attracted to both the past and the modernity of Austin and Houston.

In the course of our separate case studies of Austin and Houston, we discovered a number of differences as well as similarities. Perhaps the differences are most immediately apparent as a result of the two tales we have conveyed here. For one thing, Austin and Houston are radically different cities. The former is still a relatively small city and probably will forever remain best known not for its industry but as the home to the University of Texas and as the capital of Texas. Houston, in contrast, is a large, booming metropolis that has undergone several significant economic metamorphoses and today stands as one of America's major cities. In addition, we approached our two case studies differently. Orum was primarily concerned with an inductive approach to his data, seeking to build up to a series of major conclusions and inferences about the nature and explanations of Austin's growth over the course of about 150 years. Feagin, in contrast, sought to examine some current neo-Weberian and neo-Marxist theoretical insights in the light of empirical discoveries about the rise and fall of Houston over roughly the same period of time. These two different styles of approaching a case study of a city are, we believe, equally legitimate, but they will provide a somewhat different slant on the matter of what happened in the course of the city's history. Readers and practitioners must judge for themselves which of the two approaches fits most comfortably with both their own theoretical leanings and their own concern with uncovering the facts about the hows and whys of urban growth.

Yet, there are also a number of important ways in which our studies are similar to each other, ways that underscore the very character of what a good case study of a city can be. For example, one of the important similarities in our studies was our use of a holistic approach. Our examinations are holistic in the sense that they cover one bounded case in great depth and that they accent a number of interrelated dimensions of that city considered both simultaneously and diachronically. Our case studies are also open-ended concerning the issues examined and the methodologies employed. As each of us proceeded, new questions opened up that we had not anticipated, and new methodological procedures were discovered as well. In case studies there is much that cannot be anticipated. This is a major advantage over conventional quantitative studies, which must work with existing data, often from official governmental sources. We were able to modify our research studies to gather data from new sources and on new topics, which we discovered as we proceeded in our multiyear studies. Our case studies were longitudinal; we were able to look at a broad sweep of the history of our cities. We also encountered similar methodological problems in the course of our research. Perhaps the most important was that of empirical and theoretical generalization.

However much we believed our cases to carry some weight in assessing rapidly expanding cities other than Austin and Houston, we discovered real limits to how far those generalizations could be extended. Like the anthropologist, the sociologist (or political scientist or economist) who examines a single case in detail is naturally confined to what can truthfully be said about his or her particular entity. Sometimes, this seems to matter very little. A political scientist who studies the origins of the Communist Revolution of 1949 in China in order to speak about revolutions generally is clearly less handicapped. Over the past couple of hundred years, there have been only a handful of such revolutions, and to study one in detail may produce insights of great significance, if only because there are so few instances of such revolutions in history. Yet, obviously, this does not hold true for a study of a single, rapidly expanding American city. There are literally dozens of such cities today. To what degree can the inferences from Austin and Houston claim also to be inferences about, let us say, Phoenix? Or Santa Fe? Or even Indianapolis? There are different ways of reaching such a judgment. For example, if we are interested in learning whether rapid growth has promoted the same kind of political conflict between pro-growth and anti-growth forces in some of these other cities, we can look at secondary sources and other writings on these cities. We can also consult some of the local newspapers. Though all of this may take some time, at least it would enable one to learn whether the social and political phenomenon of rapid urban growth shares similar features from one city to another.

But such a judgment covers only the surface of our concern. After all, we believed that we were drawing empirical inferences that would explain the continuing growth in the city and that would help account for the rapid growth in the 1970s and 1980s. Since we chose the method of the case study precisely because a sample of many cases did not lend itself to detailed investigation, particularly detailed historical investigation, would we not have to undertake researches of equal intensity to discover how universal the truths were we discovered in Austin and Houston? Yes, and no. If we are honest, then we must say that there is no recourse to assessing the validity of inferences other than to assess the fruits of similar histories of comparable cities. Unfortunately, there are not many such histories around. But there are shortcuts. There are some good histories that, although they are not focused exclusively on matters of growth, as ours were, still provide important insights into the agents and forces that can help account for growth. Robert Fogelson (1967), for example, has written an excellent history of Los Angeles, covering the early years through 1930. And Bayrd Still (1948) has written an especially comprehensive history of Milwaukee, down to 1940. Such histories as these furnish enough information to determine whether the inferences we drew about events, institutions, and actors in Austin and Houston carry weight to a larger class of American cities. Furthermore, our examination of these other sources has revealed that claims about the importance of water problems in Austin and Houston paralleled the situation of scarce water in cities across the nation, such as Los Angeles.

By use of such comparative historical materials, then, we believe it is possible to set parameters on the substantive validity of what we found. Thus, we can assert that, in the most general terms, some cities that expand must face environmental obstacles of extraordinary proportions—like Austin and Los Angeles. Likewise, we believe it is also possible to draw attention to those factors in Austin, such as the battle between the New Dealers and the free enterprisers and such as the prominent role of the New Deal advocates, that, at least in degree if not in kind, were specifically unique to that place. In brief, by drawing into one's sphere of observation the available materials on comparable situations of urban growth, one is able to distinguish between those elements that are general and those that are particular.

Nevertheless, there is no substitute, particularly in realms where one seeks, as we did, some fresh understanding of an old issue, for the intensive study of a single case. Our research has alerted us to the role of growth visions and other critical matters in a way that no research, using census or other quantitative evidence, could have. Our studies have revealed the importance of human actors, both state and market entrepreneurs, in a way that no previous work has. Finally, our detailed work, long and laborious though it was, instructed us in the critical importance of contextual, global, and environmental circumstances. In the final analysis, we were able to suggest new theoretical ideas about urban development and also to hazard theoretical generalizations that may or may not hold up for other cities. Our goal, at least in part, was theoretical honing and generalization, not the statistical generalization of urban studies grounded in demographic data collected by others.

There are, then, advantages and drawbacks to the study of the single case. The drawback is that if one is studying an instance of a much larger set of phenomena, such as cities, one may be limited in what one can assert. But, as we suggest, there are ways around this problem. Ultimately, we came to believe, the richness of detail and the new facts thereby discovered more than made up for the problem of random sampling and statistical generalization. Among the major advantages too is that we stayed close to the data itself, to the everyday urban experience, throughout the process, whereas most researchers engaged in statistical generalization stay far removed from their urban data. In this sense, then, case study work is more empirical—literally, closer to "experience"—than is quantitative work.

References

Abu-Lughod, Janet I. 1971. *Cairo*. Princeton, N.J.: Princeton University Press.

Bernard, Richard M., and Bradley Rice, eds. 1983. *Sunbelt Cities*. Austin: University of Texas Press.

Dahl, Robert A. 1961. *Who Governs? Democracy and Power in an American City*. New Haven: Yale University Press.

Domhoff, G. William. 1983. *Who Rules America Now?* Englewood Cliffs, N.J.: Prentice-Hall.

Fogelson, Robert. 1967. *The Fragmented Metropolis: Los Angeles, 1850–1930*. Cambridge: Harvard University Press.

Hoffecker, Carol E. 1983. *Corporate Capital: Wilmington in the Twentieth Century*. Philadelphia: Temple University Press.

Hunter, Floyd. 1953. *Community Power Structure: A Study of Decision-Makers*. Chapel Hill: University of North Carolina Press.

Jones, Robert. 1982. *Town and Country Chaos*. London: Adam Smith Institute.

Judd, Dennis R. 1984. *The Politics of American Cities: Private Power and Public Policy*. Boston: Little, Brown.

Lynd, Robert S., and Helen Merrell Lynd. 1929. *Middletown: A Study in American Culture*. New York: Harcourt, Brace.

———. 1937. *Middletown in Transition: A Study in Cultural Conflicts*. New York: Harcourt, Brace.

McComb, David. 1981. *Houston: A History*. Austin: University of Texas Press.

Mollenkopf, John. 1983. *The Contested City*. Princeton, N.J.: Princeton University Press.

Molotch, Harvey. 1976. "The City As a Growth Machine: Toward a Political Economy of Place." *American Journal of Sociology* 82 (September): 309–32.

Olien, Roger M., and Diana Davids Olien. 1982. *Oil Booms: Social Change in Five Texas Towns*. Lincoln: University of Nebraska Press.

Orum, Anthony M. 1991. "Apprehending the City: The View from Above, Below, and Behind." *Urban Affairs Quarterly*. Forthcoming.

Still, Bayrd. 1948. *Milwaukee; The History of a City*. Madison: State Historical Society of Wisconsin.

Stone, Clarence. 1976. *Economic Growth and Neighborhood Discontent: System Bias in the Urban Renewal Program of Atlanta*. Chapel Hill: University of North Carolina Press.

Warner, W. Lloyd. 1963. *Yankee City*. New Haven: Yale University Press.

David A. Snow and

Leon Anderson

4 Researching the Homeless

The Characteristic Features and Virtues of the Case Study

This chapter sketches the contours of a case study of unattached homeless men and women living in and passing through Austin, Texas, in the mid-1980s. Its objective is twofold: to articulate and illustrate what we take to be the central characteristics of the case study method; and to underscore its utility for studying marginal groups and certain perspectives and processes that typically elude the grasp of other methodologies. We begin with an overview of the context, procedures, and objectives of our study. We then position our research in relation to the problem of homelessness more generally and to the plethora of studies conducted on today's homeless. This should provide a partial rationale for why we proceeded as we did. Next, we elaborate what we regard as the defining characteristics of the case study method by reference to our research. This discussion, which constitutes the bulk of the chapter, will illuminate our research as well as provide a more thoroughgoing understanding of the case study. Finally, we will briefly discuss the issue of generalizability as it applies to the case study method and to the study of marginal groups such as the homeless.

Overview of Context, Procedures, and Objectives

During the decade between 1975 and 1985, Austin, Texas, was one of the Sunbelt's shining boomtowns, with its population nearly doubling during this period and its economic fortunes expanding at the same rate. This double-edged growth did not shelter the city from the problem of homelessness, though, as its very prosperity and development seemed to spawn a growing number of local homeless as well as attract even much larger numbers from other cities and states.

Although estimates of the size of the city's homeless population varied widely, ranging from a low of around 650 (Baumann et al. 1985) to a high of 4,000 (Austin–Travis County Health Department 1984), there is no mistaking the dramatic growth in this population during the first half of the 1980s. This growth was clearly reflected in the increase in services provided between 1979 and 1984 by the local Salvation Army downtown lodge, by a private agency for the poor called Caritas, and by the Texas Employment Commission. In the case of the Salvation Army, the number of different people served from 1979 through 1984 jumped from 4,928 to 11,271, an increase of 128 percent. That the vast majority of these individuals were indeed destitute and undomiciled is suggested further by the quantum jump in lodgings and meals provided by the Salvation Army during the same period—from 16,863 to 156,451, an 828 percent increase. Caritas experienced an even more phenomenal increase (1,602 percent) in the services it provided during this period, and the Texas Employment Commission witnessed a 72 percent increase in day labor applicants between 1982 and 1984. Even though there is some duplication in services, both within and across agencies, the rate of increase of homeless individuals served by each agency was so robust that the conclusion is unmistakable: whatever the exact number of homeless living in or passing through Austin in the mid-1980s, the city experienced a dramatic growth in the size of that population since the late 1970s.

It was this pool of homeless street people that was the focus of the case study we conducted between 1984 and 1986. Our primary research interest was not so much with their demographics and backgrounds as with three other considerations: the repertoire of material, interpersonal, and psychological subsistence strategies and routines the homeless fashion or appropriate to facilitate their survival; the variation in the use of these strategies across the homeless; and the array of factors that constrain and shape these survival strategies and routines. In short, we were most interested in the subculture of street life as it is lived and experienced by the homeless. We pursued these focal concerns in a triangulated manner by utilizing a number of researchers and procedures to tap a variety of data sources to build several complementary and supplementary data sets.

The Rationale

During the 1980s, few other domestic issues in America have generated as much public interest and debate as the scourge of homelessness. Correspondingly, few other, if any, recent issues have commanded as much attention from social scientists and policy advocates as has that of homelessness (see Baxter and Hopper 1981; Bingham, Green, and White 1987; Hombs and Snyder 1982; Hope and Young 1986; Momeni 1989; Ropers 1988; Rossi 1989a, 1989b; Wright 1989).[1] Indeed, it is probably not too farfetched to assert that academics or researchers in the social service sector have generated reports of one kind or another on the homeless in most communities throughout the country. In a monograph overviewing many of these studies, for example, the author noted that his "working bibliography on the homeless exceeds sixty single-spaced pages of entries, of which three-quarters date from 1980 or later" (Rossi 1989b, 65). The vast majority of these more recent studies that contain primary data share two fundamental characteristics. Most are based on questionnaire surveys of the homeless or shelter providers, and most are concerned primarily with the demographics and disabilities of the homeless.

Evidence of the first tendency can be readily gleaned from perusing the research literature on today's homeless, but it is also clearly indicated by a 1985 General Accounting Office report summarizing research on the homeless. This overview identified 130 studies or reports, only 75 of which contained primary data. Thirty of the 75 were based on street and shelter surveys of the homeless; the remaining 45 reported data retrieved from shelter providers. There was not anything resembling a case study or ethnography among these studies. Clearly, there has been a proliferation of research on the homeless since 1985, but with the exception of a handful of studies—such as Kozol's *Rachel and Her Children* (1988) and Glasser's *More Than Bread* (1988)—the preponderance of this more recent research has been of the survey variety (see, for example, Baumann et al. 1985; LaGory et al. 1989; Lee 1989; Robertson, Ropers, and Boyer 1985; Ropers 1988; Rossi et al. 1987). This is not particularly surprising given the fact that the questionnaire survey has been the sociologist's primary "digging tool" since the 1950s (Benney and Hughes 1956; Denzin 1989c; Sudman 1976). Moreover, it would not be an issue if the survey were the only useful means of gathering data about different social worlds and the lives and routines of their members. Clearly, there are other research traditions that are of some utility for learning about and illuminating certain features of social life, and this is especially true for the study of marginal populations for which few, if any, reliable population parameters have been established, as is the case with today's homeless.

The tendency to focus on the demographics and disabilities or pathologies of today's homeless is also readily evident in both the popular and social science literature. Indeed, it is difficult to find current research on the homeless that goes much beyond enumeration of their demographic characteristics and of the disabilities or problems they are thought to have, such as mental illness, alcoholism, and poor health.[2] These focal concerns are congruent both with the interests and agendas of funding agencies (such as NIMH, NIH, and the Robert Wood Johnson Foundation) and with the kinds of data best procured by questionnaire surveys. The resultant findings certainly advance an understanding of the demographics and some of the presumed disabilities of the homeless, and they are of some utility to agencies interested in doing something about or for the homeless, but they tell us relatively little about life on the streets as it is actually lived and experienced. Thus, it seems reasonable to assert that survey studies of today's homeless have tended to deflect attention from questions and issues pertinent to an understanding of the nature and texture of street life, particularly from the perspective of the homeless themselves. They have tended to generate, in other words, what Geertz (1983) has called "experience distant" rather than "experience near" constructions and understandings.

Since it was the latter type of understanding we were most interested in securing, and since we were particularly interested in learning about the survival routines of the homeless and how these routines vary among them, we thought the case study would be the most appropriate research strategy. This is because case studies, as we conceive them, ideally embody the following characteristics: they are relatively holistic analyses of systems of action that are bounded socially, spatially, and temporally; they are multi-perspectival and polyphonic; they tend toward triangulation; they allow for the observation of behavior over time and thus facilitate the processual analysis of social life; and they have an open-ended, emergent quality. In the following pages, we will discuss our objectives and procedures in terms of these characteristic features of the case study.[3]

Characteristic Features of the Case Study

HOLISTIC ANALYSES OF BOUNDED SYSTEMS OF ACTION

The quintessential characteristic of case studies is that they strive toward a relatively holistic understanding of cultural systems of action.[4] By *cultural systems of action*, we refer to sets of interrelated activities and routines engaged in by one or more networks of actors within a social context that is bounded in time and space.[5] The system of action may vary considerably in scope, ranging from relatively small cliques and gangs (Anderson 1976; Horowitz 1983; Liebow 1967; Whyte 1943) to more meso-level entities, such as religious movements (Rochford 1985), nursing homes (Gubrium 1975), asylums (Goffman 1961), and ethnic enclaves (Gans 1962; Hannerz 1969; Suttles 1968), to communities (Gans 1967; Vidich and Bensman 1958; Whyte 1957) and even total societies, as in the case of those studied by the classical anthropologists (Malinowski 1961; Powdermaker 1933). The focal system of action may also vary in terms of the formality and tightness of its organization (see Goffman 1963, 198–215), but the unit of analysis for the case study is typically some system of action rather than a cross section of individuals, as in the survey.

The holistic emphasis is predicated on the contention that social actions and events can be adequately understood, to paraphrase Diesing

(1971, 138), only in relation to the whole to which they belong and their particular location in the whole system. Thus, Becker wrote that one of the primary aims of the case study is "to arrive at a comprehensive understanding of the group under study: who are its members? What are their stable and recurring modes of activity and interaction? How are they related to one another and how is the group related to the rest of the world?" (1970, 26).

Yet, Becker noted that such an objective is essentially idyllic, since it is well-nigh impossible to see and understand everything in a comprehensive manner. In reality, then, case studies tend to be selective, focusing on one or two issues or processes that are fundamental to understanding the system being studied. Thus, few studies of the homeless have taken the wide-angle approach reflected in Nels Anderson's (1923) classic case study of homeless men in Chicago shortly after the turn of the century. Instead, the tendency among earlier case studies of homeless men was to anchor analysis to a single issue or problem. Wallace (1965), for example, focused on skid row careers or types and the process of becoming a skid rower; Wiseman (1970) concentrated on the recurring relationship between skid row alcoholics and the social agencies that dealt with them; and Spradley (1970) focused even more narrowly on drinking routines of skid row "tramps" in relation to a single institution of control—the jail, or "bucket" as it was referred to by the homeless men he studied. Similarly, Hauch's (1985) more recent case study of Winnipeg's skid row is concerned primarily with the adaptive coping strategies the homeless develop. In each case, though, the focal concern was not abstracted from the context—which has long been the tendency of so much sociological research (see Mills 1959, 50–75), including the bulk of the literature on today's homeless—but was analyzed, instead, in terms of its embeddedness within the ambient context.

In practice, then, the holistic orientation manifests itself in a persistent commitment to the contextualization of social actions, events, and processes. An attempt is made to understand how a set of actions or processes are produced and reproduced or changed by examining their ongoing interaction with other elements within the particular context.

In our research, we were interested not only in the repertoire of subsistence strategies fashioned or appropriated by the homeless and in their corresponding daily routines but also in the factors that shaped and constrained these strategies and routines. Repertoires of subsistence strategies do not emerge in a random, willy-nilly manner but are the product of the interplay of the resourcefulness and ingenuity of the homeless and the local organizational, political, and ecological constraints. The number of shelters and soup kitchens in a community, and their policies regarding whom they serve and how often, have obvious implications for the sleeping and eating prospects and routines of the homeless. And community sentiment and police practices also affect the options and routines of the homeless. An understanding of the experience of homelessness and how it is managed thus requires a consideration of the local matrix of social service and control agencies and commercial establishments that deal directly with the homeless. Accordingly, we spent considerable time examining the organizational matrix in Austin. In addition to spending over four hundred hours in the field with homeless individuals, we spent another two hundred hours with agency personnel, police officers, and local political officials and activists in order to reach a more contextual understanding of street life among the homeless in Austin. These considerations take us to the second characteristic feature of case studies.

MULTI-PERSPECTIVAL ANALYSES

The contextualization of social activities, issues, and processes involves more than providing a descriptive overview of the encompassing context. It entails an effort to discern and articulate the linkage between the phenomenon of interest and the actual social world in which it is embedded and sustained or reproduced (Denzin 1989b). This means, in practical terms, that the researcher(s) consider not only the voices and experiences of the range of actors of focal concern but also the perspectives and actions of other relevant groups of actors and the interaction among them (Douglas 1976). When this occurs, the research tends to be multi-perspectival or polyphonic, which is more typically characteristic of case studies than of other modes of research.

In pursuit of a multi-perspectival understanding of street life, we attempted to identify and map the range of relevant social settings and organizations and types of homeless that together constituted the subculture of street life in Austin. By *relevant social settings and organizations*, we refer to the major institutions or agencies (e.g., the Salvation Army, the city hospital, the city police department), commercial establishments (e.g., plasma centers, labor pools, bars), and spatial or territorial niches (e.g., campsites, bridges, parks, street corners) that are central to the daily rounds, life-style, and prospects of the homeless. Social *types*, on the other hand, refer to characteristic ways of thinking and acting in a given context, ways that differ from other discernible modes of response or adaptation (see Denzin 1989b and Klapp 1964). Since we were interested in discerning and documenting the diversity of relevant settings and types of homeless as a means of tapping the range of relevant perspectives, we employed a type of nonprobability, judgmental sampling technique referred to as maximum variation sampling (Lincoln and Guba 1985). One proceeds in an almost Darwinesque fashion by sampling as widely as possible within the specified sociocultural (ecological) context until exhaustion or redundancy is reached for types of adaptation or response. We thus spent time with as many homeless as possible in the range of settings most relevant to their daily lives in Austin. In total, over six hundred hours were spent with 168 homeless men and women and with other individuals who dealt with the homeless in one capacity or another in twenty-six focal settings. From these contacts, we discerned three generic types and eight subtypes of adaptation and orientation among the homeless (see Snow and Anderson 1992) and five distinct types of organizational response to the homeless, the latter summarized in table 1. The identification both of different types of the homeless and of types of organizational responses to the homeless revealed not only different aspects and layers of street life but also its multi-perspectival character. This discovery also enabled us to gain a more thorough and multi-perspectival understanding of the experience of homelessness in particular and of the subculture of street life in general.

Here it is important to emphasize that our interest in street life as it was experienced, whether from the differing standpoints of the homeless or of the agencies that dealt with them, meant that we were primarily interested in a particular kind of perspective—what Gould and his associates (1974) referred to in their study of the heroin world as "perspectives in action" in contrast to "perspectives of action." Perspectives in action refer to accounts or patterns of talk formulated for the purpose of realizing a particular end or accomplishing a particular task in a naturally occurring situation that is part of some ongoing system of action, such as

Table 1

Organizational Responses and Perspectives
Relevant to the Homeless

Patterns of Organizational Response	Operational Perspective	Local Organizational Carriers
Accommodative	Sustenance-oriented caretaker	Salvation Army
		Private welfare agency
		Soup kitchen
		State employment commission
Restorative	Treatment-oriented caretaker	
	Medical Perspective	City hospital
		State mental health
		Detox centers
	Salvationist perspective	Assembly of God Church
		Detox centers
Exploitative	Market-oriented	Plasma centers
		Day labor
		Bunkhaus
Exclusionist/ expulsionist	NIMBY perspective	Neighborhood associations
Containment	Harassment	City police

Source: Adapted from Snow and Anderson 1991, chapter 3.

when a homeless street person panhandles a passerby. Perspectives of action, on the other hand, are constructed and articulated in response to the queries of researchers or other outsiders, such as when a street person tells a researcher about panhandling. Perspectives of action are thus produced "not to act meaningfully in the system being described, but rather to make the system meaningful to an outsider" (Gould et al. 1974, xxv). Both perspectives yield useful information, but they are of different orders. Perspectives of action are *post-factum* accounts that place the action in question within a larger normative framework, whereas perspectives in action refer to the cognitions and feelings that emerge with and are inseparable from the sequences of action that perspectives of action may be invoked to explain. The more interested researchers are in lived experience and the actual management of everyday routines, the more critical the elicitation of perspectives in action becomes to their project.

We attempted to elicit such perspectives primarily by two means: interviewing by comment[6] and listening unobtrusively to conversations among the homeless, conversations that arose naturally rather than in response to the researcher's coaxing or intervention. This relatively unobtrusive listening took two basic forms: eavesdropping, which involved listening to others within a bounded interactional encounter without being part of that encounter, such as when waiting in meal lines or in day labor offices; and a kind of nondirective, conversational listening that occurred when we engaged in encounters with two or more homeless individuals.[7] The elicitation of perspectives in action through these means enabled us, we believe, to gain a more intimate, multi-perspectival understanding of street life as it unfolded naturalistically and was actually lived or experienced.

TRIANGULATED RESEARCH

The third characteristic feature of the case study is that it calls for a triangulated research strategy. Triangulation has traditionally been associated with the use of multiple methods in the study of one phenomenon (Campbell and Fiske 1959; McGrath, Martin, and Kulka 1982; Webb et al. 1981), but Denzin has correctly noted that triangulation can occur with "data, investigators, and theories, as well as methodologies" (1989c, 236–37). Broadly conceived, triangulation thus refers to the use of multiple data sources, methods, investigators, and theoretical perspectives in the study of some empirical phenomenon.

The logic underlying triangulation is rooted in the complexity of social reality and the limitations of all research methodologies. The basic argument is that social reality is too complex and multifaceted to be adequately grasped by any single method. Consequently, rather than debate the merits of one method vis-à-vis another (they are all flawed in one way or another), one does better to combine multiple strategies so that they complement and supplement one another's weaknesses (Denzin 1989c; Douglas 1976; McGrath, Martin, and Kulka 1982; Webb et al. 1981).

Given the case study's characteristic features discussed thus far—holistic contextualization and multiple perspectives—it is clear that the case study calls for triangulated research. Indeed, most case studies with which we are familiar are triangulated at least in terms of either data sources or methodologies. Our research was triangulated in both respects.

Regarding data triangulation, Denzin (1989c, 237–39) has suggested that there are really three data points or sources: persons, situations and contexts, and time. Our research tapped all three. We have already noted two primary data sources: the homeless themselves and the array of settings, agency personnel, business proprietors, city officials, and neighborhood activists relevant to the routines of the homeless. In addition, we tracked a reasonable approximation of a random sample of 767 homeless individuals through a network of seven institutions with which they had varying degrees of contact.[8] This data source not only provided a detailed portrait of the demographics and disabilities of the homeless but also, and more important for our interests, enabled us to learn more about the institutional contacts and experiences of the homeless. Table 2 lists these agencies and the percent of the total sample that had one or more contacts with each agency.

We also gathered information on the homeless across time, both ethnographically and by tracking them. Encounters with our field sample of 168 homeless adults totaled 492, averaging 3 per person, with a high of 22. We thus had contact with many of the same homeless individuals in a range of settings over time, in some cases extending to a year or more. The tracking strategy was also longitudinal by design, tracking individuals in the institutional network well beyond a year in many cases.

Table 2

Individual Cases Tracked through Local and State Agencies

Agency	Number of Cases	Percent of Sample
Salvation Army	767*	—
Texas Employment Commission	348	45.4
Caritas (private welfare)	294	38.3
Austin Police Department	248	32.3
City hospital	181	23.6
State mental health	84	11.0
Local mental health	78	10.2

* The figure 767 refers to the number of usable cases from a sample of 800 drawn from a population of 13,881 individuals registered at least once at the Salvation Army from January 1, 1984, to March 1, 1985.

Source: Adapted from Snow and Anderson 1991, chapter 1.

In sum, our data set consisted of (1) data on homeless individuals derived from two different contexts—the streets and the institutions; (2) data on relevant agencies, commercial establishments, and ecological niches; and (3) data on the homeless across time.

As already suggested, these data sources were tapped by a mixture of methods—participant observation and informal, conversational interviewing in the case of the homeless; participant and nonparticipant observation, coupled with formal and informal interviewing, in street agencies and settings; and a systematic survey of agency records. To tap the various data sources by these means, we obviously could not use the traditional "lone ranger" approach (Douglas 1976, 192–93) to most cases studies, particularly those of the ethnographic variety. Instead, a team of researchers was developed, consisting of four individuals with different but complementary and overlapping tasks. Two members of the team were responsible for the tracking data, another assumed the role of ethnographer among the homeless, and the fourth functioned in a number of capacities—coordinating the research, negotiating access to agency records and interviewing agency personnel, and functioning as a detached observer or sideline coach for the street ethnographer.[9] Regarding the relationship between the roles of ethnographer and detached observer, it is important to note that rarely was a day or evening in the field not followed by a debriefing session that involved a discussion of field experiences, methodological and theoretical implications, and the development of plans for subsequent outings. A conscious and reflective enactment of these two roles enabled us to maintain involvement and detachment at the same time, thereby facilitating the management of the insider/outsider dialectic characteristic of ethnographic case studies.[10]

In his recent critique of traditional ethnography, as well as more conventional positivistic research strategies, Rosaldo (1989) argued that researchers should try to position themselves in a number of different ways in relation to their objects of research so as to gain a variety of angles of vision or perspective. What he is calling for, it seems, is the kind of multiperspectival strategy discussed earlier. Our response to this directive, as described above, was to triangulate our research in terms of informants, situations, and researchers. Only a team approach to the case study allows for such multidimensional triangulation, and it is in this respect that we think our study is somewhat unique among studies of today's homeless.[11]

CAPTURING SOCIAL PROCESSES

The fourth characteristic of case studies is that they allow for the analysis of actual social processes more than do other modes of research. Unlike cross-sectional studies that entail the sampling of random units at a single point in time, the case study is longitudinal in the sense that it is conducted over a period of time. This facilitates the possibility of capturing and analyzing events and happenings, interactions and relationships, and groups and institutions as they emerge and evolve across time. The case study enables one not only to grasp change as it unfolds but also to acquire a clearer fix on the mechanisms and interactions that affect the change. Such processual analysis, as Rosaldo has noted, "shows how ideas, events, and institutions interact and change through time" (1989, 92–93). It should not be surprising, then, that much of what we know about social processes, particularly at the more meso and micro levels of analyses, comes from case studies of such processes.[12]

Although the ongoing flow of actions and events is most often referred to merely as process, other analogous concepts include natural history, value added, stages, and career. Within sociology, the career concept seems to have the greatest currency. Its referent is expanded beyond occupational trajectories to the passage of people or lines of action through specifiable strands or phases of life. According to Goffman, "the perspective of natural history is taken" as "unique outcomes are neglected in favor of such changes over time as are basic and common to members of a social category, although occurring independently of them" (1961, 127). Thus, in his classic case study of the asylum, Goffman wrote of the "moral career of the mental patient" (1961). Similarly, Becker (1963) discussed career contingencies in becoming a marijuana user, Luckenbill (1986) examined the careers of homosexual prostitutes, and Shover (1983) analyzed the later career stages of property offenders.

In our research on the homeless, we also invoked the career concept to capture processes of adaptation, identity transformation, and transition from one empirically grounded type of homeless person to another. The important point, though, is not so much the conceptual utility of the career concept as the utility of the case study method for grasping such social processes. Because we conducted our research over time, we were able to track homeless individuals both ethnographically and institutionally in a panel-like fashion. This longitudinal character of our research thus enabled us to observe not only different patterns of adaptation with variation in length of time on the streets but also the actual process of drift or transition from one pattern or type of adaptation to another. We recorded not only beginnings and transition points, then, but also what was transpiring in between and what events and happenings were affecting these changes. Cross-sectional surveys can tap variation in behavior and cognitions at different points in time within a bounded system of action, of course. But only truly longitudinal methodologies, such as the case study, allow for the observation of the same real-life units of analysis across a specifiable period of time, whether the unit be individuals, small cliques and groups, organizations, or communities. And it is this feature of the case study that is one of its distinguishing characteristics.

OPEN-ENDED RESEARCH AND SERENDIPITOUS FINDINGS

The final characteristic feature of case studies is that they tend to have an open-ended, emergent quality that facilitates the discovery of both unanticipated findings and data sources. Merton conceptualized this as the "serendipity" pattern or component of research and defined it as "the discovery, by chance or sagacity, of valid results which were not sought for" (1968, 157). Here we would add that the notion of serendipity be extended to include the discovery of novel data sources as well as unexpected findings. What is particularly important about such fortuitous observations is that they provide the occasion not only for "developing a new theory or for extending an existing theory," as Merton emphasized (1968, 158), but also for probing deeper into social and psychological terrain that heretofore has only been skimmed on the surface or sidestepped altogether.

This serendipity pattern surfaces on occasion in all manner of research, but we suspect that it is a more common feature of case studies, particularly of the historical and ethnographic variety. This is because such case studies often begin with a broad, general set of questions or understandings about the phenomena under investigation and then become more focused as the research progresses. Initially, they are rather like exploratory geological expeditions, with more focused probes occurring after the contours of the landscape have been mapped. Consequently, new or unanticipated events, relations, or processes, as well as data caches, frequently surface with a turn of the corner. And these unexpected observations often lead, in turn, to the formulation of new questions and foci for investigation, thus making for a dynamic, recursive research process.

This process was a central feature of our research on the homeless, since several of the eventual focal concerns were not fully anticipated at the outset of our fieldwork. On entering the field, we initially coded our observations broadly, as indicated by the twenty-six focal settings and thirty cultural domains that emerged.[13] In time, however, it became clear that some of the settings and domains were more central than others to the lives and daily routines of the homeless. This was clearly indicated by the variation in the number of data entries contained in each respective category.[14] In short, some of the files "bulged" with data, and others did not. And it was these bulging files that became the foci of our analysis.

One such file pertained to self and identity concerns and focused our attention on the nonobvious issue of how a "sense of personal significance and meaning is generated among individuals who have fallen through the cracks of society and linger at the very bottom of the status system" (Snow and Anderson 1987, 1337–38). We label the issue as *nonobvious* because it has seldom been a topic of research among students of the homeless or of other individuals congregated at the very bottom of status systems. As noted earlier, the preponderance of research on today's homeless has focused on their demographics and disabilities, with little to no attention devoted to their inner life. Thus, when we began our research, the cognitive life of the homeless was not a focal concern. Yet, it emerged as a central issue in a serendipitous fashion, since a portion of the talk we were privy to concerned identity-related issues. Moreover, the implications of these unanticipated findings raised interesting questions about the relationship among role, self, and identity and, more particularly, about Maslow's (1962) well-known hierarchy of needs.[15]

In addition to the unanticipated emergence of such focal concerns, the possibility of institutionally tracking the homeless surfaced only after we had been in the field for several months. Initially, we had thought we would conduct only an ethnographic case study. In time, however, the study broadened methodologically as we became aware of the possibility of tracking the homeless and then took the steps necessary to compile the previously mentioned tracking sample.

Thus, just as a number of focal concerns and theoretical issues emerged unexpectedly after we initiated the study, so we also discovered an unanticipated data source. The important point here is that these fortuitous occurrences took place during the research rather than at the outset, and redirected the research accordingly. Such unanticipated observations and turns are most likely to occur in the course of research that is more open-ended and broadly conceived at the beginning of the research endeavor. Since case studies are characterized by this open-ended, emergent feature more than other modes of research, it follows that the serendipity pattern is also more likely to be a characteristic feature of the case study.

The Issue of Generalization

In the preceding pages, we have provided a rationale for conducting a case study of the homeless, we have identified what we take to be the five central features of the case study, and we have elaborated on those features in terms of the objectives and procedures of our case study of the homeless living in or passing through a single southwestern community in the mid-1980s. In the course of our discussion, we have also suggested a number of strengths or virtues of the case study: it contextualizes social action; it facilitates multi-perspectival and processual analysis; and it often leads to the discovery of unanticipated findings and data sources. At the same time, the case study, as we have conceptualized it, is encumbered by a number of dilemmas. As noted earlier, all methods are flawed in some fashion or another, and those flaws typically flow from the very characteristics of the respective methods. If the case study is to be truly multi-perspectival, triangulated, and oriented to the unfolding and development of events and behaviors across time, for example, then it is obviously a rather time-consuming and labor-intensive methodology. Additionally, its contextual embeddedness and its emergent quality make the standardization of procedures across cases a complicated, if not impossible, task. But the most frequently cited shortcoming of all is the case study's presumed lack of generalizability. It is this vexing issue that perpetually hovers, like an ominous cloud, over any case study, so we address this issue head-on in this final section of the chapter.

From the standpoint of conventional, positivistic social science, with its emphasis on the development of abstract laws that facilitate prediction and control, the production of generalizable findings is its most basic activity. Indeed, such generalizations constitute the base on which a system of laws and theorems is constructed. Kaplan, in *The Conduct of Inquiry*, tells us what such a generalization should look like. It "must be truly universal, unrestricted as to time and space. It must formulate what is always and everywhere the case, provided only that the appropriate conditions are satisfied" (1964, 91). .

Given that such generalizations can only be ahistorical and context-free, it follows that case studies, with their commitment to the contextualization of social action and processes, are of little utility from the vantage point of standard positivistic social science. But are there not other criteria or yardsticks that can be used to assess the quality of social scientific research? Are the findings that emerged from the case study we conducted limited only to the site of the research? Are there no virtues of social science research other than generalizable, context-free findings? Is the traditional positivistic conception of generalization the only one worth pursuing?

Many scholars think not. In fact, at least two other approaches to the issue of generalization have been proposed. In the first case, Yin (1984) has distinguished between statistical generalization (the enumeration of frequencies within a population) and analytic or theoretical generalization. "The short answer" to those who criticize case studies for the lack of generalizability, Yin wrote, "is that case studies, like experiments, are generalizable to theoretical positions and not to populations or universes" (1984, 23). Yin went on to consider the ways in which case studies can clarify theory, which is, after all, the broader and more significant issue.

The second alternative approach has been elaborated by Stake (1978), among others. Stake argues for a more intuitive, empirically grounded, context-specific generalization that he refers to as "naturalistic." He wrote, "Case studies will often be the preferred method of research because they may be epistemologically in harmony with the reader's experience and thus to that person a natural basis for generalization" (1978, 5). What Stake appears to be saying is that the data generated by case studies are often likely to resonate experientially or phenomenologically with a broad cross section of readers and thereby facilitate a greater understanding of the phenomenon in question.

Although such an understanding may not facilitate prediction or control, it is still a kind of knowledge worth pursuing because, to borrow from Geertz, it puts "us in touch with the lives of strangers" and thereby "renders others accessible" and enlarges "the universe of discourse" (1973, 14, 16). Geertz was referring to "thick description," of course. But such description not only bears a striking family resemblance to Stake's notion of naturalistic generalization; it is also the very kind of research enterprise that enhances the prospect of naturalistic generalization. Denzin has made this linkage in his essay on "interpretive interactionism" (1989b) and argues that naturalistic generalization via thick description is what we should strive for in the first place. Whether this should be the primary or only goal of social science is clearly a matter for debate, but there seems to be little question that the kind of knowledge associated with "naturalistic generalization" is clearly worth pursuing. If it was not, then many case studies that are counted as classics—such as Whyte's *Street Corner Society*, Liebow's *Tally's Corner*, and Gans's *Urban Villagers*—would not be so regarded.

We would argue, then, for a more expanded conception of generalization, one that includes the standard kind of abstract, aggregate-level generalization as well as the kinds associated with the notions of analytic generalization and naturalistic generalization and the kindred processes of thick description and interpretive interactionism. Moreover, we would argue further that this latter type of generalization is especially important when considering marginal subcultures and populations such as the homeless, illegal aliens, ethnic and racial minorities, certain classes of deviants, and the stigmatized in general. This is so not only because marginal populations do not lend themselves readily to standard, cross-sectional research procedures but also because the kinds of questions and measures associated with those procedures are not so likely to be relevant to the routines and experiences of marginal group members to begin with. Additionally, and perhaps most important, the generation of information that facilitates naturalistic generalization about such populations reduces the distance between us and them and thereby undermines the basis for misunderstanding and dehumanization. Such information is clearly worth having and too important for social scientists to sidestep. Therein, we think, lies one of the major virtues of the case study. It may not be the only avenue to such knowledge, but it is more likely than other modes of research to generate that knowledge.

Notes

1. It should be noted here that homelessness is hardly a new phenomenon. Instead, it constitutes an old chapter in American history, one that has generated a rather voluminous literature. For a sampling of this earlier literature, see Anderson 1923; Sutherland and Locke 1936; Bogue 1963; Wallace 1965; Spradley 1970; Wiseman 1970; and Bahr and Caplow 1973. For an overview of this earlier literature, see Bahr 1973, and for a comparison of the findings of this literature with today's, see Rossi 1989a, 1989b.

2. Clearly there are discussions of the causes of homelessness, focusing primar-

ily on extreme poverty and the decline in affordable housing (see Hope and Young 1986, chapters 5–7; Ropers 1988; Rossi 1989a, chapter 7; and Wright 1989, chapter 3). But discussions of the homeless themselves have focused almost exclusively on demographics and pathologies, such as mental illness, alcoholism, and health problems (see, for example, Lamb 1984; Momeni 1989; Rossi et al. 1987; Rossi 1989a; and Wright 1989).

3. Not all definitions of the case study emphasize each of these characteristics, although most include at least several of them. Diesing (1971) essentially equates the case study method with participant observation, a definition that is also accepted by Strauss (1987) and Burgess (1983). A somewhat different definition is provided by Yin (1983), who recognizes three essential aspects of case studies: they research (1) contemporary phenomena, (2) in a real-life context, (3) using multiple sources of evidence. Yin's view of case studies is broader than Diesing's and does not preclude the possibility of case studies that do not entail ethnographic research. We concur with Yin's broader definition while, at the same time, emphasizing that ethnographic observation frequently constitutes a central component of case study research. For an extensive annotated bibliography of the case study, see Yin 1983.

4. The phrase *cultural systems of action* is used to distinguish human systems from other systems that exist independent of human experience and activity. For an early and still relevant discussion of this distinction, see Znaniecki 1934.

5. By positing cultural systems of action as the focal unit of analysis for the case study, we are obviously distinguishing the case study from the life history or biographical approach, which takes the individual as the focus of analysis. The two methods share similar epistemological roots and concerns but differ in terms of their respective units and levels of analyses. For a discussion of the life history–biographical method, see Bertaux 1981; Bertaux and Kohli 1984; Denzin 1989a; and Plummer 1983.

6. *Interviewing by comment* refers to an attempt to elicit information verbally from an informant by making an intentional statement rather than by asking a direct question. Comments can vary, just as questions do, in the degree to which they are focused or unfocused and in their level of specificity or generality, ranging, for example, from general and commonplace statements of puzzlement or bewilderment, such as, "I don't get it" or "I don't understand," to more focused statements that cast others into a specific identity or role, such as, "He sure looks like a greenhorn" or "I didn't think you were a regular Sally (Salvation Army) user." For a discussion of interviewing by comment as a supplementary data-gathering technique, the rationale and logic underlying its use, and the variety of forms that comments can take, see Snow, Zurcher, and Sjoberg 1982.

7. Although it might be argued that the information secured during such encounters represented more of a reaction to the researcher's presence than a naturally occurring phenomenon among the homeless, our field experiences suggest that this is not the case. Some of the homeless were apprised of the field research-

er's true status, but they typically lost sight of it as the researcher continued to spend time on the street with them. This forgetfulness was forcefully illustrated one night when the field researcher gave an ill, homeless woman a ride to a health clinic. On the way back from the clinic to the abandoned warehouse where she was going to spend the night, she asked, "Are you sleeping in your car these days or down at the Sally?" The researcher had explained his situation to this woman many times during the previous two and a half months, but she had forgotten and/or not fully believed what he had told her. This should not be surprising, however, in light of the dramaturgical thesis that individuals tend to respond to and identify others more in terms of their proximate roles or actions than in terms of their claims to the contrary.

8. For a discussion of the construction of this sample and the underlying rationale, see Snow 1989, 7–16, and Snow et al. 1986.

9. See Snow, Benford, and Anderson 1986 for a discussion of several of these research roles.

10. For discussions of this chronic tension, from various points of view, see Pollner and Emerson 1983; Merton 1972; and Rosaldo 1989.

11. One other notable contemporary study of homelessness utilized a triangulated methodology: Cohen and Sokolovsky's research on Bowery men (1989). The study was based on two structured questionnaires, systematic participant observation, and casual observation in the Bowery over several years.

12. See, for example, Becker 1963; Becker et al. 1961; Denzin 1987a, 1987b; Glaser and Strauss 1968, 1971; Lindesmith 1947; and Sudnow 1978.

13. By *cultural domains*, we refer to categories of meaning, events, and problems that constitute the social world and life-style of the homeless (e.g., drinking and alcohol, drugs, food and eating, sleeping and shelter, social relationships, work) and that were discerned by the previously discussed procedures. For further discussion of the concept of cultural domains, see Spradley 1980, esp. 88–99.

14. By *data entries*, we refer to single bits or pieces of information relevant to any single focal setting, cultural domain, or homeless individual. The focal settings, cultural domains, and homeless individuals constituted the coding categories that emerged over time. The data entries, extracted from the field notes, varied from a single sentence to several pages in length and were assigned to one or more of the coding categories.

15. For a discussion of these issues, see Snow and Anderson 1987, 1365–69.

References

Anderson, Elijah. 1976. *A Place on the Corner*. Chicago: University of Chicago Press.

Anderson, Nels. 1923. *The Hobo: The Sociology of the Homeless Man.* Chicago: University of Chicago Press.

Austin–Travis County Health Department. 1984. *Robert Wood Johnson Grant Application: Health Care for the Homeless.* Austin, Tex.: Austin–Travis County Health Department.

Bahr, Howard M. 1973. *Skid Row: An Introduction to Disaffiliation.* New York: Oxford University Press.

Bahr, Howard M., and Theodore Caplow. 1973. *Old Men Drunk and Sober.* New York: New York University Press.

Baumann, Donald J., Cheryl Beauvais, Charles Grigbsy, and D. F. Schultz. 1985. *The Austin Homeless: Final Report Provided to the Hogg Foundation for Mental Health.* Austin, Tex.: Hogg Foundation for Mental Health.

Baxter, Ellen, and Kim Hopper. 1981. *Private Lives/Public Spaces: Homeless Adults on the Streets of New York City.* New York: Community Service Society.

Becker, Howard S. 1963. *Outsiders: Studies in the Sociology of Deviance.* New York: Free Press.

———. 1970. *Sociological Work: Method and Substance.* Chicago: Aldine.

Becker, Howard S., Blanche Geer, Everett C. Hughes, and Anselm Strauss. 1961. *Boys in White: Student Culture in Medical School.* Chicago: University of Chicago Press.

Benney, Mark, and Everett C. Hughes. 1956. "Of Sociology and Interview: Editorial Preface." *American Journal of Sociology* 62:137–42.

Bertaux, Daniel, ed. 1981. *Biography and Society: The Life History Approach in the Social Sciences.* Beverly Hills: Sage.

Bertaux, Daniel, and Martin Kohli. 1984. "The Life Story Approach: A Continental View." *Annual Review of Sociology* 10:215–37.

Bingham, Richard D., Roy E. Green, and Sammis B. White, eds. 1987. *The Homeless in Contemporary Society.* Newbury Park: Sage.

Bogue, Donald J. 1963. *Skid Row in American Cities.* Chicago: Community and Family Study Center, University of Chicago.

Burgess, Robert G. 1983. *In the Field.* London: Allen and Unwin.

Campbell, Donald T., and Donald W. Fiske. 1959. "Convergent and Discriminant Validation by the Multitrait-Multimethod Matrix." *Psychological Bulletin* 56:81–105.

Cohen, Carl I., and Jay Sokolovsky. 1989. *Old Men of the Bowery: Strategies of Survival among the Homeless.* New York: Guilford.

Denzin, Norman K. 1987a. *The Alcoholic Self.* Newbury Park: Sage.

———. 1987b. *The Recovering Alcoholic.* Newbury Park: Sage.

———. 1989a. *Interpretive Biography.* Newbury Park: Sage.

———. 1989b. *Interpretive Interactionism.* Newbury Park: Sage.

———. 1989c. *The Research Act.* 3d ed. Englewood Cliffs, N.J.: Prentice-Hall.

Diesing, Paul. 1971. *Patterns of Discovery in the Social Sciences*. Chicago: Aldine.

Douglas, Jack D. 1976. *Investigative Social Research*. Beverly Hills: Sage.

Gans, Herbert. 1962. *The Urban Villagers: Group and Class in the Life of Italian-Americans*. New York: Free Press.

———. 1967. *The Levittowners: Ways of Life and Politics in a New Suburban Community*. New York: Pantheon Books.

Geertz, Clifford. 1973. *The Interpretation of Cultures*. New York: Basic Books.

———. 1983. *Local Knowledge: Further Essays in Interpretive Anthropology*. New York: Basic Books.

Glaser, Barney G., and Anselm L. Strauss. 1968. *A Time for Dying*. Chicago: Aldine.

———. 1971. *Status Passage*. Chicago: Aldine.

Glasser, Irene. 1988. *More Than Bread: Ethnography of a Soup Kitchen*. Birmingham: University of Alabama Press.

Goffman, Erving. 1961. *Asylums: Essays on the Social Situations of Mental Patients*. Garden City, N.Y.: Doubleday Anchor.

———. 1963. *Behavior in Public Places*. New York: Free Press.

Gould, Leroy C., Andrew L. Walker, Lansing E. Crane, and Charles W. Lidz. 1974. *Connections: Notes from the Heroin World*. New Haven: Yale University Press.

Gubrium, Jaber E. 1975. *Living and Dying at Murray Manor*. New York: St. Martin's Press.

Hannerz, Ulf. 1969. *Soulside: Inquiries into Ghetto Culture and Community*. New York: Columbia University Press.

Hauch, Christopher. 1985. *Coping Strategies and Street Life: The Ethnography of Winnipeg's Skid Row Region*. Winnipeg: Institute of Urban Studies.

Hombs, Mary Ellen, and Mitch Snyder. 1982. *Homelessness in America: A Forced March to Nowhere*. Washington, D.C.: Community for Creative Non-Violence.

Hope, Marjorie, and James Young. 1986. *The Faces of Homelessness*. Lexington, Mass.: Lexington Books.

Horowitz, Ruth. 1983. *Honor and the American Dream: Culture and Identity in a Chicano Community*. New Brunswick, N.J.: Rutgers University Press.

Kaplan, Abraham. 1964. *The Conduct of Inquiry*. San Francisco: Chandler.

Klapp, Orrin E. 1964. *Symbolic Leaders: Public Dramas and Public Men*. Chicago: Aldine.

Kozol, Jonathan. 1988. *Rachel and Her Children: Homeless Families in America*. New York: Crown.

LaGory, Mark, Ferris J. Ritchey, Timothy O'Donoghue, and Jeffery Mills. 1989. "Homelessness in Alabama: A Variety of People and Experiences." Pp. 1–20 in *Homelessness in the United States: State Surveys*, edited by Jamshid A. Momeni. Westport, Conn.: Greenwood Press.

Lamb, Richard H., ed. 1984. *The Homeless Mentally Ill: A Task Force Report of the American Psychiatric Association.* Washington, D.C.: American Psychiatric Association.

Lee, Barrett A. 1989. "Homelessness in Tennessee." Pp. 181–203 in *Homelessness in the United States: State Surveys,* edited by Jamshid A. Momeni. Westport, Conn.: Greenwood Press.

Liebow, Elliot. 1967. *Tally's Corner: A Study of Negro Streetcorner Men.* Boston: Little, Brown.

Lincoln, Yvonna S., and Egon G. Guba. 1985. *Naturalistic Inquiry.* Beverly Hills: Sage.

Lindesmith, Alfred R. 1947. *Opiate Addiction.* Bloomington, Ind.: Principia Press.

Luckenbill, David F. 1986 "Deviant Career Mobility: The Case of Male Prostitutes." *Social Problems* 33:283–96.

McGrath, Joseph E., J. Martin, and R. Kulka. 1982. *Judgment Calls in Research.* Beverly Hills: Sage.

Malinowski, Bronislaw. [1922] 1961. *Argonauts of the Western Pacific.* New York: E. P. Dutton.

Maslow, Abraham H. 1962. *Toward a Psychology of Being.* New York: Van Nostrand.

Merton, Robert K. 1968. *Social Theory and Social Structure.* Enlarged ed. New York: Free Press.

———. 1972. "Insiders and Outsiders: A Chapter in the Sociology of Knowledge." *American Journal of Sociology* 78:9–47.

Mills, C. Wright. 1959. *The Sociological Imagination.* New York: Oxford University Press.

Momeni, Jamshid A., ed. 1989. *Homelessness in the United States: State Surveys.* Westport, Conn.: Greenwood Press.

Plummer, Kenneth. 1983. *Documents of Life.* London: Allen and Unwin.

Pollner, Melvin, and Robert M. Emerson. 1983. "The Dynamics of Inclusion and Distance in Fieldwork Relations." Pp. 235–52 in *Contemporary Field Research: A Collection of Readings,* edited by R. B. Emerson. Boston: Little, Brown.

Powdermaker, Hortense. 1933. *Life in Lesu: The Study of a Melanesian Society in New Ireland.* New York: W. W. Norton.

Robertson, Marjorie J., Richard Ropers, and Richard Boyer. 1985. *The Homeless of Los Angeles County: An Empirical Evaluation.* Los Angeles: Basic Shelter Research Project, School of Public Health, University of California.

Rochford, E. Burke, Jr. 1985. *Hare Krishna in America.* New Brunswick, N.J.: Rutgers University Press.

Ropers, Richard H. 1988. *The Invisible Homeless: A New Urban Ecology.* New York: Human Sciences Press.

Rosaldo, Renato. 1989. *Culture and Truth: The Remaking of Social Analysis.* Boston: Beacon Press.

Rossi, Peter. 1989a. *Down and Out in America: The Origins of Homelessness.* Chicago: University of Chicago Press.

———. 1989b. *Without Shelter: Homelessness in the 1980s.* New York: Priority Press.

Rossi, Peter H., James D. Wright, Gene A. Fisher, and Georgianna Willis. 1987. "The Urban Homeless: Estimating Composition and Size." *Science* 235 (March 13):1336–41.

Shover, Neal. 1983. "The Later Stages of Ordinary Property Offender Careers." *Social Problems* 31:208–18.

Snow, David A. 1989. *The Homeless Street People of Austin: A Team-Field Study in the Mid-1980s.* Austin, Tex.: Hogg Foundation for Mental Health.

Snow, David A., and Leon Anderson. 1987. "Identity Work among the Homeless: The Verbal Construction and Avowal of Personal Identities." *American Journal of Sociology* 92:1336–71.

———. 1992. *Down on Their Luck: A Case Study of Homeless Street People.* Berkeley: University of California Press. Forthcoming.

Snow, David A., Susan G. Baker, Leon Anderson, and Michael Martin. 1986. "The Myth of Pervasive Mental Illness among the Homeless." *Social Problems* 33:407–23.

Snow, David A., Robert D. Benford, and Leon Anderson. 1986. "Fieldwork Roles and Informational Yield: A Comparison of Alternative Settings and Roles." *Urban Life* 14:377–408.

Snow, David A., Louis Zurcher, and Gideon Sjoberg. 1982. "Interviewing by Comment: An Adjunct to the Direct Question." *Qualitative Sociology* 5:285–311.

Spradley, James. 1970. *You Owe Yourself a Drunk: An Ethnography of Urban Nomads.* Boston: Little, Brown.

———. 1980. *Participant Observation.* New York: Holt, Rinehart, and Winston.

Stake, Robert E. 1978. "The Case-Study Method of Social Inquiry." *Educational Researcher* 7:5–8.

Strauss, Anselm L. 1987. *Qualitative Analysis for Social Scientists.* New York: Cambridge University Press.

Sudman, Seymour. 1976. "Sample Surveys." *Annual Review of Sociology* 2:107–20.

Sudnow, David. 1978. *Ways of the Hand.* New York: Alfred A. Knopf.

Sutherland, Edwin, and Harvey Locke. 1936. *Twenty Thousand Homeless Men.* Chicago: J. B. Lippincott.

Suttles, Gerald D. 1968. *The Social Order of the Slum.* Chicago: University of Chicago Press.

U.S. General Accounting Office. 1985. *Homelessness: A Complex Problem and the Federal Response*. Washington, D.C.: U.S. General Accounting Office.

Vidich, Arthur, and Joseph Bensman. 1958. *Small Town in Mass Society: Class, Power, and Religion in a Rural Community*. Princeton, N.J.: Princeton University Press.

Wallace, Samuel. 1965. *Skid Row As a Way of Life*. Totowa, N.J.: Bedminister Press.

Webb, Eugene J., Donald T. Campbell, Richard D. Schwartz, Lee Sechrest, and Janet Belew. 1981. *Nonreactive Measures in the Social Sciences*. 2d ed. Boston: Houghton Mifflin.

Whyte, William Foote. 1943. *Street Corner Society: The Social Structure of an Italian Slum*. Chicago: University of Chicago Press.

Whyte, William H. 1957. *The Organization Man*. Garden City, N.Y.: Doubleday.

Wiseman, Jacqueline. 1970. *Stations of the Lost: The Treatment of Skid Row Alcoholics*. Chicago: University of Chicago Press.

Wright, James D. 1989. *Address Unknown: The Homeless in America*. New York: Aldine de Gruyter.

Yin, Robert K. 1983. *The Case Study Method: An Annotated Bibliography*. Washington, D.C.: COSMOS Corporation.

———. 1984. *Case Study Research: Design and Methods*. Beverly Hills: Sage.

Znaniecki, Florian. 1934. *The Method of Sociology*. New York: Farrar and Rinehart.

R. Stephen Warner

5 Oenology

The Making of *New Wine*

In the late spring of 1975, I conceived the idea of conducting a field study of certain social processes centered in the Presbyterian church in the coastal community of Mendocino, California. Thirteen years later, in May 1988, *New Wine in Old Wineskins: Evangelicals and Liberals in a Small-Town Church* was published by the University of California Press. In October 1989, *New Wine* received the Distinguished Book Award of the Society for the Scientific Study of Religion. The present chapter accounts for this extended, ultimately successful, project.

The Case in Point

New Wine is at a one level a social history of a rural Protestant congregation from the late 1950s to the early 1980s, a history noteworthy in part for its ironies. At the end of the 1950s, Mendocino Presbyterian Church was a kind of elevated social club for WASPs, but in 1962 a militant, young Chinese-American pastor was called to the pulpit and turned the congregation's attention, a bit grudgingly, toward social justice for American minorities and Asian peasants. This activist thrust was continued in the late sixties by his successor, who reached out to new kinds of social outcasts, hippies escaping the deterioration of San Francisco's Haight-Ashbury district and young men escaping the military draft. This pastor harnessed the evangelical energies of a lay elder of the church to offer refuge on his ranch to such representatives of the counter-culture, but this enterprise—called Antioch Ranch—over time became a radically evangelical religious congregation itself, a church within the church. It was more the religiously conservative message of the Jesus movement that attracted the counterculture than the politically liberal thrust of the church's 1960s pastors, and hippie Christians began filling the pews by the end of the decade.

When the pastorate was vacated again in 1972, these Christians' num-bers, enthusiasm, and testimonies to changed lives encouraged evangeli-cal activists in the church to bring a minister of their own stripe to the pulpit. Thus in 1973, Mendocino Presbyterian called a graduate of Fuller Theological Seminary to be its pastor, and under his evangelical regime the church became a legend of success (in membership and finances) among California Presbyterians. Yet the evangelical pastor and the evan-gelical leader of the radical movement that had paved his way immedi-ately locked horns in a struggle that was not resolved for five years, end-ing in a Pyrrhic victory for the pastor. Despite his religiously conservative message (or actually because of it), the church met the goals of sixties liberal pastors better in the late seventies than it had before. By the early 1980s, the Mendocino Presbyterian could rightly call itself in its newslet-ter "an evangelical church with a social conscience."

The story is remarkable also for its characters, including the succession of church pastors: Peter Hsu, champion of civil rights, friend of bohe-mian artists, and first nonwhite pastor of a white Presbyterian church in California (1962–66); Mark Kimmerly (1967–72), social ethicist, un-official pastor to the hippies, and (later) single parent; Eric Underwood (1973–83), evangelical preacher and everyone's favorite friend; Bruce Douglas (1979–84), Peace Corps alumnus and Underwood's associate for youth ministry; and standing behind them all, Frederick Althorpe (1931–35 and 1952–57), revered pastor emeritus. There are evangeli-cals like Larry Redford, the leader of the Antioch Ranch fellowship and chair of the committee that called Underwood, but soon Underwood's adversary; Larry's poetic wife, Sue; Jeannie and David Baker, devoted parents and homesteaders, lieutenants and neighbors to the Redfords; and Eleanor Kearney, the born-again wife of one of the town's wealthiest citizens. Add counterculture veterans like Arturo de Grazia, potter and theologian; Ben Moss, the principal of the Christian school and fanatical

Jew for Jesus; Therese, German-American queen of the hippies and worker for Christ; and Laurie, hippie musician and diehard pagan.

Framing the story of these men and women and their common ground in the church is a theoretical analysis of two contemporaneous trajectories of American Protestantism since World War II: the cultural ascendancy of the liberal main line in the 1950s ceding to the resurgence of conservative evangelicalism in the 1970s; and the charismatic enthusiasm generated first by the social movements of the 1960s and then by the Jesus movement of the 1970s. Joining the frame and the historical chronicle is a thread of autobiography, my own trajectory as a citizen of academia and admirer of William Sloane Coffin's at Yale, then field researcher and friend of Eric Underwood's in Mendocino, then again teacher of the sociology of religion in Chicago. The book is filled out with an extensive index, a glossary of terms for non-Protestant readers, and four pages of acknowledgments (at the end) to those who helped me complete it. The whole production is 350 pages long.

I hope (and believe) that case studies are becoming a more respectable social science genre, but the first responses to the project when I brought it to the attention of potential publishers were discouraging. A prospectus and covering letter written in 1982, when the outline of the book was at last clear in my mind, caught the eye of editors at two trade houses known for their social science lists, but they eventually found the extensive detail on one case too much to bear. A religion editor at another trade house liked my writing enough to spare me a half hour of his valuable time, but he couldn't believe that I really meant to spend nearly four hundred pages on one church, and he tried to talk me into doing ten pages each on twenty case congregations. When I showed a completed manuscript to editors at several university presses in 1985, two were still unconvinced that the unorthodox, novelistic presentation of my findings could pass muster with their boards. But Stanley Holwitz, the chief of the Los Angeles office of the University of California Press, sent the manuscript immediately to two knowledgeable outside readers, and after some additional crafting, it was on its way to publication. In the July 1989 issue of the book review journal *Contemporary Sociology*, Wade Clark Roof cited *New Wine* as a "fitting example" of a new genre, the "rich, burgeoning literature" of congregational studies (Roof 1989, 595). Although I can claim no credit for the substantial funding now being provided for congregational studies by the Lilly Endowment and other foundations and did not benefit from such funding for my work on *New Wine*,[1] I felt my vision of this particular case study to be vindicated at last.

Methodological Triangulation in Fieldwork

New Wine employs four methods, three of which—participant observation, interviews, and archival research—are written about in the book's methodology chapter and will be discussed here for the way that each supplemented the other's limitations. The fourth, and in some ways the most crucial for wrapping up the project, was the writing itself.

PARTICIPANT OBSERVATION

I moved to an apartment in Mendocino in May 1976 and, supported by my savings, lived there until late December. During these seven months the bulk (but by no means all) of my field research was conducted. My entrée to the community was relatively easy, since my former wife, whom I call "Jane" in the book, was a member of the Presbyterian church and of Larry Redford's Antioch group. Through her, I had met some of the principals in the church on previous visits, including Underwood and the Redfords, and had been assured of their willingness to undergo my study.

When I arrived in 1976, I was thus prepared to hold Friday nights open for Antioch meetings and Sundays for church services and coffee hours. I soon found that I could do additional observation in a prayer meeting on Thursdays and (since I can sing baritone) at choir rehearsal on Wednesdays. On first Mondays, I made a habit of community meetings, not directly connected to the church. More important, I joined in work parties and weekend camp-outs with the Antioch group (I had brought my tent and sleeping bag with me to Mendocino in hope of such opportunities) and shared summer picnics with the church congregation. Since Mendocino is a small town, full of gossip, I expected that my frequent errands to the bank, post office, and grocery store and my occasional forays to concerts, bars, and dance halls would yield important information, and I was not disappointed. Later, I was invited to meetings of the Rotary club and the church's board of elders.

Following the advice of Rosalie Wax, Howard Becker, and John Lofland, I took extensive notes, about an hour of writing for every hour of observation, not knowing what use might be made of all the detail I recorded. When I came to write the book, I found invaluable the cultural oddities in my early notes, recorded by one new to the field and to evangelicalism, and the local social color in the later notes, a product of informed and compulsive hobnobbing. The passages in the book that give me the most pleasure are the fruit of my own watching and listening.

Participant observation yields rounded research findings, something that is particularly important in ideological organizations like churches. Living in Mendocino, seeing members of the church and Antioch group in leisure and work settings as well as in formally defined religious events, made it possible for me to gauge the quotidian relevance of religious profession. Inside their homes, I saw carefully embroidered religious mottoes, sentimental paintings of Jesus, and sleek wooden crosses, along with cookbooks, dried flowers, and stereo systems. Around town, I overheard casual references to the work of the Lord in someone's life and peevish remarks about Holy Joes from someone else. Scrubbing a kitchen alongside Antioch people for a needy member of the fellowship, I found that "Praise God!" and "Hallelujah!" could have precisely the syntactical function and situational usage of casual profanity. I saw firsthand the evangelicals' dedication to and deviation from their ideals.

The corresponding pitfall of participant observation is the temptation to suppose that the period of one's fieldwork supplies an adequate sample of the phenomenon under investigation, freeze-framing social process to a static model.[2] Classic ethnographies did this, presenting cultural patterns in the present tense as "the way it is" among the subject aborigines, as if nonliterate societies had no history. That I did not succumb to the temptation to use my Mendocino data in this manner is attributable not only (as we shall see) to the availability of archival data and my familiarity with such historically sensitive ethnographic models as *The Death and Rebirth of the Seneca* by Anthony Wallace, *The Joyful Community* by Benjamin Zablocki, and *The Survival of a Counterculture* by Bennett Berger, but also to the fact that, even before embarking on the study, I knew of Mendocino as a place that took people (like Jane) through many changes.

From 1969 to 1989, with the exception of four years, I traveled to

Mendocino at least once every year, first of all to visit my son, later to conduct research, and most recently to keep in touch with old friends. Along the way I've seen many people come and go, have children and grow old, turn on, drop out, and climb back up. I knew that some charismatic Christians in 1976 had recently been dope-smoking hippies, and I watched some of them become upstanding Presbyterians. Because of Jane's twin involvement with Redford's fellowship and Underwood's church, I saw close up the tensions that would inevitably bring change to their symbiotic system, as constituents gravitated from the radical movement to the more settled institution. I knew intuitively that no snapshot could properly portray Mendocino's Christian community.

Another benefit of full-time participant observation is that the researcher can use his or her own experience as data. Writing of Malinowski in the Trobriand Islands, Clifford Geertz remarked: "There is a lot more than native life to plunge into if one is to attempt this total immersion approach to ethnography. There is the landscape. There is the isolation. . . . There is the memory of home and what one has left. There is the sense of vocation and where one is going. And, most shakingly, there is the capriciousness of one's passions, the weakness of one's constitution, and the vagrancies of one's thoughts" (Geertz 1988, 77; see also Clifford 1988, 34–35). I felt what it was like in Mendocino to be alternately chilled by fog and exhilarated by clean, crisp, sunny air; awed by dark forests and wistful for city life and television; worried about my landlady's water supply, my car's brakes, and my own livelihood and soul; lonely for like-minded company and thrilled by rooms full of song. Moreover, unlike Malinowski, I had pitched my tent among people of my own race and language, from whom I was alien only by reason of a simple profession of religious faith, and the possibility of going native was ever present. Maintaining emotional and analytic distance from my people (without veering over into a defensive pretense that I was essentially different from them)[3] was a chronic concern.

I had many friends in the world abroad who kept track of me by phone and letter, and I took up friends' offers to host me when I had time to get away for the four-hour drive down to San Francisco. I heeded advice to allow time for an extended vacation midway in my fieldwork and had three weeks off in early fall. Above all, like Bruno Bettelheim in Buchenwald, I found that my note-taking was the therapeutic exercise I needed to maintain equanimity. My fears, doubts, dreams, and afterthoughts, thus tamed, became material for later analysis.

INTERVIEWS

I questioned people directly, more or less formally, in more or less structured formats, for several kinds of information. I wanted to know what young people thought of their conversions and of speaking in tongues, and what old-timers thought of the new evangelical pastor and his protégés and of his liberal predecessors and theirs. I wanted people of all ages to recount their experiences with the world outside and with the church and the Antioch group. Some interviewees used the opportunity to witness to me with their testimonies, whereas others were clearly uncomfortable with the questions I asked.[4] As time went on and I learned more about the community and its history, I asked some respondents for quite specific items of information, for example to elaborate on cryptic references in minutes of meetings held a decade or more ago. Some people sought me out to tell me their side of some dispute, as both Eric Underwood and Ben Moss did when they took sharply opposed sides on the "elopement" of a high school girl, who had been a member of the Antioch group, with her similarly underage boyfriend.

Since I did not tape-record my interviews, I could not reproduce long sequences of extemporaneous vernacular speech for publication and had to rest content with tape-recorded sermons, newsletter prose, and the bits and pieces of verbatim speech that I could scribble in my notepad as an interview proceeded. Yet respondents may have been more frank with me in the absence of a tape recorder (see Warner 1988, 75–78), and because I had to return to my desk immediately after the interview to make sense of the scribbles, the substance of the interview was entered into my field notes and my memory earlier and more securely than if I had relied on later transcriptions. Since other scholars were looking at new evangelical and charismatic Christian cultures at about the same time I was, I can now refer to their work (e.g., Harding 1987; Neitz 1987; Rose 1987; Ammerman 1987) for accounts of respondents' discourse superior to my own.

Native speech, even as truncated, gives flavor and color to ethnography. Its absence means that the published report is a "controlling discourse always more or less that of the author" (Clifford 1988, 47). The danger with interviews is that subjects' perspectives are likely to be self-serving and their recall flawed. Moreover, when one has found a particularly articulate informant, there is the temptation to rely on him or her for the definitive reading of the culture at hand, as if the group enjoyed an unreflective, monolithic consensus. Since my people were English-speaking and since ideological differences among them were obvious, I had less need and less inclination to rely on any one of them as local guide than if I had been an utter foreigner immersed in a culture thoroughly opaque to me. It was thus forced on my consciousness that "informants are specific individuals with real proper names" (Clifford 1988, 51).

For instance, on an early visit to Mendocino (August 1975), Jane and her husband invited me to listen to a local radio gospel hour. I heard a member of their Antioch group, a folksinger named Josh, introduce a new composition by saying, "The Lord gave me this song." Later that day, when I met Eric Underwood to ask if he had objections to my doing a study of his church, I mentioned Josh's remark. Eric said, "The Lord gave Josh the gift to write the song," and I heard at once a difference between the rhetoric of the charismatics and that of the neoevangelicals in Mendocino. Moreover, I had my own observations and my access to local archives to control for respondents' partial perspectives. I never imagined that there was only one Christian culture in Mendocino.

ARCHIVES

When one has observed and interviewed in the field for a finite period of time and has returned to one's home office with an accumulation of notes to analyze, a collection of classic ethnographies to emulate, and the encouragement of colleagues to tell what it was like, it can seem most salient that one has been in another world, whose distinct way of life is what one's home world needs to understand. Some of the best contemporary ethnographies do just this, giving voice to previously strange beliefs and customs, where the object of the case study is the level of human action called *culture*. As I looked over my notes during my mid-field vacation, things in Mendocino struck me as too complicated for that, and even if I had planned to complete an ethnography of the Antioch group, my project would have been spoiled by the group's disintegration before my eyes. I realized that I had dropped for a brief moment into an intricate, open-ended ballet of persons, social organizations, and religious cultures that, in order to comprehend, I would have to follow backward and forward in time. So my case study became less of an ethnography and more of a social history, and I began to read what archival materials were available to me when I returned to the field in October 1976.

Archival research is a high-flown term for an activity that took shape for me on election day, when I looked over voter rosters posted at polling places to find which political parties the church and Antioch people belonged to. Under this general rubric, which Eugene Webb and his colleagues (1981) have called "traces" and "the running record," I must include the tape-recorded worship services, newsletters, and newspapers I began receiving by mail before I moved to Mendocino and the census records I consulted in my university library years later.

To fill in what I had not heard preached from the Mendocino pulpit in the 1960s, I used one of Peter Hsu's books, written shortly after he left the community, and Mark Kimmerly's master's thesis, completed just before he arrived. Laurie, a musician and Berkeley alumna, lent me a copy of a term paper she had written in 1970 on the topic of Therese's hippie commune, where she had lived until it (and its patroness) were taken over by radical Jesus people. A member of the choir lent me her copy of a fifty-page souvenir history of the church, which had been prepared for its first centenary in 1959 and which featured particularly revealing photographs of church life in the 1950s. Underwood lent me a chaotic stack of weekly church attendance records dating back to 1959, which he had found in the office files. By all odds the most valuable archives were the minutes of the Mendocino church "session," or board of governing elders, to which I was allowed access by formal vote, and the church's annual reports, widely distributed to all attendees at annual potluck suppers. I eventually read the minutes for 1957 through 1982 and relied on them as the foundation for the chronology of the narrative.

But archival records are not self-sufficient. Not only were the minutes of the session soporific, they were also expurgated of much contextual information necessary for decades-later interpretation, context that would have been understood by those privy to them a few weeks after the meeting recorded, or embarrassing to them, or both. N. J. Demerath and Rhys Williams remarked, apropos of their historical study of church-

state relationships in Springfield, Massachusetts, that "the written tran-
script is merely the recording of motions, seconds, and votes. Verbatim
debate is missing altogether." Perfunctory resolutions get more space
than "the hottest political topics of the day" (1987, 10–11). Thus, had
not an interviewee already volunteered information about a tumultuous
sex scandal in 1965, I might have passed right over a reference in the
contemporaneous minutes to a person's unstated "activities . . . that have
led to difficulties over the past few months" (Warner 1988, 96). (Indeed,
Eric Underwood told me that when, as the new pastor getting acquainted
with the church, he ran into the same reference, he had to ask an old-
timer confidante what had happened and who had been involved.) Similarly, interviews with Mark Kimmerly and Peter Hsu helped me decipher
the session's delicately phrased misgivings about their social activism in
the mid-1960s.

Denominational archives (which I consulted in a seminary library as
part of a brief survey of membership trends in California Presbyterian
churches, a survey reported in chapter 8 of *New Wine*), similarly require
supplementation with personal and contextual memories, which, in the
case of national denominational affairs, may well be published (e.g., Fry
1975). It is presumably this kind of methodological triangulation that led
the reviewer Erling Jorstad, a historian, to praise *New Wine* as a "break-
through," a "significant addition" to "religious history (religion as influenced by its social setting)," in place of the earlier "church history"
(1989, 657).[5]

Implicating the Reader through Desk Work

My financial, professional, and psychological investments in
the Mendocino project were so compelling and the data I accumulated
there so rich that I did not doubt on my departure whether I had something to publish. Family and friends encouraged me, and both the sociologist Howard Becker and the pastor Mark Kimmerly insisted that I had
an obligation to report what I had found. I was aware that "writing it
up" usually takes far longer than finding "it" out in the first place, that
"desk work" is more protracted than "fieldwork."[6] But for me the usual
agonies of writing when fieldwork is over were compounded by the fail-

ure of my initial conceptualization and my ignorance of the literature I would therefore need to read. As a political sociologist, I had long wanted to conduct an empirical study of consensus building, and I had gone to Mendocino originally to see how the heirs of sixties activism could accommodate themselves to seventies evangelicalism, which, to judge from the church's organizational success, they evidently had done. I had presupposed that the two Protestant theological parties—evangelicalism and liberalism—would be well represented among Mendocino's laity, but it became apparent during my first months in the field that I was wrong. The conflict I had intended to study did not exist in Mendocino. A salvage job was in order.

I also became acutely aware that whatever I had to say could be read by the English-speaking, literate, and quite sophisticated people of Mendocino, a community of a few thousand with several bookstores and four or five local newspapers. I faced practical worries about challenges to my expertise and my legal right to publish. "Sociologists, caught in their own society, must write about matters over which they are, at best, dubious authorities and therefore subject to continual challenge (in both scholarly and lay circles). Informants, research advisors, friendly and hostile peers, journal editors, libel lawyers, governmental authorities, and suspicious members of studied groups may all know a good deal about the social worlds represented by sociologists in their writing" (Van Maanen 1988, 23). But I brooded more about my moral standing next to the people of Mendocino, in which respect I am evidently typical of a new generation of ethnographers. "One of the major assumptions upon which anthropological writing rested until only yesterday, that its subjects and its audience were not only separable but morally disconnected, that the first were to be described but not addressed, the second informed but not implicated, has fairly well dissolved" (Geertz 1988, 132). Eventually, I asked several principal actors to read and comment on chapters dealing with them. I also glossed over a few affairs, the details of which might still cause pain to living persons.

The decision to write a historical narrative brought into question my earlier unthinking acceptance of the sociological folkway that makes Muncie into Middletown, Newburyport into Yankee City, and Candor into Springdale. The religion editor who had wanted me to write twenty case histories set me to thinking that "Port Madera," the pseudonym for

Mendocino I had been using, might present a gratuitous barrier to the acceptance of the book as a piece of history as well as sociology, and I began to explore the possibility of taking the wraps off the name of the community. Historians rightly think of sociological data as being located in space and time. On the other hand, historians ordinarily lack the sociologist's privilege and burden of writing about people who are alive, read books, and have feelings and lawyers.

If we are to write real social history, we need some kind of personal names. Real, prickly, idiosyncratic people do things like preach sermons, teach Sunday school, struggle for civil rights, and label each other as sinners. It is real people who provide the intersection between various timeless cultural ideals and the flow of events, and we have to know who they are from one year to the next. We want to know that the same fellow (I call him Bobby Houston) who found in a Jesus Movement commune the fundamental resocialization he craved later introduced Esalen-Institute meditation techniques to an evangelical prayer group; that Ben Moss, the Christian school principal, formerly taught in New York City public schools; and that Peter Hsu became a denominational executive and seminary professor after his sojourn in Mendocino. A name is an identity, an index of actors' continuity across temporal, social, and cultural divides. One reason the book took me so long to write is that there was no simple solution to protecting the dignity of the subjects in the story while providing the reader with a textured narrative. Without the narrative, there would be no book, because the book is not primarily a study of a culture but of a social institution. (This much is a lecture to sociologists and anthropologists.) In the end, I used proper names for places and public figures and pseudonyms for the churchpeople of Mendocino, and the book addressed its subjects and implicated its audience.[7]

My first finding was that Protestant liberalism had all but disappeared from Mendocino with the departure of Hsu and Kimmerly. The polar positions from which consensus would have to have been forged in Mendocino may have coexisted in American Protestant culture at large but did not exist in the local setting. Having amassed a mountain of data and developed a stubborn conviction that I was onto something, I took time out to learn what was for me a new field, the sociology of religion, which I thought might help me to see how my presuppositions had gone awry. By the time I learned that the reigning literature in that field also gave me little help (it too assumed that Protestant liberalism extended from its cosmopolitan center deeper into the social fabric than subsequent empirical research found to be true), I was quite convinced that I had a message to share of broader import than the story of one small-town church and its people. Yet that story was the indispensable grounding of whatever message I did have, and I resolved to tell it to the best of my ability.

> The ability of anthropologists to get us to take what they say seriously has less to do with either a factual look or an air of conceptual elegance than it has with their capacity to convince us that what they say is a result of their having actually penetrated (or, if you prefer, been penetrated by) another form of life, of having, one way or another, truly "been there." And that, persuading us that this offstage miracle has occurred, is where the writing comes in. . . . Ethnographers need to convince us . . . not merely that they themselves have truly "been there," but . . . that had we been there we should have seen what they saw, felt what they felt, concluded what they concluded. (Geertz 1988, 4–5, 16)

Chapters 4 through 7 and 9 through 12 narrate the trajectory of the church, and the cultural currents that so affected it, from 1959 to 1979. Though the narrative is somewhat more detailed for events subsequent to my research (chapters 9–12) than those before (chapters 4–7), I use my own observational voice when possible to flesh out data I collected from archives and oral histories, giving descriptions of places and persons figuring in earlier times as I may have encountered them elsewhere or later (e.g., Warner 1988, 102, 109, 122–23, 136–38, 161, 170–72).[8] Having been chilled through to the bone for a winter week in 1975 when I stayed in an unheated room in the drafty old house on the headlands where Jane and her family lived, I knew why Carolyn Kimmerly demanded that the church's manse be remodeled before she and her husband would arrive in 1967. Having held summer jobs in my undergraduate years as a forest fire-fighter and having seen remote rural buildings reduced to ash before our crew could arrive, I knew how some hippie communards must have felt as their community center, a great old barn, burned to the ground on Halloween night in 1970.

Instances of the particular inform chapters devoted to the general, unfamiliar characters reappear until they are known, and cosmopolitan references stand out in parochial chronicles. Key actors, such as Underwood and Redford, appear in detail in the first, mostly theoretical, chapters so that the reader can anticipate where the story will lead as it follows their careers. Other characters, like Arturo de Grazia and David Baker, appear early (1968 and 1969 in chapters 4 and 5) and pop up often later (1972 and 1976 in chapters 6, 7, 10, 11, and 12) until their stories, along with many other threads of the narrative, are rounded off in an epilogue (to 1986). I took care to weave into the narrative those references to happenings of the times that readers will likely remember: California's Fair Housing Law of 1962, the Rumford Act (which Peter Hsu defended in a series of debates on the Mendocino coast); the songs of Malvina Reynolds (who performed at a 1968 Poor People's March support rally in the church's social hall); the alleged involvement of Angela Davis in a Marin County courthouse shoot-out (which split the national Presbyterian Church when its staff contributed $10,000 in its name to her defense fund); the Christmas bombing of North Vietnam in 1972 (condemned from the local church pulpit by a student minister); Jim Jones's rural commune (which was nearby in Mendocino County and often in the news in 1976); the Ford-Carter election (which was prayed over in Antioch meetings); the 1984 Beirut kidnapping of Benjamin Weir (who spoke to a church potluck during my visit); the advent in the 1970s of sinsemilla technology in the cultivation of marijuana (which changed the economy of Mendocino and Humboldt counties).

The more I worked on this story and the conceptual frame distinguishing evangelicals (Underwood and Redford) from liberals (Hsu and Kimmerly) and movements (civil rights and Antioch Ranch) from institutions (electoral politics and Mendocino Presbyterian Church), the more I became convinced that I had stumbled upon an important sociological discovery in Mendocino, a discovery about American society at large. To put it a little too bluntly, I discovered there not an isolated subculture called evangelicalism but the fact that the academic culture in which I was steeped (along with many of my potential readers) had itself become alienated from a broad spectrum of conservative religion with far more adherents and an equal claim to the legacy of the American cultural mainstream. I criticized academics' and Protestant liberals' unexamined assumption of cultural privilege in a brief essay written two years after my main fieldwork and published in 1979, and *New Wine* restated this critique with far more authority, depth, and nuance. The final draft of the book stands with those who "have rejected discourses that portray the cultural realities of other peoples without placing their own reality in jeopardy" (Clifford 1988, 41).

The key rhetorical device was to present myself, the researcher, as a prototypical representative of academic culture who was surprised to find out in the field that, when it came to evangelicals, there was little "separating 'them' from me" (Warner 1988, 73). This statement is made explicit in the theory and methods chapters, but it is continually insinuated throughout the book.

The history that chronicles the Mendocino church from the 1950s to the 1970s (chapters 4–7 and 9–12) and my role in its narration (chapter 3) is bracketed by statements (ibid., 64, 289) of the gulf between academe and conservative religion, a gulf that I attribute as much to academic ignorance as to evangelical isolation. To do this, I give evidence of my own well-socialized status as a liberal California Presbyterian in the 1950s (ibid., 50, 56, 68), as a veteran of political action at Berkeley in the 1960s (ibid., 15, 46, 241), as an expositor of big-name sociological theorists at Yale in the 1970s (ibid., 65, 67, 72, 76, 79, 289–90), as a teacher of sociology of religion in Chicago in the 1980s (ibid., 36, 296), as a college professor (ibid., 76, 83, 295) with many good friends and colleagues in academia (ibid., 70, 74, 78, 87, 183, 308, 310, 341–43), and as a long-time resident of college towns across the country (ibid., 15, 202, 296, 303–4)—an educated, cosmopolitan, modern man generally knowledgeable in matters religious but as astonished as the rest of the intelligentsia by the events of 1976 that earned it the journalists' label "year of the evangelicals," events that we might have anticipated had we been better informed.

The narrative also shows Mendocino evangelicals' openness to multifaceted relationships with me. These portrayals appear not only in the explicitly autobiographical methods chapter but throughout the book, from beginning to end. I recount Mendocinoans' recognition of my presence. They greet me (ibid., 72), tell me about their spiritual gifts (ibid., 134), offer me information and other favors (ibid., 78–80, 258, 260), pray for me (ibid., 42), witness to me (ibid., 299), confide in me (ibid., 236), wish they hadn't said things to me (ibid., 235–36), express impolite opinions to me (ibid., 38, 41, 234, 253, 284), and read drafts of my book (ibid., 236, 254). I depict my own participation in meetings and encounters as one among them (ibid., 38, 75, 171, 181, 202, 220, 243, 323). I sing songs, take notes alongside Sue Redford, tell about living in Chicago, overhear complaints addressed to others, and carry a Bible (but do not offer prayers or take communion). They are shown relating to me as my son's father, as a sociological researcher, as a potential convert, and as an eligible male (ibid., 70, 73–75, 86). I acknowledge that I had my favorites among them (ibid., 72, 76–77, 226, 265–66, 282); I document my own emotions at being among them (ibid., 73–74, 78, 85–87, 222); and I offer a few gratuitous opinions on what I lived through (ibid., 39, 276, 287).

Lest this theme of personal sociological enlightenment appear too relentless, I speak of other facets of myself known to the people of Mendocino and orthogonal to the divide between evangelical and academic cultures: a bearded, gray-haired male with strong ties to his family, a backpacker, amateur musician, and cook. I acknowledge limits on my knowledge, including scenes that I did not experience, questions that I did not ask, and information that people refused to give me (ibid., 80, 84, 92, 119, 143, 218, 240, 249). To judge from the responses, I feel the desk work was a success.[9]

From the Particular to the General

I intended that the dense particularity and sustained narrative design of the book should give it broad appeal as well as certain authority. An elaborate story is an aid to the imagination (Coles 1989). The sheer number of images comprising it makes the chances high that some of them will enter the reader's memory and be embedded in a unique mnemonic context. With such attention-holding properties, a story can more readily provoke intellectual surprise by confronting settled ideas and paradigmatic theories. Given richness of narrative detail, the theories at risk are greatly varied, and the narrative design should thus militate against the reduction of the findings to a single evanescent theoretical issue.[10] In this manner, I believe that stories can have more general import than theories in the pluralistic intellectual world we inhabit.[11]

Nonetheless, when one's book is one of hundreds published per year in even a subfield of the discipline and when potential readers' resources of money and time are finite, one must somehow capture their attention. A quick and sure means of communicating the general import of one's case study is to signal particular scholarly communities through special terminology (e.g., *rational choice*) and abbreviated citations (Van Maanen 1988, 26–28). These devices efficiently indicate one's sophistication, and as a long-time teacher of sociological theory, I have many at my disposal. But they tend to exclude far more potential readers than they alert. At the risk of being dismissed by some colleagues and talking down to others, I used jargon and citations sparingly in *New Wine* and usually explicated their meaning when I did. Many of my signals appeared as chapter epigrams, where, it seems to me, authors' crypticism is customarily indulged by readers. I hoped social theorists would notice the quotations from Marx, Weber, Burke, Shils, Geertz, Stinchcombe, Collins, and Alberoni; sociologists of religion, those of Herberg, Kelley, and Tipton; religionists, those from the Bible, hymnody, and Luther; and literary types, those from Bellow and Dickens. And I hoped other readers would not be distracted.

More problematic, because harder to carry off efficiently and unambiguously, was connecting the case study to substantive topics of broad interest. One such connection occurred to me soon after I left the field. Archival records revealed that the membership and financial well-being of Mendocino Presbyterian had swelled under the religiously conventional, community-conscious leadership in the 1950s (as had that of the denomination as a whole), dwindled under the liberal pastorates in the 1960s (again repeated at the national level), and mushroomed under the evangelical regime of the 1970s (when national attention had shifted from the still declining mainline churches to the similarly burgeoning religious Right). If the Mendocino church was hardly a typical Presbyterian church, perhaps it was a uniquely situated mirror for American Protestantism in general. Taking care not to attribute the organizational decline of the 1960s at either the local or the national level to the coincident clerical liberalism, I drew on a large literature to argue from my first draft to the last that the church did indeed recapitulate the trajectory of American Protestantism for a quarter century. Although I have never been pleased with the writing of that part of the book (chapter 1, alas), the claim of generality was credible to experts in the field.[12]

Given the attention being paid in the media and at conferences to the conservative religious resurgence, I was sure that evangelicals should appear somewhere in the title, but I disregarded the implicit incentive to paint them in lurid tones. Although I interviewed one person who had ferociously punitive attitudes and who insisted on calling himself a "fanatic," as well as others whose absorption in the occult rendered them "spiritually immature" among their brethren, my overwhelming impression was that the evangelicals of Mendocino were well-adjusted citizens of the modern world who made their living in a money economy (even as they gave their businesses religious names), took advantage of modern medicine (even as they prayed for recovery), and tolerated the sins of others (even as they preached moral purity). In the long delay between my field research and the book's publication, I read a number of recently published and draft studies of evangelicalism and other brands of religious conservatism (especially Neitz 1987; Ammerman 1987; Hunter 1983; Roof 1978; Richardson, Stewart, and Simmons 1979; and Caplow, Bahr, and Chadwick 1983), studies that influenced the phrasing of my findings. My relatively benign portrayal of contemporary evangelicalism has raised some eyebrows but has garnered approval elsewhere.[13]

A third general topic, and the most interesting to me, has yet to be noticed by reviewers. Mendocino, though a small, fairly remote place, is an artists' colony, tourist mecca, and haven for early retirees and other exurbanites. Its population grew rapidly in the 1970s, in part due to its magnetic appeal, for a culture of nostalgia, as the ideal type of the small town, where people are friendly, houses are unlocked, chickens are kept in the backyard, and the butcher (whose name you know) makes sausage fresh daily. Those who chose to migrate to Mendocino with these expectations I labeled "elective parochials" (Warner 1988, 87, 201–8), and I claimed that Eric Underwood's evangelical preaching was so effective in part because his theological teachings ennobled (without his conscious design) the cultural choices they had made (see chapter 9). As I worked on the book, I became aware through field trips in Chicago of other instances of this general pattern—that congregations often prosper because they affirm the local, sometimes ethnic, culture—and I happened on

Frances FitzGerald's studies of communities that have been newly sorted out by the forces of modernity she likened to a centrifuge (1986, 16). Later I proposed that the American religious system flourishes because its voluntary and pluralistic nature facilitates social sorting and group mobilization on the basis of religiously expressed cultural identities. That idea is the foundation of my next book (Warner forthcoming).

Developing the three topics above (the postwar trajectory of American Protestantism, the modernity of evangelicalism, and the interplay of congregationalism and social sorting) as general implications of the Mendocino case study was primarily a matter of accumulating sufficient citations, illustrations, and allusions from my professional reading, fieldwork, and life experience so that I could say credibly that the smaller phenomenon simulates the larger. This is implication by subsumption, and its accomplishment requires more assiduous application than analytic acuity. It is harder to demonstrate that a given case study provides evidence for or against some causal theory because in that circumstance, one must look at the simultaneous operation of two or more variables.

For example, Redford, the Antioch Ranch leader, and Underwood, the church pastor, carried on a cold war for five years, from 1973 to 1978. Why? In Mendocino, people found their personality differences the most plausible factor. Among religiously knowledgeable readers, the conflict could easily be attributed to their theological differences, the former being a charismatic evangelical, the latter a plain evangelical. Such overdetermination plagues authors of case studies. I argue that the theological differences were far greater between Redford and Kimmerly and did not cause conflict and that another factor, deeper than personality, was that Redford led a movement and Underwood an institution. The two men were, I claim, ideological allies but organizational rivals, and there wasn't room for both of them in the same church. I suspect that this explanation will satisfy sociologists, and I built it into the chronicle of the conflict process. But I did not "prove" it.

Another causal question consumed more of my analytic time. Why did the church grow so fast (attendance rate half again higher, membership nearly tripled, real-dollar per capita spending doubled) from 1973 to 1982? Churchpeople in Mendocino easily found the answer in Underwood's ministry (or the Holy Spirit working through Underwood's ministry). But there is a large empirical literature in sociology of religion (much of it brought together in Hoge and Roozen 1979), not to mention a long-standing sociological mind-set, to the effect that individuals seldom make such a difference. The population growth of Mendocino County in the back-to-the-land boom of the 1970s seemed more palpable to sociologists—or so I was advised by a granting agency in 1982.

To test that theory, I (along with an assistant whose salary was paid by the grant) gathered population data and Presbyterian church membership data for several score of northern California communities from 1960 to 1980 (and presented the results in a separate chapter moved to the middle of the book late in the editing process). We found that although the membership of the church in Mendocino was indeed correlated with changes in the surrounding community's population (and had been since the turn of the century), most other northern California communities gained population in the 1970s without their Presbyterian churches experiencing similar growth. In other words, the Mendocino church stood out for enrolling community newcomers; the other churches did not similarly capitalize on their demographic opportunities. I concluded that the Mendocino churchpeople were right, but although many Mendocino Presbyterians actually lived in Fort Bragg, ten miles away, I could not refute the alternative theory that the other northern California Presbyterian congregations faced stiffer competition from other mainline churches in their own communities. (This objection was raised by Stephen Simpler [1988], among others.) To counter that objection would require the kind of information only a fairly extensive on-site quantitative survey of sixty communities could elicit. If such a survey found, as I think likely, that there was indeed something statistically special about the Mendocino case (*New Wine* claims that the combination of Underwood's evangelical preaching and his congregation's elective parochialism was the special thing), we would have to return to the intensive case study to determine it. And that's where we came in.

There is one final pitfall of the case study that I circumvented, but I cannot recommend my path to guide others. *New Wine*, as I have said, took well over a decade to complete. I can claim other scholarly accomplishments during that period; I had other experiences that I would not have missed for the world and no doubt wasted a good bit of time. But the project was labor-intensive. Had I depended on its publication to gain tenure, I would have been out of a job. Fortunately for me, my previous work in theory was sufficient for tenure and promotion (in 1978), and *New Wine* was the product of my years as an associate professor. Yet the fieldwork that provided its inspiration and the best of its data was the work of a relatively young man of thirty-four, who had the freedom from family obligations to show up for participant observation anytime the opportunity arose and the stamina to record the results well into the wee hours. Perhaps a way could be arranged to give the youngster credit for the fieldwork and to assign the desk work to the senior.

Notes

I am indebted to Joe Feagin and Tony Orum for suggestions and encouragement, to Anne Heider for editorial criticism, and to the Institute for Advanced Study for support and stimulation. A preliminary version of the argument of the second section was presented to a seminar of the Congregational History Project, University of Chicago Divinity School, on January 26, 1989. I am grateful to the project's co-directors, James Lewis and James Wind, for their invitation.

1. Since the publication of *New Wine*, I have been invited to be a collaborator and/or consultant for several Lilly-funded projects studying religious congregations and voluntary associations.

2. See, for example, Furman 1987, chapter 4, and Gans 1962. "The refusal of communities to remain motionless before and after their portraits are sketched is a problem that has continued to plague fieldworkers" (Van Maanen 1988, 39).

3. As I believe Peshkin (1984) did.

4. But I was never as relentless as Tipton (1982); see Warner 1984, 1206.

5. From sociological reviewers: "Sociologists interested in how institutions generally adapt to changing circumstances can learn from it" (Roof 1989, 595). "His methodologically sophisticated work should be read and emulated by every sociology student" (Ammerman 1989, 276).

6. I owe the term *desk work* to Van Maanen (1988), who may owe it in turn to George Marcus.

7. During the 1988 meetings of the Society for the Scientific Study of Religion, "Peter Hsu" electrified the audience at a session devoted to *New Wine* by using his real name and introducing himself publicly from the floor during the question period. He testified to the book's veracity but complained that in my concentration on his public ministry, I had not sufficiently chronicled his quotidian doings. (He, like his successors, made sure that the church doors were locked at the end of the day.) Larry Redford was sought out in admiration by a long-lost cousin, an evangelical layman who had read the book and subsequently stumbled on Redford's true identity, but Redford's wife, Sue, had yet to read the book a year

after receiving a gift copy. Her memories of the events it recounted were still too fresh and bitter. Eric Underwood liked the book less than I would have expected, and Mark Kimmerly more. Additional follow-up to the book, based on interviews with named principals and others, is reported in Warner 1990.

8. My literary model in this regard was Tom Wolfe's *The Right Stuff*.

9. On the *narrative*: "This book contains a sparkling, richly detailed narrative" (Carpenter 1989, 29); Warner uses "the skills of a journalist and the training of a sociologist [and] tells a fascinating story" (Jorstad 1989, 657); "a minimum of jargon and a highly readable, almost novelistic style" (Blanchard 1989, 242); the narrative "is spun tightly with a novelist's skill" (Noll 1988, 3); "Warner makes the usually complex study of ethnography read like a novel" (Simpler 1988, 993); the stories "are told in this book with the gripping realism of a well-written novel" (Ammerman 1989, 276); "impossible to put down" (Kellstedt 1989, 29).

On *ethnographic authority*: "Its strong point is that it is so extensively and carefully documented that we gain a vivid sense of having 'been there.' . . . And we are there through it all" (Wuthnow 1988, 5, 6); "The story itself, then, is fascinating, but it is told by a social scientist with an eye on convincing his reader that the conclusions are valid. And the reader is convinced" (Kellstedt 1989, 30); the book is "rich with insights" and arguments are made "convincingly" (Blanchard 1989, 244); Warner "is utterly faithful to the case at hand" (Ammerman 1989, 276); the book's "fresh insights . . . contribute to evangelicalism's self-understanding" (Muether 1989, 416).

Implicating the reader through personal stories: The book "has good character development. We come away really knowing something about Larry Redford, Eric Underwood, and the others. . . . When character development is good, it also invites us to identify with the story. . . . And in subtle ways, we are changed vicariously" (Wuthnow 1988, 6); "For clergy, laity, and others interested in the field of congregation studies, *New Wine in Old Wineskins* is a tour de force" (Anderson 1989, 258).

On the *autobiographical subtext*: "This second drama is the modern novel imbedded in the more conventionally Victorian tale of the Mendocino church, with its Dickensian richness of detail and clean authorial interpretations. . . . [The subplot] contributes a vitally compelling element to the book" (Noll 1988, 3–4); "An engaging aspect of the book is its explicit autobiographical foundation. Chapter 3 is existentially, if not formally, the starting point of the book" (Anderson 1989, 256); "What we do, since we usually have the luxury of choosing our own research topics, has to have a strong dose of self-edification and personal enjoyment. . . . [I]t is clear that the study itself was profoundly important at a personal level" (Wuthnow 1988, 7); "The author's personal feelings show through vividly" (Jorstad 1989, 657).

10. Reviewers of *New Wine*, although generally positive, express varied reservations and criticisms, but their complaints are dispersed rather than concentrated. Thus Stephen Simpler (1988) wished I had said more about the Presbyte-

rian church's mainline monopoly in Mendocino and Richard Tholin (1988) that I had emphasized its WASP coloration. Lyman Kellstedt (1989) wanted more about politics and Don Browning (1989) more about psychology. Mark Noll (1989) wished I had been more systematic about the role of music in the church and fellowship, and Douglas Anderson (1989) regretted that I did not say more about northern California religiosity. William Swatos (1989) thought that the role of the pastor's wife, Vonnie Underwood, was slighted. Dallas Blanchard (1989) missed an explicit analysis of leadership styles and Clark Roof (1989) a general theory of congregational change. To me, the most telling criticism so far was Nancy Ammerman's (1989). She pointed out that I did not have enough to say about "intermediate organizational links between local congregation and larger culture" (276), and I am happy to recommend George Marsden's (1987) recent case study of Fuller Theological Seminary as a book I could have used to help close that gap.

11. A similar point has been made by John Shelton Reed about the longevity of certain half-century-old ethnographies of aspects of southern culture in the United States (Reed 1989, 10–13).

12. "To a considerable extent, the story of this particular congregation's transformation in outlook and identity is the story of American Protestantism in search of itself in the past quarter-century" (Roof 1989, 595); "Warner makes a strong case for this church as a microcosm, an ideal type, of what was happening during these and succeeding years in religion nationally" (Blanchard 1989, 244). See also Carpenter's (1989) review. Richard Tholin (1988) complained rightly that I did not make it sufficiently clear that I was writing of white American Protestantism, and Douglas Anderson (1989) thought that my portrayal of the evangelical/liberal divide was oversimplified.

13. Erling Jorstad (1989) seemed surprised by my claim that today's evangelicals are not especially radical, and Mary Jo Neitz (1989) wondered if my findings were an artifact of my self-selected Mendocino friendship network. But John Muether (1989) said that I had "a good grasp of what distinguishes evangelicalism theologically" (416); Joel Carpenter (1989) hoped that "liberal Protestants and secular academics" would get a "deeper understanding—and perhaps appreciation—of evangelicals" from the book (30); and Nancy Ammerman (1989) concluded that I showed the reader "evangelicals who are ordinary people, modern people, members of a mainline church, concerned about this world, yet convinced that the boundaries of this world are permeable to the influences of another" (276).

References

A list of published reviews of and public responses to *New Wine in Old Wineskins* appears at the end of the References.

Ammerman, Nancy. 1987. *Bible Believers: Fundamentalists in the Modern World.* New Brunswick, N.J.: Rutgers University Press.

Berger, Bennett M. 1981. *The Survival of a Counterculture: Ideological Work and Everyday Life among Rural Communards.* Berkeley: University of California Press.

Bettelheim, Bruno. 1943. "Individual and Mass Behavior in Extreme Situations." *Journal of Abnormal and Social Psychology* 38 (October): 417–52.

Caplow, Theodore, Howard M. Bahr, Bruce A. Chadwick, Dwight W. Hoover, Laurence A. Martin, Joseph B. Tamney, and Margaret Holmes Williamson. 1983. *All Faithful People: Change and Continuity in Middletown's Religion.* Minneapolis: University of Minnesota Press.

Clifford, James. 1988. "On Ethnographic Authority." Pp. 21–54 in *The Predicament of Culture: Twentieth-Century Ethnography, Literature, and Art.* Cambridge: Harvard University Press.

Coles, Robert. 1989. *The Call of Stories: Teaching and the Moral Imagination.* Boston: Houghton Mifflin.

Demerath, N. J., III, and Rhys H. Williams. 1987. "Richness vs. Rigor: Contending with History in a Community Study." Paper presented at the annual meeting of the Society for the Scientific Study of Religion, Louisville, Kentucky.

FitzGerald, Frances. 1986. *Cities on a Hill: A Journey through Contemporary American Cultures.* New York: Simon and Schuster.

Fry, John R. 1975. *The Trivialization of the United Presbyterian Church.* New York: Harper and Row.

Furman, Frida Kerner. 1987. *Beyond Yiddishkeit: The Struggle for Jewish Identity in a Reform Synagogue.* Albany, N.Y.: SUNY Press.

Gans, Herbert. 1962. *The Urban Villagers: Group and Class in the Life of Italian-Americans.* New York: Free Press.

Geertz, Clifford. 1988. *Works and Lives: The Anthropologist As Author.* Stanford: Stanford University Press.

Harding, Susan. 1987. "Convicted by the Holy Spirit: The Rhetoric of Fundamental Baptist Conversion." *American Ethnologist* 14 (February): 167–81.

Hoge, Dean R., and David A. Roozen, eds. 1979. *Understanding Church Growth and Decline, 1950–1978.* New York: Pilgrim Press.

Hunter, James Davison. 1983. *American Evangelicalism: Conservative Religion and the Quandary of Modernity.* New Brunswick, N.J.: Rutgers University Press.

Marsden, George. 1987. *Reforming Fundamentalism: Fuller Seminary and the New Evangelicals.* Grand Rapids, Mich.: Eerdmans.

Neitz, Mary Jo. 1987. *Charisma and Community: A Study of Religious*

Commitment within the Charismatic Renewal. New Brunswick, N.J.:
Transaction Books.

Peshkin, Alan. 1984. "Odd Man Out: The Participant Observer in an Absolutist
Setting." *Sociology of Education* 57 (October): 254–64.

Reed, John Shelton. 1989. "On Narrative Sociology." *Social Forces* 68
(September): 1–14.

Richardson, James T., Mary White Stewart, and Robert B. Simmonds. 1979.
*Organized Miracles: A Study of a Contemporary Youth, Communal,
Fundamentalist Organization.* New Brunswick, N.J.: Transaction Books.

Roof, Wade Clark. 1978. *Community and Commitment: Religious Plausibility
in a Liberal Protestant Church.* New York: Elsevier.

Rose, Susan D. 1987. "Women Warriors: The Negotiation of Gender in a
Charismatic Community." *Sociological Analysis* 48 (Fall): 245–58.

Tipton, Steven M. 1982. *Getting Saved from the Sixties.* Berkeley: University of
California Press.

Van Maanen, John. 1988. *Tales of the Field: On Writing Ethnography.*
Chicago: University of Chicago Press.

Wallace, Anthony F. C. 1970. *The Death and Rebirth of the Seneca.* New York:
Alfred A. Knopf.

Warner, R. Stephen. 1979. "Theoretical Barriers to the Understanding of
Evangelical Christianity." *Sociological Analysis* 40 (Spring): 1–9.

———. 1984. "Making Sense of the Seventies." *American Journal of Sociology*
89 (March): 1201–8.

———. 1988. *New Wine in Old Wineskins: Evangelicals and Liberals in a
Small-Town Church.* Berkeley and Los Angeles: University of California
Press.

———. 1990. "Mirror for American Protestantism: Mendocino Presbyterian
Church in the Sixties and Seventies." Forthcoming in *The Mainstream
Protestant "Decline": The Presbyterian Pattern,* edited by Milton J. Coalter,
Louis Weeks, and John M. Mulder. Louisville, Ky.: John Knox.

———. Forthcoming (1992). *Communities of Faith: An Essay on Religion in
the United States Today.* New York: Basic Books.

Webb, Eugene J., Donald T. Campbell, Richard D. Schwartz, Lee Sechrest, and
Janet Belew Grove. 1981. *Nonreactive Measures in the Social Sciences.*
Boston: Houghton Mifflin.

Zablocki, Benjamin. 1972. *The Joyful Community.* Baltimore: Penguin Books.

Published reviews of and public responses to Warner 1988

Ammerman, Nancy. 1989. *American Journal of Sociology* 95 (July): 275–77.

Anderson, Douglas Firth. 1989. *American Presbyterians* 67 (Fall): 255–58.

Blanchard, Dallas A. 1989. *Journal for the Scientific Study of Religion* 28
(June): 242–44.

Browning, Don. 1989. Presentation to the Congregational History Project, Chicago, January 26.

Carpenter, Joel. 1989. *Christianity Today* 33 (April 7): 29–30.

Hsu, Peter [pseud.]. 1988. Comment from floor at session during the annual meeting of the Society for the Scientific Study of Religion, Chicago, October 28.

Jorstad, Erling. 1989. *Journal of American History* 76 (September): 656–57.

Kellstedt, Lyman. 1989. *Reformed Journal* 39 (September): 29–30. (Previously published in *Religion and Politics* 5 (Summer 1989): 2–3.)

Lagerquist, DeAne. 1989. Presentation to the Congregational History Project, Chicago, January 26.

Muether, John R. 1989. *Westminster Theological Journal* 51 (Fall): 414–16.

Neitz, Mary Jo. 1989. *Sociological Analysis* 50 (Holidaytide): 419–22.

Noll, Mark A. 1988. Presentation at the annual meeting of the Society for the Scientific Study of Religion, Chicago, October 28.

———. 1989. *Evangelical Studies Bulletin* 6 (Fall): 1–5.

Roof, Wade Clark. 1989. *Contemporary Sociology* 18 (July): 594–96.

Simpler, Stephen. 1988. *Christian Century* 105 (November 2): 993–94.

Swatos, William H., Jr. 1989. *Sociological Analysis* 50 (Holidaytide): 422–24.

Tholin, Richard. 1988. Presentation at the annual meeting of the Society for the Scientific Study of Religion, Chicago, October 28.

Wuthnow, Robert. 1988. Presentation at the annual meeting of the Society for the Scientific Study of Religion, Chicago, October 28.

Gilbert Geis

6 The Case Study Method in Sociological Criminology

The age-old methods of history often have been employed as stalking-horses for debate about procedures that properly ought to be emphasized in sociology and in criminology, one of the sociological subdisciplines. Edward Gibbon, renowned for his chronicle of the decline and fall of the Roman Empire, called history "little more than the register of the crimes, follies and misfortunes of mankind."[1] This offhand characterization by the author of what has been called "the greatest work of historical research in the entire world canon"[2] presages the equally offhand manner in which many important case study criminological inquiries into humanity's lawbreaking and deviance are sometimes regarded.

Henry Thomas Buckle, an eminent early historian, insisted that a true social science should be "an induction from history" and that its primary goal should be to form the masses of facts accumulated by historians into statements of perceived regularity that allow accurate prediction.[3] Albion Small, a prominent early sociologist, maintained, however, that historians were no more than journalists whose material was out of date.[4] But Nigel Walker, a criminologist with a humanistic bent, more aptly summarized historical explanation in a manner that indicates the vital role that the case study method can play in research on lawbreakers: "Historians often want to know why people behaved in a way that seems unlikely, and they are satisfied by an account which makes it clear how they *could* have acted as they did, without demanding what would in most cases be impossible—an account which showed that what they did was inevitable."[5]

Such observations about history as it relates to criminology and the case study method cut to the core of the scientism debate. This chapter will examine some of the early jousting over the virtues of case study versus quantitative methods in criminology and then discuss the case study approach in work on homicide. Thereafter, it will examine the use of life histories in pioneering research on juvenile delinquency. Finally, case studies in the topical area of white-collar crime will be considered. I will use my own research on a major antitrust case in the early 1960s to illustrate some significant case study themes. At the end, note will be made of the striking revival of the case study method as feminist writers have moved prominently into research on the characteristics of crime by women.

Stouffer and Attitudes toward Prohibition

A key question concerning case studies is this: Should criminology strive for mathematical precision, deriving its core working procedures from the natural sciences, or does its optimal development require a strong infusion of humanistic concerns, such as those that characterize historical research? And, presuming that some measure of both approaches is necessary, what should be the proper proportions and in what order should they be introduced into the brew? In this debate, it must be recognized that if method is allowed to dictate the choice of subject and the selection of information, what can be scrutinized becomes dictated by the limitations of the selected method. The more numerically precise an approach, the less range and depth it typically offers. Much more can be seen and heard than can be measured; and words can express considerably more of the nuances of feeling and experience than can numbers. By limiting the field of inquiry to the measurable, investigators often fall prey to Huntington Cairns's criticism that "the history of social theory is too largely a record of generalizations wrung from insufficient facts."[6]

Half a century ago, the virtues of the case study method as opposed to numerical techniques were set out in an inquiry undertaken to demonstrate the opposite point. For his 1930 Ph.D. dissertation, Samuel Stouffer—who later, while on wartime leave from the Harvard faculty, would produce his monumental study *The American Soldier* (1949)—chose the issue of Prohibition to conduct, as his title indicates, *An Experimental Comparison of Statistical and Case Study Methods in Attitude Research*. Subjects were 238 undergraduates who registered their views on Prohibition, completed an attitude inventory, and wrote a one-thousand-word autobiographical essay describing their experiences and feelings with respect to drinking and to prohibition laws. The attitude scale was found to predict Prohibition and personal drinking habits as well as the essays.

Stouffer took the results to be a tribute to the strength of attitude scales—simple, quick, cheap, "fairly valid."[7] He might have added that attitude inventory work also is easier and that in times of perilous tenure and advancement for university professors, such considerations can prevail over more demanding techniques of inquiry. But the difficulty with Stouffer's work, though it was meticulously done, was that both the scale and the essay were constructed—the latter in terms of questions the students had to answer in their writing—so that neither approach could have left much doubt about whether the respondent favored Prohibition and personally drank. In this sense, the study preordained the result it supposedly was seeking to determine.

Stouffer, though exalting attitude scales, gracefully conceded that the case histories "gave clues to connecting links which escape the statistical worker who is limited to a consideration of the relationship expressed in abstract mathematical symbols." He also noted, quoting Charles Cooley, that "the phenomena of life are often better distinguished by pattern than by quantity."[8] "Measurement," Cooley had written, "is only one kind of precision."[9] Four years later, William Ogburn would add to the debate the observations that "the role of statistics is often that of making exact something already known" and that "it seems true that the discipline of statistics helps little in the initial step of discovery, even though it may be of importance in the final step." Ogburn also suggested that the case study method is appropriate for the investigation of phenomena such as crime more than, say, the phenomena of economics.[10]

The Criminological Enterprise

In criminology, the tension between case study work and mathematical inquiries has persisted throughout the subdiscipline's history. More than most other fields of sociological study, criminology has a strong meliorative streak. Most criminologists seek to learn what causes crime so that it can be controlled, though they also may desire to improve the lot of offenders and to refocus enforcement on targets other than lower-class, minority group members. These motifs are often best advanced by dramatic illustrations rather than by correlative conclusions. For this, among other reasons, case study methods have played a particularly prominent role in criminological scholarship.

CASE STUDIES OF HOMICIDE

A brief review of the study of homicide provides a clear lesson about the limits of statistical inquiry uninformed by comprehensive case study work. Homicide is a particularly opportune form of behavior about which to aggregate numerical information concerning such matters as the characteristics of offenders and victims and the circumstances of their lethal encounter. Homicides also can be analyzed cross-nationally, primarily because definitions are relatively stable and because it can be presumed that a very large percentage of the offenses became known to the authorities.[11] Difficulties arise, however, because there are so many varieties of homicide—infanticide, gang killings, automobile fatalities, among others—that much of the richness of the data is lost when aggregated.

Acts of homicide, at the same time, arouse an almost prurient fascination and concern with their details. Such elements are lost in statistical analyses. Their omission may be defended as allowing a calmer and more dispassionate consideration of the subject. Yet, the essence of a true understanding of homicides abides in a comprehension of the perceptions of the offenders, the verbal exchanges that precede the killings, the often casual method in murder. For this reason, a book such as Henry Lundsgaarde's *Murder in Space City* (1977), which mingles detailed case materials with arithmetical summaries of categories and dispositions, continues to be very heavily cited by scholars trying to capture the essential nature of death-dealing behavior.

In his analysis of homicides that he characterizes as "righteously enraged slaughters," Jack Katz used the large body of case study material on homicide, including such "fictional-non-fiction" works as Norman Mailer's *The Executioner's Song*, Joseph Wambaugh's *The Onion Field*, and Truman Capote's *In Cold Blood*, to derive telling insights into the components of murder. Katz sees the typical homicide as a self-righteous act undertaken to defend what the killer defines as communal values, and he relied on case study reports to document the "sensual attractions of doing evil," setting forth the following thesis:

> Whatever the relevance of antecedent events and contemporaneous social conditions, something causally essential happens in the very moments in which a crime is committed. The assailant must sense, then and there, a distinctive constraint or seductive appeal that he did not sense a little while before in a substantially similar place. Although his economic status, peer group relations, Oedipal conflicts, genetic makeup, internalized machismo, history of child abuse, and the like remain the same, he must suddenly become propelled to commit the crime. Thus, the central problem is to understand the emergence of distinctive sensual dynamics.[12]

Put another way, Katz is emphasizing here that the precursors of lawbreaking typically nominated as "causal" in statistical studies are always in place but that they cannot adequately explain why at one time, but never on innumerable similar occasions, they produce the homicide. "It is not necessary to constitute the field back to front," Katz observed. "We may begin with the foreground, attempting to discover common or homogeneous criminal projects to test explanations for the necessary and sufficient steps through which people construct given forms of crime."[13]

LIFE HISTORIES OF JUVENILE DELINQUENTS

The study of juvenile delinquency is a criminological area with a long history of distinguished case study work. Delinquency studies dominate criminology, and theories based exclusively on the acts of young offenders far outshadow in number and sophistication those tied to adult offenders. The presence of extensive case study material on juveniles undoubtedly has contributed to the vitality of these theoretical developments.

Life history documents produced by a delinquent with the prompting and direction of the researcher have been particularly prominent in the study of delinquency. The gathering of life histories as sociological fare first was pioneered by W. I. Thomas, a University of Chicago sociologist, best remembered today as coauthor of the classic study of Polish peasants in their homeland and after immigrating into the United States.[14] Thomas, like his department colleagues, took advantage of the fact that his university was one of the few major institutions of higher learning then located in a large city. Chicago's sociologists assiduously explored some of the shabbier aspects of the city to produce an array of brilliant monographs that combined journalistic acumen with sophisticated sociological insight.[15]

Many of these studies dealt with criminological themes, though the legal definitions of what was being examined played a secondary role to descriptive portrayals of the milieu in which personal and behavioral matters were embedded. Two contributions by the Chicago sociologists had a particularly strong impact on the application of the case study method to criminological research. The first, *The Gang*, by Frederic Thrasher (1927), illustrated the power of a case study to generate for years to come a fruitful line of scientific inquiry.[16] The second, represented by a series of autobiographies by juvenile delinquents—"the boy's own story," the contributions were called—indicates both the strengths and the weaknesses, as well as the almost inevitable ultimate failure, of a line of life history inquiry that overrelies on the idiosyncratic experiences and talents of the people who produce the material. Today, life histories have virtually disappeared as a tool in the sociological research kit; but it is worth scrutinizing their moment in the sun to try to determine why this is so and whether the loss is to be regretted.

The Jack-Roller (1930). The subject of delinquency in the studies conducted by faculty and associates at the University of Chicago devolved to Clifford Shaw and Henry McKay, both graduates of the sociology department though neither holding his Ph.D. because of an inability (or unwillingness) to pass the foreign language requirement. Shaw was gregarious, charismatic, a leader; McKay was soft-spoken, modest, retiring. Both men were rural products, part of the great migration from the surrounding countryside into the hub city of the Midwest.

At the Institute for Juvenile Research, in addition to his ecological studies with McKay, Shaw collected autobiographical statements by delinquents. From among the eighty-nine such documents, he chose three for book publication: *The Jack-Roller* (1930), *The Natural History of a Delinquent Career* (1931), and *Brothers in Crime* (1936).

The Jack-Roller, the hardiest survivor of the three (it remains in print today), may be taken as prototypical of the genre. In it, Stanley told of his intense hatred for a stepmother, his constant efforts as a youth to escape home by running away, and his involvement with other boys in "jackrolling," that is, robbing drunks. Shaw made various efforts to redeem Stanley, including several foster home placements. But Stanley felt ill at ease in the sometimes splendid settings into which he was placed, and he often got into difficulty in a series of menial jobs because of his chronic inability to suffer the smallest slight, real or imagined.[17] Ultimately, Shaw found Stanley a job as a traveling salesman, a job that appeared to provide the freedom from supervision and the ability to use his extraordinarily ingratiating personality to its best. Forty years later, located in Los Angeles, Stanley added to his life history the report that he had continued to remain out of prison, though he had spent some time in a mental hospital. He remained excruciatingly touchy about any infringement on his emotional territory: he would explode if he thought that he had in any way been slighted.[18]

The Jack-Roller, combined with its sequel *The Jack-Roller at Seventy* (1982) by Jon Snodgrass, offers an unusual opportunity to appraise the life history method as a technique of scientific inquiry. Shaw had claimed that life histories can contribute to the treatment of a delinquent, a position that today has to remain as unfounded as assertions on behalf of the "talking therapy" of psychiatry. In a review of *The Jack-Roller*, Kimball Young made the telling criticism that life histories tend to focus attention on the personal attributes and conditions of the subjects and to divert attention from "all those institutional formulations which would remove the major causes of such behavior: illness, low standards of living, unemployment, and all the rest."[19]

Howard Becker (1966), in his thoughtful introduction to the paperback reissue of *The Jack-Roller*, mourned that qualitative work like it was now devalued and in short supply. He pointed out that life histories, among their other virtues, can disprove hypotheses and can suggest variables that were overlooked in other work. Becker also maintained that Shaw had strengthened his life histories by offering to their writers specific guidelines concerning what should be taken up. It could be argued, contrariwise, that this kind of leading-the-witness tactic removes an important element of innocence from the documents and colors the story.

There is, in addition, an inherent problem that bears on all life histories by lawbreakers: the representativeness of the cases. The fact that Stanley was able to produce a compelling document distinguishes him from almost all other juvenile delinquents. Besides, in order to be publishable, the story usually has to have drama and, in particular, has to convey information that adds something to readers' understanding of the phenomenon. It is very likely that the remaining eighty-six life histories accumulated by Shaw never found their way into print either because they were too tedious or, just as likely, because they had an inevitable sameness to them. Thrasher granted as much when he wrote that a case described by Shaw in *The Natural History of a Delinquent Career* was "typical in this respect of hundreds and thousands of other cases in American cities."[20]

It might have been more valuable for criminological work not to have collected a massive file of life histories by delinquents (though these assuredly could be put to good use) but rather to have gathered complementary stories from each of the major participants in the same events. Undoubtedly, such products would not duplicate the astonishing complexity of the different views of what persons had experienced in common as set forth in the sequential volumes of Lawrence Durrell's fictional Alexandria quartet. But they would provide data of unusual importance. It may be that how a protagonist views reality *is* for analytic purposes the same as reality, but it would be a major step forward to learn how others perceive that same slice of reality in which they are participants or onlookers.

A particularly perceptive evaluation of the value of criminological life histories such as *The Jack-Roller* has been offered by Solomon Kobrin, who noted that Max Weber defined the distinctiveness of the social sciences as residing in the importance of the meaning that actors attach to their social behavior. Weber then added, in favor of greater recourse to personal documents, that a theory of social control and deviance cannot be fully developed without incorporating into it the sociopsychological processes that link the factors of social structure, at both the macro and the small group levels, to forms of concrete behavior.[21]

CASE STUDIES OF WHITE-COLLAR CRIME

Organized and white-collar crime are the two precincts of criminological inquiry that have been particularly dominated by the case study approach. There are a number of reasons why this is so. For one thing, neither category concerns criminal activity that is so labeled in any statute book: both terms are the creation of criminologists intent on finding a proper designation for an array of illegal behaviors that appear to have structural and behavioral similarities. This definitional uniqueness—combined with characteristics of the behaviors themselves—has largely foreclosed attempts to put together much in the way of comprehensive numerical analysis because official data do not correspond to the criminological categories. Also, for both forms of behavior, access to many important sources of information is precluded by the power, secrecy, and relative imperviousness to quantitative studies of people and organizations that commit these kinds of lawbreaking. Few criminologists would be incautious enough to invade the territory of Mafia members or ingratiating enough to penetrate the lairs of corporate enterprises in order to administer questionnaires.

Since most of my own work has dealt with white-collar crime, I will focus on it rather than organized crime for a further analysis of case study contributions to criminology. Edwin H. Sutherland's classic statement on white-collar crime, coming as his presidential address to the American Sociological Society in 1939, combined mostly case study material with a few numerical items to support twin conclusions: first, that theoretical postulations in criminology were patently inadequate because of their failure to account for crimes by people in positions of power; and second, that a large amount of lawbreaking by people of high social status, crime committed in the course of their occupations, was not being attended to satisfactorily.[22]

Almost a decade later, in *White Collar Crime*, Sutherland expanded on these two points. He provided an inventory of the amount of corporate lawbreaking that had been officially acted on by agencies of the federal government. Absent illustrative material to buttress his theme about the widespread existence of corporate, business, and political crime, he then presented an array of case histories, largely derived from students, regarding petty commercial shenanigans, matters that were oddly discordant with his major focus on corporate wrongdoing.

That such case materials, carefully gathered from classroom essays and intelligently organized and interpreted, are able to provide the backbone for a powerful sociological study would later be demonstrated by Paul Blumberg's *The Predatory Society* (1989). In Sutherland's hands, the case studies seem little more than the padding of material insufficient to sustain a book-length manuscript.

Subsequent work on white-collar crime, following Sutherland's pioneering influence, illustrates the power of the case study method and the difficulties and distortions introduced when, in accord with the imperatives of the quantitative putsch, the subject is placed into a numerical fold.

The Heavy Electrical Antitrust Cases. Soon after the publication of Sutherland's *White Collar Crime*, a number of major case studies on different aspects of the phenomenon appeared, including Frank Hartung's (1950) study of violators of the wartime meat-rationing regulations, Marshall Clinard's (1952) investigation of offenders against the wartime Office of Price Administration controls, and Donald R. Cressey's (1953) monograph based on interviews with embezzlers held in federal prisons. Then, for a number of reasons, prominent among them the fear engendered among scholars contemplating "radical" academic research during the reign of Senator Joseph McCarthy and the House Committee on Un-American Activities,[23] the study of white-collar crime virtually ceased between 1964 and 1975. The work I did on the heavy electrical equipment antitrust prosecutions during this time[24] was one of the few exceptions to the reign of silence on the subject.

This antitrust case became a landmark event in the annals of white-collar crime for several reasons. First, it involved many prominent business executives from well-known corporations such as General Electric, Westinghouse, and Allis-Chalmers. Second, the jail sentences imposed on seven of the defendants, though only thirty days, represented uncharacteristically tough and punitive responses. Third, the antitrust conspiracy generated a large amount of public record material, including several appellate court decisions on the civil side, and extensive Senate hearings marked by the penetrating cross-examinations of Senator Estes Kefauver of Tennessee, at the time a leading Democratic party presidential prospect.

Timing and other logistic difficulties represent especially troublesome issues for criminologists desiring to carry out case studies on matters that involve criminal court proceedings. The Sixth Amendment guarantees a researcher access to the courtroom under most circumstances, an opportunity that to date has not been adequately exploited by social scientists, though popular writers have produced some extremely good interpretative reporting of the dynamics of criminal trials. Unfortunately, few participants, officials or others, who are scheduled to take part in a trial will talk with an outsider beforehand, partly because to do so might jeopardize their case (the researcher could be subpoenaed to tell what was said), partly because it is considered unethical (a principle much breached when media advantage is sought), and mostly because the sub judice status of the case provides a good excuse not to have to be bothered discussing it with outsiders. Then, almost all cases ultimately are settled out of court, and the researcher loses the opportunity to glean the excellent case study material that would have become available during the trial contest.

The heavy electrical equipment antitrust case, however, was not settled rapidly and quietly, though the defendants ultimately pleaded nolo contendere in large part because they feared a trial or a guilty plea would jeopardize their position and that of their employer in the forthcoming civil suits. My newspaper clipping file indicates that my interest in the case began from the moment the indictments were announced. The fact that a Senate subcommittee later decided to investigate the matter thoroughly as a precursor to recommended reforms of the Sherman Antitrust Act was my marvelous good luck. In later years, I often would form an early interest in one or another white-collar crime case only to have it evaporate: defendants died, U.S. attorneys changed, or most often, the matter was settled quickly and quietly through negotiations that took place well beyond my research reach.

The tools available to work on the antitrust case three decades ago were strikingly less satisfactory than those available now. Today's researchers undoubtedly are bored by old-timers recounting the primitive nature of technical equipment available during their youth, much as kids traditionally bewail their grandparents' recitals of barefoot walks to school through snowbanks. Yet, it seems worth noting that it was not that long ago that, absent xerox machines, a colleague and I spent the better part of two years laboriously typing hundreds of newspaper stories from historical archives in Oklahoma, Texas, and Maine, preparatory to writing a case study book about the settling of the all-Negro town of Boley, Oklahoma, and the migration therefrom in 1914 to the Gold Coast in Africa.[25] It never remotely occurred to us that we might take a quick jet trip to Accra to gather crucial site material bearing on the outcome of the hegira. For one thing, there were no jets; for another, the cost and the absence of grant sources ruled out the quest for this archival information.

The same was true regarding the antitrust research. There were no tape recorders and no travel possibilities, and the costs of duplicating legal briefs and other court filings were well beyond my means. On the other hand, several things had helped to prepare me for this kind of case study work. Journalism classes in college and several years as a newspaper reporter provided important tools. Perhaps the subtlest was an attitude that conveyed to people that they were somehow "obligated" to answer questions that often verged on the impertinent. Doggedness in the pursuit of information and the idea that both sides ought to be allowed to have their say were two other derivatives of my newspaper training. I also had voraciously read autobiographies of prominent journalists, and I had had deeply implanted in me the ethos (though sometimes my practice falls short of the preaching) of fairness and "objectivity" in regard to facts, and accuracy concerning quotations, the spelling of names, and references to sources—matters that too often are dealt with rather cavalierly by social scientists. Though I found the journalism training invaluable (despite the drawbacks in terms of thinking theoretically and ideologically), I would not have anticipated that with the rise in investigative journalism, and the improved education of reporters, in time some particularly comprehensive and sophisticated sociology would begin to appear in the columns of the nation's leading newspapers.

My first move in dealing with the antitrust cases was to subscribe to the local newspapers in the towns where the major corporate offenders were located: the *Sharon* (Pa.) *Herald* for Westinghouse, and the *Schenectady* (N.Y.) *Union-Star* for General Electric. Both would supply excellent insights on local opinions about the defendants, who, not surprisingly, were portrayed as pillars of the community. The Schenectady daily, for instance, carried an extraordinarily disingenuous statement issued by the most highly placed defendant, a statement that likely would have been forestalled by the corporate public relations arm had he tried to direct it through the firm to a national outlet. In it, the General Electric vice-president, after expressing his appreciation for the "confidence and support" of his neighbors, noted that he had been sentenced for conduct "interpreted" as "being in conflict with the complex antitrust laws."[26] The statement was particularly useful to me as counterpoint to a depiction of the flagrant nature of the conspirators' behavior in obvious and knowing violation of the antitrust laws.

I also used the telephone a good deal, another habit acquired from newspaper days. Person-to-person calls at times will tease some of the most difficult-to-reach individuals into answering questions. I talked at some length with the sentencing judge and built up what today would be called a network among persons involved in or also studying the case.

Among my best sources of information were attorneys on both sides. I had taught myself reasonably well how to do legal research, a tool that can open up to a social scientist an absolute gold mine of information. Law review articles pour forth by the thousands each year, almost every one with a thorough examination of its subject and a comprehensive array of footnotes that often supply a useful beginning inventory of the relevant scholarship on the subject. Appellate court decisions, in which judges usually set out in some detail what happened and then justify why they ruled as they did, offer another wondrous lode of sociological case data. I also tend to collect briefs from attorneys because these represent the product of long hours of digging and of thought, though little of their content may find its way into the formal court decision.

But by far my primary source material for the case study of the heavy electrical antitrust case was the two-volume hearing report produced by the Senate Subcommittee on Antitrust and Monopoly of the Committee on the Judiciary. I twice read through the several thousand pages of testimony and cross-examination and became thoroughly absorbed in the human and criminological drama that unfolded. Senator Kefauver was a masterful interrogator. He would lull the corporate executives, typically southerners like himself, into a sense of ease by initiating folksy exchanges about the fortunes of their home state university football teams. Then he would clobber them with shrewd and penetrating questions about their conspiratorial actions. Though the hearings at times frustratingly failed to provide the kind of information I wanted on matters central to the sociological study of white-collar crime, they were flush with excellent data and insights and filled with vivid, revealing responses to the tough questions.

I found it criminologically intriguing, for instance, that whereas violators filed false travel claims so as to mislead their superiors regarding the sites of their meetings with competitors, they never asked for expense money to places more distant than those they had actually gone to—on the theory, apparently, that whatever else was occurring, it would not do to cheat their employer. One witness's answer to a committee attorney was so revealing that John Conklin (1977) later would use the phrase italicized below as the basis for the title of an overview book on white-collar crime:

Committee attorney: "Did you know that these meetings with competitors were illegal?"

Witness: "*Illegal? Yes, but not criminal.* I didn't find that out until I read the indictment. . . . I assumed that criminal action meant damaging someone, and we did not do that. . . . I thought we were more or less working on a survival basis in order to try to make enough to keep our plant and employees."[27]

After reviewing what had taken place during the antitrust conspiracy, I was able to return to a number of Sutherland's broadly painted hypotheses to see how this material dovetailed with them. Some, such as the importance of learning and associational patterns as precursors to lawbreaking, stood up very well. Others were not supported, particularly Sutherland's insistence that the claims of people in the highest echelons of the corporation—claims that they were unaware of the wrongdoing—deserved no credence. I had begun with a strong bias in favor of Sutherland's view. Perhaps the General Electric president was a superb actor or perhaps I was gullible, but I ended up convinced that he was innocent of foreknowledge of what had been going on. Also, others, most notably Alan Dershowitz in a student note in the *Yale Law Journal*, insisted that the media downplayed the case,[28] but my judgment agreed with that of the defendant who lamented: "They have never laid off a second. . . . They don't use the term 'price fixing.' It is always 'price rigging' or trying to make it as sensational as possible."[29]

Looking back, I regret that a decade or so later I did not interview the main players in the heavy electrical antitrust conspiracy to try to determine what they would say after the passage of time and under more relaxed conditions. Were they angry? Remorseful? What lessons had they learned? Would they still pretend that their lawbreaking was nothing but a misunderstanding? I will never know now whether they would have talked with me, but I will always be sorry that I did not make the effort. In research, as in life, one of the most important axioms, one that I honor but too infrequently obey, lies in the words of Supreme Court Justice Byron White: "It's nothing to come to an important job and be smart. The key is what you spend your time on."[30]

WHITE-COLLAR CRIME QUANTITATIVELY

The inexorable press for more and better quantitative data if a criminologist hopes to publish his or her findings in a quality (note the verbal irony here) journal is demonstrated by the recent appearance of two articles in the *American Sociological Review*. These represent virtually the only occasions, in several decades, that the subject of white-collar crime has penetrated so preeminent a scholarly bastion.[31] Both articles are carefully researched and well reasoned. At the same time, they illustrate the compromises that sometimes are made—and perhaps have to be made—in order to translate ideas emerging from sophisticated case study material into quantitative form.

Sutherland, on the basis of his materials, had maintained that the criminal justice system was notably lenient in the manner in which it dealt with white-collar offenders. He believed that this could be traced to a class homogeneity between those who passed judgment and those who were judged—they shared the same values, saw economic offenses similarly, had gone to the same high-status schools, belonged to the same country clubs, and worshipped at the same churches. Other scholars and practitioners routinely echoed Sutherland's position. For instance, Robert Ogren, a federal prosecutor, has noted: "White-collar crimes may be more vicious, calculated, and exploitative than street crimes, which are punished far more severely."[32]

The two recent quantitative articles in the *American Sociological Review* attempted to shed light on the common wisdom expressed by Sutherland and others. Both utilized large data sets available from cases handled by the federal district courts, and both sought from these figures to determine the severity of sentences for various categories of offenders. In both instances, the nature of the data forced the researchers to jettison key elements of the definition of white-collar crime. At the same time, the fact that the concept of white-collar crime has had a long and highly regarded sociological tradition upon which they wished to build led them to tie their findings to that tradition, despite the definitional problems. We can observe, in these efforts, how tensions between the constricting demands of quantitative work and the insights of the case study method can produce results that may pass each other in the dark.

Education and White-Collar Crime: The Hagan Study. John Hagan, Ilene Nagel (Bernstein), and Celesta Abonetti divided offenders appearing in selected federal courts into groups in terms of whether they had committed a white-collar or a common crime and whether or not they had a college education. Holding constant items such as age, sex, employment status, ethnicity, prior felony convictions, and maximum possible sentence, the researchers found no evidence that college-educated offenders were sentenced more leniently for white-collar crimes than less-educated offenders were for common crimes.[33]

Restricted to the fact situation examined, the conclusion is not without interest. But as an attempt truly to respond to the issue of discrepant sentencing raised by Sutherland, the results can be misleading. For one thing, the common crimes dealt with in federal courts are highly idiosyncratic. For another, the operationalization of white-collar offender status solely in terms of college education seems inappropriate. Assuredly, Sutherland was regrettably remiss about providing a firm definition of white-collar crime,[34] but there is no question that the concept he worked with has to do with status and power, matters not necessarily correlated with a college education. Many people have college degrees, but relatively few have the kind of corporate, business, or political power that concerned Sutherland. To investigate Sutherland's claim of judicial partiality adequately would require a much stricter delineation of a cohort of white-collar offenders and a comparable group of common offenders tracked at least from the time that the cases came to the attention of the court. For many of us, the fact that President Nixon was pardoned for his offenses and the fact that the congressional committee investigating the Iran-Contra crimes decided beforehand to assiduously avoid raising the issue of the impeachment of President Reagan (since he was near the end of his term and since committee members felt the country should not have to endure the strain of another Nixon-like debacle) provide at least a strong suggestion that power may prevail in the disposition of white-collar crime.

Status and White-Collar Crime: The Wheeler Study. The second quantitative investigation of the sentencing of white-collar offenders tackled the definition issue in quite another manner. Stanton Wheeler, David Weisburd, and Nancy Bode sought to determine whether, for the same white-collar offense, people with greater social status received tougher sentences. Those involved in what was called white-collar crime, however, included a heavy representation of very low status offenders. About one-third of the women and one-fourth of the men convicted of postal fraud, credit fraud, and false claims and statements, for instance, apparently were unemployed.[35] In the end, the conclusion that the higher-status white-collar offenders received tougher sentences, noteworthy as the finding may be for the sample examined, is not a persuasive adjudication of Sutherland's theme. Susan Shapiro has also noted of the findings that "unmeasured variables that prevent offenders from escaping the enforcement process may also explain the results."[36]

DILUTING CASE STUDY INSIGHTS AND FINDINGS

The study of white-collar crime, illustrated by the sentencing research, provides an example of some of the difficulties involved in attempting to translate rich case study materials into statistical form. Sutherland's work represents a ground-breaking piece of case study research; in Robert Yin's typology of case study work, Sutherland's is a *revelatory* inquiry, in the sense that it opened up to scrutiny a phenomenon previously unexplored and one largely unsusceptible to satisfactory understanding through the use of statistical techniques.[37] Given the persuasive scientism of the time at which he was writing, Sutherland made a valiant, though awkward, effort to camouflage the character of his work, proclaiming in the opening sentence that the book was intended to reform criminal theory, and nothing else. Time would clearly tell that this was about the least of its accomplishments: the greatest was to demonstrate by case study methods an ability to focus attention on a neglected realm of consummate social and scientific importance.

Sutherland scattered in his work a striking array of ideas that have remained largely unaddressed during the more than five decades since he first enunciated the concept of white-collar crime. Part of the difficulty is that case study material will rarely be published today by any of the leading social science journals, though book publication, for those with the patience and the skill, is very much in order for comprehensive case studies of important criminal episodes and issues.

Attempts to extend a field of inquiry essentially tailored for case study work into a state-of-the-art numerical research effort can, of course, produce an operational definition of the phenomenon that sharpens our understanding of it; but, and more likely, it probably will blunt nuances in order to reduce the concept to proportions that are more readily manageable numerically, and in the process the original postulation will lose a good deal of its deeper meaning. In the sentencing studies, we see an additional pitfall: the definition is established not in terms of the inherent nature of the phenomena being studied but rather in terms of the data that happen to be available.

Conclusion

Criminology is a social science enterprise that particularly lends itself to case study work. If nothing else, much of criminal behavior is inherently dramatic, and its elements often are unknown and fascinating to those who look on from outside. In addition, the "dark figure"—those offenses that do not become known to the authorities—seriously hinders attempts to gain a representative sampling of criminals and criminal acts on the basis of which confident quantitative generalizations may be rendered. Case study depictions of gang behavior, courtroom proceedings, prison riots, and similar material offer an arena of investigation that should have wide appeal to sociologists concerned with discovering regularities and significant meaning in the variegated events that constitute illegal behavior and in the manner in which the social system responds to such behavior.

In this regard, the notable resurgence of the case study method that has marked the appearance and growth of the feminist emphasis in criminology merits special attention. Kathleen Daly and Meda Chesney-Lind have called on scholars who seek to understand crimes by women to get their "hands dirty, and to plunge more deeply into the social worlds of girls and women." They noted that feminist criminologists, "like criminologists of the past (from the 1930s to the 1960s), seek to understand crime at close range, whether through biographical case studies, autobiographical accounts, participant observation, or interviews."[38] This difference between male and female criminological scholars, Daly and Chesney-Lind stressed, is not related to such invidious gender distinctions as female "math anxiety" but rather to a greater interest among the feminists in "providing texture, social context, and case histories; in short, in presenting accurate portraits of how adolescent and adult women become involved in crime."[39]

As they carry out their research, sociological criminologists would do well to bear in mind the observations made by Jerome Michael and Mortimer Adler after their comprehensive review of work in the subdiscipline, observations that are largely as sound today as they were when first recorded in 1932. "Most of the quantitative research . . . is not only insignificant," they wrote, "it is also unnecessary and pretentious." They insisted that such work had little practical utility and that "accurate nonquantitative descriptive knowledge . . . is sufficient for practical purposes." Much of quantitative criminology was found by Michael and Adler to be pretentious because it was imitative of what was "mistakenly supposed to be scientific method."[40] To this point, in more general terms, Clive Entwistle has added the following comment:

The sociologist likes to think of himself as a "scientist" in the sense that a physicist or a chemist is a scientist. Indeed, in his anxiety to assume that authoritative role, he has proved himself most willing to jettison every unquantifiable element in the field of human studies. He does not throw out the baby *with* the bath water—he throws out the baby and keeps the bath water for hard chromatographic analysis. The baby is held to be described by the results.[41]

Notes

1. Gibbon, *The Decline and Fall*, 1:69. Gibbon's comment is a paraphrase from Voltaire's *L'Ingénu*, 146.
2. Burgess, "Mr. Gibbon," 36.
3. Buckle, *History of Civilization*, 1:34.
4. Bannister, *Sociology and Scientism*, 51.
5. Walker, *Behaviour and Misbehaviour*, 13.
6. Cairns, *Law and the Social Sciences*, 20.
7. Stouffer, *Statistical and Case Study Methods*, 50.
8. Ibid., 52.
9. Cooley, "Case Study of Small Institutions," 124.
10. Ogburn, "Limitations of Statistics," 19.
11. See, for instance, Archer and Gartner, *Violence and Crime*.
12. Katz, *Seductions of Crime*, 4.
13. Ibid., 312.
14. Thomas and Znaniecki, *The Polish Peasant*.
15. See, for instance, Wirth, *The Ghetto*, and Zorbaugh, *The Gold Coast and the Slum*.
16. The subtitle of Thrasher's work—*A Study of 1,313 Gangs in Chicago*—illustrates the whimsical, if not bawdily irresponsible, tone of this bygone period. Obviously, Thrasher had not made a precise count of the number of gangs within his study provenance. The number 1,313 was derived from the address of a notorious brothel in Chicago.
17. Cf. Foreman, "The Theory of Case Studies."
18. Snodgrass, *The Jack-Roller at Seventy*.
19. Young, book review, 474.
20. Thrasher, "Juvenile Delinquency," 129–30.
21. Kobrin, "The Uses of the Life-History Document."
22. Sutherland, "White-Collar Criminality."
23. See Schrenker, *No Ivory Tower*.
24. Geis, "The Heavy Electrical Equipment Antitrust Cases."

25. Bittle and Geis, *The Longest Way Home*.
26. *Schenectady Union-Star*, February 7, 1961.
27. Geis, "The Heavy Electrical Equipment Antitrust Cases," 144.
28. Dershowitz, "Increasing Community Control."
29. Geis, "The Heavy Electrical Equipment Antitrust Cases," 149.
30. Quoted in Navasky, *Kennedy Justice*, 439.

31. The June 1990 issue of *American Sociological Review* did publish a piece by Susan Shapiro which proposed a redefinition of the concept and theory of white-collar crime. Such articles, as well as quantitative material, represent the kinds of pieces to which the journal now is hospitable, as opposed to case studies.

32. Ogren, "The Ineffectiveness of the Criminal Sanction," 965.

33. Hagan, Nagel (Bernstein), and Abonetti, "The Differential Sentencing of White-Collar Offenders."

34. Braithwaite, "White-Collar Crime."
35. Daly, "Varieties of White-Collar Crime," 775.
36. Shapiro, "The Road Not Taken."
37. Yin, *Case Study Research*.

38. Daly and Chesney-Lind, "Feminism and Criminology," 519, 517. Examples cited include Rosenbaum, *Women on Heroin*; Campbell, *The Girls in the Gang*; and Miller, *Street Women*.

39. Ibid.
40. Michael and Adler, *Crime, Law, and Social Science*, 315.
41. Entwistle, book review, 19.

References

Archer, Dane, and Rosemary Gartner. 1984. *Violence and Crime in Cross-Cultural Perspective*. New Haven: Yale University Press.
Bannister, Robert C. 1987. *Sociology and Scientism: The American Quest for Objectivity*. Chapel Hill: University of North Carolina Press.
Becker, Howard S. 1966. Introduction to *The Jack-Roller: A Delinquent Boy's Own Story*, by Clifford R. Shaw. Chicago: University of Chicago Press.
Bittle, William, and Gilbert Geis. 1964. *The Longest Way Home: Chief Alfred C. Sam's Back-to-Africa Movement*. Detroit: Wayne State University Press.
Blumberg, Paul. 1989. *The Predatory Society: Deception in the American Marketplace*. New York: Oxford University Press.
Braithwaite, John. 1985. "White-Collar Crime." *Annual Review of Sociology*, volume 11. Palo Alto: Annual Reviews.
Buckle, Henry T. 1903. *History of Civilization in England*. 2 vols. London: Grant Richards.
Burgess, Anthony. 1988. "Mr. Gibbon and the Huns." *New York Times Book Review* (February 28), 1, 36–37.

Cairns, Huntington. 1935. *Law and the Social Sciences*. New York: Harcourt Brace.

Campbell, Anne. 1984. *The Girls in the Gang: A Report from New York City*. New York: Blackwell.

Clinard, Marshall B. 1952. *The Black Market: A Study of White Collar Crime*. New York: Holt.

Conklin, John E. 1977. *"Illegal but Not Criminal": Business Crime in America*. Englewood Cliffs, N.J.: Prentice-Hall.

Cooley, Charles H. 1927. "Case Study of Small Institutions As a Method of Research." *Publications of the American Sociological Society* 22:123–32.

Cressey, Donald R. 1953. *Other People's Money: A Study in the Social Psychology of Embezzlement*. New York: Free Press.

Daly, Kathleen. 1989. "Gender and Varieties of White-Collar Crime." *Criminology* 27 (November): 769–93.

Daly, Kathleen, and Meda Chesney-Lind. 1988. "Feminism and Criminology." *Justice Quarterly* 5 (December): 497–535.

Dershowitz, Alan. 1961. "Increasing Community Control over Corporate Crime." *Yale Law Journal* 71 (September): 289–306.

Entwistle, Clive. 1987. Book Review. *New York Times Book Review* (December 31), 19.

Foreman, Paul. 1948. "The Theory of Case Studies." *Social Forces* 26 (May): 408–19.

Geis, Gilbert. 1967. "The Heavy Electrical Equipment Antitrust Cases of 1961." Pp. 139–50 in *Criminal Behavior Systems*, edited by Marshall B. Clinard and Richard Quinney. New York: Holt, Rinehart and Winston.

Gibbon, Edward. [1776] 1932. *The Decline and Fall of the Roman Empire*. 2 vols. New York: Modern Library.

Hagan, John, Ilene H. Nagel (Bernstein), and Celesta Abonetti. 1980. "The Differential Sentencing of White-Collar Offenders in Ten Federal Court Districts." *American Sociological Review* 45 (October): 802–20.

Hartung, Frank E. 1950. "White-Collar Offenses in the Wholesale Meat Industry." *American Sociological Review* 56 (July): 25–34.

Katz, Jack. 1988. *Seductions of Crime: Moral and Sensual Attraction of Doing Evil*. New York: Basic Books.

Kobrin, Solomon. 1982. "The Uses of the Life-History Document for the Development of Delinquency Theory." Pp. 153–65 in *The Jack-Roller at Seventy: A Fifty-Year Follow-Up*, by Jon Snodgrass. Lexington, Mass.: Lexington Books.

Lundsgaarde, Henry P. 1977. *Murder in Space City*. New York: Oxford University Press.

Michael, Jerome, and Mortimer J. Adler. 1932. *Crime, Law, and Social Science*. New York: Harcourt Brace.

Miller, Eleanor M. 1986. *Street Women*. Philadelphia: Temple University Press.

Navasky, Victor S. 1971. *Kennedy Justice*. New York: Atheneum.

Ogburn, William F. 1934. "Limitations of Statistics." *American Journal of Sociology* 40 (July): 12–20.

Ogren, Robert W. 1973. "The Ineffectiveness of the Criminal Sanction in Fraud and Corruption Cases: Losing the Battle against White-Collar Crime." *American Criminal Law Review* 11 (Summer): 959–88.

Rosenbaum, Marsha. 1981. *Women on Heroin*. New Brunswick, N.J.: Rutgers University Press.

Schrenker, Ellen W. 1986. *No Ivory Tower: McCarthyism and the Universities*. New York: Oxford University Press.

Shapiro, Susan P. 1985. "The Road Not Taken: The Elusive Path to Criminal Prosecution for White-Collar Offenders." *Law and Society Review* 19 (2): 178–217.

———. 1990. "Collaring the Crime, Not the Criminal: Reconsidering the Concept of White-Collar Crime." *American Sociological Review* 55 (June): 346–65.

Shaw, Clifford R. 1930. *The Jack-Roller: A Delinquent Boy's Own Story*. Chicago: University of Chicago Press.

———. 1931. *The Natural History of a Delinquent Career*. Chicago: University of Chicago Press.

———. 1936. *Brothers in Crime*. Chicago: University of Chicago Press.

Snodgrass, Jon. 1982. *The Jack-Roller at Seventy: A Fifty-Year Follow-Up*. Lexington, Mass.: Lexington Books.

Stouffer, Samuel A. [1930] 1980. *An Experimental Comparison of Statistical and Case Study Methods in Attitude Research*. New York: Arno.

Stouffer, Samuel A., et al. 1949. *The American Soldier*. 4 vols. Princeton, N.J.: Princeton University Press.

Sutherland, Edwin H. 1940. "White-Collar Criminality." *American Sociological Review* 5 (February): 1–12.

———. 1949. *White Collar Crime*. New York: Dryden.

Thomas, William I., and Florian Znaniecki. 1918–20. *The Polish Peasant in Europe and America: Monograph of an Immigrant Group*. Chicago: University of Chicago Press.

Thrasher, Frederic. 1927. *The Gang: A Study of 1,313 Gangs in Chicago*. Chicago: University of Chicago Press.

———. 1933. "Juvenile Delinquency and Mercenary Crime." Pp. 126–52 in *Crime for Profit: A Symposium on Mercenary Crime*, edited by Ernest D. MacDougall. Boston: Stratord.

Voltaire, François M. A. [1767] 1964. *L'Ingenu* (The child of nature). Translated by John Butt. Baltimore: Penguin Books.

Walker, Nigel. 1977. *Behaviour and Misbehaviour: Explanations and Non-Explanations*. Oxford: Basil Blackwell.

Wheeler, Stanton, David Weisburd, and Nancy Bode. 1982. "Sentencing the

White-Collar Offender: Rhetoric and Reality." *American Sociological Review* 47 (October): 641–59.

Wirth, Louis. 1928. *The Ghetto*. Chicago: University of Chicago Press.

Wolfgang, Marvin E. 1958. *Patterns in Criminal Homicide*. Philadelphia: University of Pennsylvania Press.

Yin, Robert K. 1989. *Case Study Research*. Rev. ed. Newbury Park: Sage.

Young, Kimball. 1930. Book Review. *American Journal of Sociology* 36 (November): 474.

Zorbaugh, Harvey W. 1929. *The Gold Coast and the Slum: A Sociological Study of Chicago's Near North Side*. Chicago: University of Chicago Press.

Christine L. Williams

7 Case Studies and the Sociology of Gender

In the last two decades, sociologists "discovered" gender. Starting in the 1970s, the mainstream sociology journals began regularly publishing articles that took into account differences between men and women, challenging the widespread presumption that men's social life—in particular, white men's social life—constituted the "normal" or "universal" human experience. Today, it is rare that an issue of the *American Journal of Sociology* or the *American Sociological Review* fails to contain at least one article addressing gender differences.

Feminist sociologists are not satisfied with this transformation, however. In "The Missing Feminist Revolution in Sociology," the authors lamented that "feminist sociology . . . seems to have been both co-opted and ghettoized, while the discipline as a whole and its dominant paradigms have proceeded relatively unchanged" (Stacey and Thorne 1985, 302). Simply "adding women in" to our regression tables and equations has not increased theoretical acuity about gender or revealed the male biases that plague sociological research. On the contrary, introducing "gender" as a variable into quantitative research has actually done disservice to the interests of a "feminist revolution in sociology." The quantitative methodologies dominant in mainstream social science impose severe limits on our ability to understand and appreciate gender as a sociological construct.

In this essay I will discuss some of the main features of the feminist critique of quantitative methods, and the case for qualitative research in the sociology of gender. However, I will not argue that one approach is inherently superior but that different questions are best addressed using different methodological approaches. In my view, qualitative methods are best suited to address questions of meaning and interpretation, whereas quantitative methods are more appropriate for describing what large groups of individuals actually do or have done to them. The problem with most research in the sociology of gender is not that it is quantitative per se but rather that quantitative techniques are used to describe the meanings that individuals associate with sex differences. The opposite problem—using qualitative methods to describe general patterns of behavior—is equally troublesome, yet not as prevalent due to the underrepresentation of this type of research in the mainstream journals.

The contrasting strengths of quantitative and qualitative methods led me to take the case study approach in my own research. I define *case study* as the in-depth study of a specific group or individual chosen to represent—even exaggerate—social conflicts that our theories suggest are experienced in the wider society. The case study design allows the researcher to combine descriptive, quantitative methods with the qualitative techniques for uncovering the meanings associated with gender identity. After giving an overview of the feminist critique of quantitative methods, I will describe my recent case studies of women in the U.S. Marine Corps and men in the nursing profession in an effort to combine the strengths of the two approaches. I will try to show how these two "extreme" cases can reveal more about the social construction of gender than a large, randomly selected, national survey.

The Feminist Critique of Quantitative Methods

The vast majority of quantitative research that deals with gender does not advance insight or understanding into the meanings of gender differences and the ways they are created and maintained. In fact, more often than not, this type of research contributes to the perpetuation of harmful stereotypes about men and women by giving them an aura of scientific objectivity. In this section, I will review four problems characteristic of quantitative gender research: (1) collapsing the sex-gender distinction; (2) exaggerating minor differences; (3) reifying existing stereotypes; and (4) decontextualizing gender.

COLLAPSING THE SEX-GENDER DISTINCTION

Beginning in the 1970s, feminists introduced a distinction between *sex* and *gender: Sex* refers to the biological and anatomical differences between males and females, differences that we are born with (or develop); *gender* refers to the meanings, beliefs, and practices associated with these differences (commonly referred to as *masculinity* and *femininity*). The main reason for introducing this distinction is to insist that differences in men's and women's social behavior are culturally elaborated and socially learned, not given in nature (Scott 1986, 1054).

This insight is for the most part lost in research that simply adds women into the analysis. In the mainstream sociology journals, it is common to see individuals' sex (i.e., whether they are male or female) treated as an independent variable in equations meant to describe and ultimately predict human behavior and attitudes. The following example is from an article entitled "Race Differences in the Timing of Adolescent Intercourse" published in the *American Sociological Review*: "Mothers' education and the respondent's sex have net *effects* [on adolescent intercourse]. Both low maternal education and *being male* increase by roughly three-fourths the likelihood of intercourse" (Furstenberg et al. 1987, 517, emphasis added). The implication is that biological sex actually *causes* changes or differences in the dependent variables under examination: change the respondents' genitals, and their behavior changes. Our societal double standard drops from view as "being male"—not the social organization that rewards promiscuity in males and punishes it in females—is deemed responsible for differences in intercourse. To counteract this biological reductionism, some researchers have changed their sex variable into gender simply by coopting the term.[1] This confusion between sex and gender collapses the original theoretical distinction, for here again gender is determined entirely by the shape of the genitals.

Of course, all social scientists should be wary of making causal claims about the social world, but even the most careful researchers fall into this conceptual trap when significant correlations are found among variables. In a critique of the top journals in sociology, Norval Glenn wrote: "Many people who do read the [social science] journals are likely to be misled by unwarranted conclusions about cause and effect. . . . Many social scientists, including many active researchers, seem to share the illusion that we know more than we do know" (1989, 119–20). If sociologists mislead people into believing that sex "causes" variations in human social behavior, feminists are back to square one in the fight against biological determinism.

EXAGGERATING MINOR DIFFERENCES

A second deficiency of quantitative research is its tendency to exaggerate differences between men and women. Quantitative researchers tend to concentrate on difference, focusing on the "tails of distributions and not their centers" (Epstein 1988, 37). Findings of equality are not headlined in articles. Even when the overwhelming evidence suggests similarity, the few dimensions of difference are highlighted. Thus, we are told that women are more Democratic than men—even though there is only an eight-point difference in voting behavior—obscuring the fact that the majority of men and women vote for the same candidates (Richardson 1986, 163). We are told that males are better at math than females, even though, again, there are plenty of girls who score better than boys on standardized math tests (Marini 1988, 376–77). And so on. Often these findings are "statistically significant," which is usually assured whenever a large, random sample has been used. But this practice of highlighting statistically significant, although minor, differences between men and women lends credence to the belief that men and women occupy totally dichotomous, nonoverlapping social worlds, which clearly they do not. The result is that differences are exaggerated, similarities ignored.

Margrit Eichler has called this focus on sexual dichotomies "a form of scholarly gender apartheid" (1988, 119). Some standard quantitative procedures in sociology, she argued, create the impression that men and women are discrete categorical groups. For example, quantitative researchers often utilize statistical tests of significance to document gender differences. This entails using the null hypothesis—usually the hypothesis that *no* differences exist—and then trying to reject it. According to Eichler, this procedure typically "results in an affirmation of the existence of a difference. In a cumulative sense, this may have a very peculiar effect. . . . [It] is likely to exaggerate sex differences over similarities. In other words, it will exaggerate the importance of gender as a categorical variable. Wherever techniques have this effect, we are dealing with a case of sexual dichotomism in methods" (1988, 123–24). She recognizes, rightly, that there is nothing inherently sexist about statistical tests of significance. However, they can be used in a sexist manner, by highlighting findings of difference over the overwhelming similarity and overlap that exist between men and women.

REIFYING EXISTING STEREOTYPES

A third problem with the quantitative treatment of gender is that it tends to reify existing stereotypes about men and women. Perhaps the most egregious example of this is found in the "M-F" scales, which are used with great frequency in journals such as *Sex Roles* and *Social Psychology Quarterly*. These scales attempt to measure quantitatively individuals' masculinity and femininity by averaging "scores" on questionnaires composed of personality attributes considered appropriate to each sex.[2]

In the most popular of these scales—the Bem Sex Role Inventory (BSRI)[3]—the following characteristics are deemed masculine: "acts as a leader, aggressive, ambitious, analytical, assertive, athletic, competitive, defends own beliefs, dominant, forceful, has leadership abilities, independent, individualist, makes decisions easily, masculine, self-reliant, self-sufficient, strong personality, willing to take a stand, willing to take risks." The following are considered feminine characteristics: "affectionate, cheerful, childlike, compassionate, does not use harsh language, eager to soothe hurt feelings, feminine, flatterable, gentle, gullible, loves children, loyal, sensitive to needs of others, shy, soft-spoken, sympathetic, tender, understanding, warm, yielding." Respondents rank themselves on each characteristic, using a seven-point scale ranging from "never or almost never true" to "always or almost always true." These responses are then averaged, and an overall masculinity and femininity "score" is computed (Eichler 1980, 63–66).

A cursory examination of these items reveals how the researchers uncritically accept the enormous sexist bias of our cultural stereotypes. It is extremely degrading to see femininity cast in such negative terms—childlike, flatterable, gullible—in contrast to the positive portrayal of masculinity—defends own beliefs, independent, strong personality. Furthermore, the implication is that a failure to "measure up" (or down, in the case of femininity) makes one *less* masculine or feminine. But in reality, no one can possibly conform to these stereotypes. The masculine man described by the tests is Donald Trump; the feminine woman is Zsa Zsa Gabor. These are not real people, they are oppressive cultural stereotypes. The M-F tests merely gauge our compliance with unattainable hegemonic ideals, further reifying these stereotypes.

Another problem with these "objective-type" tests is that they fail to register ambivalence as well as the situational contexts in which gender is experienced. Fitting one's personality along a continuum of responses always damages the self: contradictory answers are "averaged away," not taken as indicators of internal conflicts; shades of meaning and interpretation are dismissed as irrelevant "noise" or random error. Yet it is precisely these ambiguities that should interest us about gender, for they indicate the ongoing negotiated process of gender identity formation and maintenance. R. W. Connell has attributed the widespread popularity of this approach to gender to a "drastic reification": "If this research has been popular, and people feel they recognize themselves in dimensional accounts . . . , it is, perhaps, because the process of reification is so far advanced as to make recognition of qualitative diversity threatening. Fear, not of 'otherness' so much as of the riotous exuberance of motive and imagination that is a possibility in sexual life, can be a powerful motive in a world partly reified already" (1987, 174–75). The tests provide us with "scientific" moorings in a world in flux, renewing confidence in stereotypes that are being challenged by feminists and threatened by social change.

DECONTEXTUALIZING GENDER

My fourth criticism of quantitative approaches to the study of gender is their tendency to decontextualize the subject matter. Quantitative researchers tend to make categorical statements about men and women, statements that obscure or hide the variation in the experience of gender by different social groups and in different contexts. Looking at aggregate characteristics of *all* men and *all* women obscures significant differences and makes gender seem like a more universal, normative experience than it is. It is likely that *masculinity* and *femininity* mean different things to upper-class whites, middle-class Chinese-Americans, and lower-class Dominican immigrants and that the relationships between men and women in these different groups qualitatively differ. It is also likely that what a female marine defines as *feminine* varies from the definition preferred by a suburban housewife. As Elizabeth Spelman has noted, "If what characterizes the relationship between white men and white women does not characterize the relationship between Black men and white women, or between white men and Black women—then it is misleading to talk simply of relationships between 'men and women,' for whether what we say is true is going to depend on which men and women we are talking about" (1988, 107).

Even more problematic than making categorical statements about gender, however, is the tendency in quantitative research to "control" variation in the meaning of gender by comparing men and women of the same group, as if doing so provides a truer or purer picture of the effects of gender on people's behavior. But by comparing only white middle-class men and women, sociologists are as unable to generalize to the experience, attitudes, and behaviors of all men and women as they would be if they looked only at lower-class Hispanic men and women. Again to quote Spelman, "Simply because race and class are kept constant doesn't mean they have no effect. To talk about gender differences where race and class are constants is to talk about gender differences in the context of class and race similarity; but far from freeing us from the context of race and class, keeping them constant means they are constantly there" (1988, 104).

The overwhelming bulk of quantitative research on gender ignores social context, literally whitewashing distinctions of meanings that are situationally constructed and maintained. In the interest of distilling some pure essence of gender, sociologists often obliterate racial, class, and cultural context.[4] As Judith Stacey and Barrie Thorne noted, "Reducing social life to a series of measurable variables diminishes the sense of the whole that is crucial to theoretical understanding of social, including gender, relationships. The use of gender as a variable, rather than as a basic theoretical category, is a prime example of the co-optation of feminist principles" (1985, 307–8).

These four problems I have identified with quantitative methodologies—collapsing the sex-gender distinction, exaggerating minor differences, reifying existing stereotypes, and decontextualizing gender—have led some gender sociologists to eschew their use altogether. Dorothy

Smith, for example, has argued that a "Sociology for Women" must involve ethnographic or other qualitative techniques. To explicate the social organization underlying everyday life, she maintained, the sociologist must go back to real people in concrete situations and to their descriptions of their experience (Smith 1979).

Although I do not agree that quantitative methods are useless, the qualitative approach to gender issues is able to avoid many of these problems besetting quantitative studies. In the next section of this chapter, I will discuss the qualitative component of my own case study research in an effort to overcome the methodological limitations already discussed. I will review the rationale for the design of my study and illustrate how in-depth interviewing research can escape the problems I have described. Finally, I will examine the limitations that I believe are characteristic of qualitative research.

Case Study Design

Before I describe my study, a brief discussion of the theoretical issues that inspired it is needed. I have already mentioned the feminist distinction between sex and gender. The idea is that any differences between men and women—aside from the purely anatomical and reproductive ones—are socially constructed and maintained.[5] Given that gender differences are the product of society, therefore, I wondered *how* these differences are constructed and, furthermore, *why* they are constructed.

Feminist theorists have suggested several alternative ways of conceptualizing the social construction and maintenance of gender. At the outset of my research I considered the various contrasting and conflicting explanations: Is gender coercively enforced on men and women, as some radical feminists suggest? Is it the by-product of ritualistic practices and macrostructural forces—such as job segregation by sex—as suggested by socialist feminists? Or is gender a socialized identity, as psychoanalytic feminists claim? I decided to design an empirical study that would allow me to observe all three levels of gender reproduction—laws and restrictive policies, formal and informal practices, and socialized personality differences—in a comparative context.

I was drawn to the study of men and women in nontraditional occupations on the presupposition that the processes involved in maintaining and reproducing gender differences in these contexts would be more obvious and visible than in instances where men and women conformed to traditional roles. Here I was following in the long tradition of social theorists who have examined the "abnormal" or extreme cases in order to inform "normal" processes.[6] However, I was prepared to find that men and women who crossed over into the jobs of the other sex were not properly gender identified. In other words, popular stereotypes and mainstream sex-role theory had prepared me to expect that women in "men's jobs" might in fact be masculine, and men in "women's jobs," feminine. But such a finding, I thought, would also shed light on the theoretical debates occurring within the feminist literature.

The Marine Corps and the nursing profession seemed like ideal case studies for my research project for several reasons. First, they are closely associated with masculinity and femininity and have roughly equal proportions of "nontraditional" workers in them—just under 5 percent. Second, both occupations have histories of limiting the participation of the "opposite" sex, and archival materials are available to examine the exclusionary policies directed against male nurses and female marines. And finally, the occupations themselves formed boundaries for my sample selection. By limiting my study to these two self-enclosed, identifiable groups, I could compare and contrast experiences of men and women subject to the same or similar rules, practices, and expectations.

The study itself combined in-depth interviewing, participant observation, and archival research.[7] In what follows, I show how the qualitative data are far more appropriate for addressing questions of meaning and interpretation than are quantitative data.

Far from collapsing sex and gender, in-depth interviewing and participant observation highlighted the enormous energy that goes into creating gender differences. For example, female marines take makeup and poise classes in the course of their basic training. They are required to wear makeup (eye shadow and lipstick are the minimum acceptable amount), and they are taught the proper "feminine" ways to smoke cigarettes, drink beer (always from a glass), and address senior male officers at parties. According to one recruit, the Marine Corps made her into "a more feminine person" than she had been before:

They're constantly on you for appearance. To be feminine, to walk feminine. The whole time I've been here they've reminded me not to walk so masculine with my arms out to the side. They really want you to hold your head high, have good posture, good appearance. Hygiene is the upmost. . . . I think it's great. I did not even expect it. I wanted to come in here and be a lean, mean fighting machine. . . . I never wore make-up, never brushed my hair. . . . I didn't keep it in a nice, feminine, attractive style they wanted.

Drill instructors bragged to me about their "successes" in turning raw recruits into proper, "feminine" ladies.

Male nurses face comparable expectations that they demonstrate suitably "masculine" qualities—including ambition, leadership abilities, and camaraderie with male physicians. One nurse complained that doctors often sought him out to chat about their mutual interests (boat building, in this case), which he resisted out of fear of alienating his female colleagues. A nursing student, who described himself as "not overly ambitious," related this story: "I had one doctor tell me that he was glad to see more men go into nursing because they were more decisive. He said that to my face, and didn't see that there would be anything weird about saying it." These expectations may become self-fulfilling prophesies, actually constructing the differences attributed to natural dispositions. The qualitative approach, then, allowed me to discover some of the ways that gender differences are made to seem natural, when clearly they are not. Men and women do not behave in certain ways because their sex somehow compels them. Rather, gender differences are constructed by subjecting men and women to different social expectations and environments.

Earlier I argued that quantitative research tends to exaggerate differences between the sexes. Qualitative research tends to do the opposite. When confronted with the reality of men's and women's everyday lives, the observer is impressed by their overwhelming similarity. Granted, I did choose particular cases that highlighted overlap—female marines are doing "men's work," and male nurses "women's work," after all. But these cases made it clear that men and women can do the work we associate with the natural capabilities of the opposite sex. There is nothing inherently "masculine" about the Marine Corps: One marine I interviewed compared it to her experience of attending Catholic boarding school. Likewise, there is nothing inherently "feminine" about nursing: A nurse described his training as comparable to—in fact, harder than—a medical internship. Once again, the enormous effort that goes into distinguishing the two sexes is evident. People consider the same activity "feminine" when done by a woman, and "masculine" when done by a man.

This was perhaps most apparent during World War II, when the national emergency sparked a radical reorganization of the sexual division of labor. A nursing shortage prompted some men to rally in favor of permitting men to join the all-female nursing corps of the army and navy. But far from arguing the case for integration and equality, these men stressed the unique contributions they, as men, could make to the war effort:

> [There is a] need for realistic planning by nursing to provide representative nursing care for men patients with special provisions in urology [and psychology]. . . . It was urged that the objectives set up should include careful selection of men student nurses, assurance for the student and his advisers that nursing offers him a field in which as a graduate he will find opportunity for leadership and supervision, teaching, and other nursing activities where well-qualified men nurses are needed. (Quoted in Williams 1989, 40)

Now, as then, gender distinctions persist in spite of actual similarity. Studies that focus on difference miss the intervening reinterpretation process that creates invidious distinctions and the impression of dimorphous male and female worlds.

In the previous section I argued that quantitative research tends to reify existing stereotypes about men and women, a process that can be seen most clearly in the M-F tests that gauge individuals' compliance with a set of objectified norms. In my own research I confronted an extreme example of this: One widely used personality scale—the Minnesota Multiphasic Personality Inventory—uses interest in nursing as an indicator of femininity!

Male nurses and female marines are aware of the stereotypes and find them oppressive and offensive. One nurse told me he was considered "gay 'til proven otherwise" by nearly everyone he met. And a marine described an occasion when a man she had met in a bar responded skeptically about her occupation when she disclosed it, convinced that female marines could not possibly be attractive, feminine-looking women.

Perhaps the most extreme example of confrontation with negative stereotypes I encountered was the "defeminization testing" of drill instructors by their commanding officer. Here is how one of the tests was described to me:

> I was told that [a Marine Corps captain] was going to ask us questions on, more or less, the defeminization of women in recruit training. . . . We went into this big conference room, and he asked us questions like "Did drill instructor school make you change your voice in any way to sound more masculine?" . . . I guess because they're worried about us sounding like men. . . . He asked us questions like "did we feel any less feminine when we were on the drill field?" All the questions revolved around femininity, or us being feminine. . . . We gave it to him. Some of the women even cried because a lot of the questions he asked you really had to dig deep into yourself and tell him. . . . It finally came to the point that the D.I.'s were getting kind of upset and we told him, "Sir, I don't understand where you're coming from. Why are you asking us this?"

Female marines and male nurses bristle under the weight of the dominant cultural stereotypes about masculinity and femininity. They respond in various ways—including overconformity with the norms. (One nurse told me he was straight three times during the interview!) What quantitative measures omit is the reflexivity of social norms; they miss the ambiguity or process behind the answers to survey questionnaires. Individuals may be well aware of the dominant cultural stereotypes of masculinity and femininity: male nurses *know* that nursing is considered feminine work; female marines *know* that combat is considered masculine by most people. However, the fact that they do not conform personally to these stereotypical notions does not mean that they lack a gender identity they call "masculine" or "feminine." Men and women respond to and reinterpret gender norms, accepting or rejecting certain tenets without abandoning their masculine or feminine identities.

I also charged that quantitative measures of gender ignore ambivalence and uncertainty by averaging away disparate responses or attributing them to random variation. The real strength of qualitative research, I believe, is in revealing discrepant, often contradictory, beliefs that signal internal conflicts. One nurse inadvertently revealed his double standard against women when he disparaged his female colleagues for their lack of commitment to nursing and then explained that he would quit nursing "anytime" if something better came along. A new recruit revealed substantial internal confusion when I asked her to explain what she meant by her expression, "feminine marine":

> [The drill instructors] are always stressing when each is appropriate [the rough Marine Corps demeanor or femininity]. When marching in formation in our cammie greens [camouflage outfits], it's the hard type. When we are in our skirts, or out to dinner, or speaking with a superior officer, it's our feminine type. They just tell us when to use it and where to use it and how to use it.

> CW: What's the proper way to act when it's feminine?

> It's military but . . . it's a hard feminine style. It's hard to explain. Like when we're marching, the woman part drops out. It's just recruits out marching, slamming our heels down on the deck. When we're not in our cammies or out marching, it's put on your makeup and say yes or no, and don't bend down with your knees apart. I don't know, it's hard to explain, I'm having a hard time here. . . . The military's always there. . . . You're a woman at all times, but I guess there's time when you just let it shine out a bit more.

Quantitative measures often give the impression of static certainty in individuals' beliefs, attitudes, and personalities. My experiences in the field suggest the opposite: Views are constantly in flux, typically inconsistent, often ambivalent.

Finally, quantitative research that treats gender as a variable often decontextualizes it by removing social settings and group membership ties in the interests of abstractly defining "pure" gender differences. My study confirms the need to examine gender in social context. Different social groups have unique ways of construing gender differences, which may or may not conform to the hegemonic cultural norms.

The dominant cultural images of men as aggressive and analytic, women as tender and yielding, had little resonance with the marines I interviewed. One recruit, for example, described women as "the real brains behind the Marine Corps." Another told me that women may be better suited for combat than men: "I think women are just as good fighters as male marines are, sometimes they might be better because they have their own disguise. I mean, what man is going to think, 'What woman is going to be fighting, is going to be killing people?'"

Interestingly, the male nurses I interviewed did not venture far from the dominant cultural stereotypes of masculinity in their descriptions of themselves and their work. But they did recast their nursing work in masculine terms, stressing the technical elements, physical strength requirements, or administrative responsibilities of their jobs. For example, one nurse told me, in response to a question about differences between male and female nurses, "Some women feel threatened by men who are aggressive in nursing. I mean aggressive in their care. . . . For instance, when I was working in orthopedics, I was aggressive with patients who would not want to get out of bed because their leg hurts. I would say, 'You have to get out of bed, you need to walk.' So I set my foot down."

The meanings and behaviors associated with masculinity and femininity vary depending on the context. These significant variations will elude us as long as our emphasis in research is on distilling some "essence" of gender difference apart from everyday, lived experience.

The qualitative approach can be used, therefore, to escape many of the methodological problems besetting quantitative studies of gender. As a method, however, it is also limited. The final section of the chapter will describe some of the shortcomings of qualitative research and make the argument in favor of combining the two approaches in case studies.

Qualitative Caveats

The information garnered from qualitative research does have limitations. Since most sociologists have been trained in statistical procedures, often we raise questions about central tendency, questions that qualitative data are poorly equipped to answer. For example: "How frequently does X occur?" "How many people experience X?" "How do most people respond to X?" The appropriate method to address this type of question is quantitative, typically a randomly administered survey.

A fallacy often found in qualitative studies is the use of quantitative descriptions of their nonrandom samples. Even the use of percentages to describe the sample's behaviors must be resisted (e.g., "40 percent of the sample did X; 60 percent did Y"), for this use of numbers lends a false impression of generalizability to the larger population.

Misuses of numbers are, in part, the product of confusion about the appropriate goal of qualitative research, which is to describe as truthfully as possible individuals' definitions of their situations, and the meanings they attribute to their behaviors. Quantitative approaches, on the other hand, should be used to describe what large groups of people do or what others have done to them. In my own research, for example, quantitative techniques were needed to answer the questions: "What proportion of male nurses work in administrative specialities?" "Are female marines promoted at similar rates to male marines?" In-depth interviews and ethnographic research were needed to discern how male nurses and female marines thought and felt about the nontraditional gendered contexts in which they worked and whether they tried to promote or mitigate gender distinctions in the workplace.

The opposite fallacy occurs when users of quantitative methods attempt to answer questions of meaning and significance with measures of central tendency. Survey questionnaires are frequently designed to do just this, that is, to disclose the most common or typical values and attitudes of a population. If my previous discussion has been convincing, it should be clear that these techniques are incapable of answering such questions without falling into the four methodological quagmires I have detailed. How can a national survey measure how women define femininity without reifying existing stereotypes? How can a survey be designed that would preserve the social context of each respondent? Can a statistical analysis of a survey avoid attributing variation to sex and not to the social processes of gender reproduction? How can ambivalence or conflict be registered in responses to standardized questions? Each of these questions should severely limit our confidence in even the simplest survey measure of people's beliefs.

Does this mean we cannot know more than what a limited sample of individuals think or feel about their situations? I think so. This is precisely why I advocate using the case study design. Because of the inherent size limitation in most qualitative studies, it makes sense to limit the sample to a specific group of individuals subject to the same or similar constraints on their behavior. But it then follows that case studies must be carefully selected for their illustrative, theoretical value. The researcher must carefully confront the question: What can the insights and experiences of this particular group (or this particular individual) tell us about the general theoretical problem before us? In my study, I reasoned that if gender is socially constructed, as feminist theory suggests, these processes will be most apparent in contexts where individuals confront cultural stereotypes of their activities as appropriate only to the opposite sex. Female marines and male nurses have their work cut out for them if they want to be considered "appropriately" gendered; the stereotypes of the masculine marine (John Wayne, Rambo) and the feminine nurse (Florence Nightingale) must be counteracted somehow if they are to remain secure in their gender identity. What male nurses and female marines do to "vindicate" their masculinity and femininity probably would not be unlike what more "traditional" workers do, although they may be more aware of what is at stake in their compliance with particular norms. Thus, I reasoned, by studying these two groups, we can possibly gain insight into the gendering process in general. The test of this, of course, is whether the findings strike a chord of recognition with those in other contexts.

Regardless of the merits of this particular study, my point is that sociologists must provide this sort of account to justify their selection of cases to study. Otherwise they can be "unbounded," making it difficult to cull out theoretical insights about underlying social patterns.

Carefully chosen case studies, then, give the researcher the opportunity to combine the advantages of both methodological approaches for a broader understanding of gender than either one is capable of providing alone. However, a resurgence in the popularity of qualitative research is unlikely until a major stumbling block is removed from the researcher's path: the "problem" of reliability. I will conclude, therefore, with a few comments about reliability and validity.

In sociology textbooks, it is common to find quantitative methods characterized as yielding more "reliable" data, that is, more consistent information than that yielded by qualitative studies. Good reliability means that different researchers using the same research instrument are likely to obtain the same responses from the population. Qualitative data, on the other hand, are considered to have greater "validity," that is, they are more likely than quantitative data to reflect truthfully what happens in the social world.

The dominance of quantitative methodology in sociology has meant that the criterion of reliability has been given priority over validity in evaluating research. For example, Jerome Kirk and Marc Miller have noted, "As a means to the truth, social science has relied almost entirely on techniques for assuring reliability, in part because 'perfect validity' is not even theoretically attainable. Most nonqualitative research method-ologies come complete with a variety of checks on reliability, and none on validity" (1986, 21). In certain areas, in fact, a veritable obsession with reliability has taken over. Some social psychologists, for example, have begun using video display terminals to run their experiments, thus eliminating any human contact with the subject, which might bias their results (Sherif 1987, 46). The implication is that "pure" data on human social behavior can be obtained only outside of real human social contexts!

Reliability has been overrated in sociology, and it is time for the pro-fession to reevaluate the importance of reliability as a governing principle in our research. It certainly is not as important as validity. After all, per-fect validity entails perfect reliability, but the converse is not true (Kirk and Miller 1986, 21). Furthermore, it is not impossible to obtain reliable results in qualitative research. By strictly adhering to guidelines for docu-menting context and procedures, one can achieve reasonable certainty about the conditions under which others might observe the same find-ings. Yet it is not clear how quantitative research may enhance theoretical validity without qualitative studies. A major rethinking of these issues might persuade the discipline to develop more tolerance about combining qualitative and quantitative approaches in case studies.

The sociology of gender has made enormous theoretical and empirical strides in the past twenty years. I believe that the greater acceptance of qualitative methodologies among feminist theorists has contributed to the growth and development of the field. Time has come for the "feminist revolution" to venture into the mainstream, outside of the study of gen-der per se, and to broaden the horizons of sociology generally.

Notes

I would like to thank the following people for their helpful comments: Ben Agger, Joe Feagin, Debra Umberson, and Mary Waters.

1. Examples may be found in Terance D. Miethe, Mark C. Stafford, and J. Scott Long, "Social Differentiation in Criminal Victimization: A Test of Routine Activities/Lifestyle Theories," *American Sociological Review* 52, no. 2 (April 1987): 184–94; Bert Klandermans and Dick Oegema, "Potentials, Networks, Motivations, and Barriers: Steps toward Participation in Social Movements," *American Sociological Review* 52, no. 4 (August 1987): 519–31; and Von Bakanic, Clark McPhail, and Rita J. Simon, "The Manuscript Review and Decision Making Process," *American Sociological Review* 52, no. 5 (October 1987): 631–42. These examples were all chosen arbitrarily.

2. The attributes are selected from a long list provided to a large group of respondents (typically college students) who are asked whether each attribute is commonly considered desirable in men or women (Eichler 1980, 66).

3. Sandra Bem introduced this scale in a 1974 article, "The Measurement of Psychological Androgyny," *Journal of Consulting and Clinical Psychology* 42:155–62. As an indication of its popularity, the *Social Science Index* lists under the "Bem Sex Role Inventory" eighty-eight articles published between 1978 and 1988, including twenty-five articles from 1986 to 1988. Another indication of the continued popularity of the scale is from the *Social Science Citation Index*. The SSCI lists over one thousand citations to the original 1974 article from 1980 to 1988, including ninety-four citations in the 1988 edition.

4. Elliot Mishler (1986) recently made a similar point about the study of social class. He wrote:

> Interpreting differences in the frequency among social classes of a particular response to a specific question depends on the assumption that the question "meant" the same thing to all respondents. . . . Excluded from this line of reasoning is the possibility of variation among subgroupings in their understandings of questions and in the intentional meanings of answers [and] how these are, in turn, related to variation in sociocultural frameworks of language and meaning. There is little consideration of the problem that comparison groups may only partially share a common culture and that they in other respects may represent quite different subcultures. The particular combination of such partial overlaps would have a marked effect on responses and on the meaning of subgroup differences. When this is not recognized as a problem, however, it plays no specific role in the interpretation of findings. (1986, 5–6)

The same point may also be made with regard to gender, race, or any other grouping of individuals on the basis of a social attribute.

5. Even biological differences are considered meaningless outside of a social context. In fact, some feminist theorists—especially those influenced by La-

can—insist that biological differences are constructed through social discourse. See Judith Butler, "Variation on Sex and Gender," in *Feminism As Critique*, edited by Seyla Benhabib and Drucilla Cornell (Minneapolis: University of Minnesota Press, 1987), 128–42.

6. Durkheim and Freud both utilized this approach. In the study of gender, this tactic has been employed by Harold Garfinkel and Robert Stoller, both of whom studied transsexuals to derive insight into the social construction of gender in "normal" people.

7. A detailed description of the methodology can be found in Williams 1989, 144–50.

References

Connell, R. W. 1987. *Gender and Power: Society, the Person, and Sexual Politics*. Stanford: Stanford University Press.

Eichler, Margrit. 1980. *The Double Standard: A Feminist Critique of Feminist Social Science*. New York: St. Martin's Press.

———. 1988. *Nonsexist Research Methods: A Practical Guide*. Boston: Allen and Unwin.

Epstein, Cynthia Fuchs. 1988. *Deceptive Distinctions: Sex, Gender, and the Social Order*. New Haven: Yale University Press; New York: Russell Sage Foundation.

Furstenberg, Frank F., S. Philip Morgan, Kristin A. Moore, and James L. Peterson. 1987. "Race and the Timing of Adolescent Intercourse." *American Sociological Review* 52, no. 4 (August): 511–18.

Glenn, Norval D. 1989. "What We Know, What We Say We Know: Discrepancies between Warranted and Unwarranted Conclusions." Pp. 119–40 in *Crossroads of Social Science*, edited by Heinz Eulau. New York: Agathon Press.

Kirk, Jerome, and Marc L. Miller. 1986. *Reliability and Validity in Qualitative Research*. Sage University Paper Series on Qualitative Research Methods, volume 1. Beverly Hills: Sage.

Marini, Margaret Mooney. 1988. "Sociology of Gender." Pp. 374–93 in *The Future of Sociology*, edited by E. F. Borgatta and K. S. Cook. Newbury Park: Sage.

Mishler, Elliot G. 1986. *Research Interviewing: Context and Narrative*. Cambridge: Harvard University Press.

Richardson, Laurel. 1986. *The Dynamics of Sex and Gender*. 3d ed. New York: Harper and Row.

Scott, Joan W. 1986. "Gender: A Useful Category of Historical Analysis." *American Historical Review* 91, no. 5 (December): 1053–75.

Sherif, Carolyn Wood. 1987. "Bias in Psychology." Pp. 37–56 in *Feminism and Methodology*, edited by Sandra Harding. Bloomington: Indiana University Press.

Smith, Dorothy E. 1979. "A Sociology for Women." Pp. 135–87 in *The Prism of Sex: Essays in the Sociology of Knowledge*, edited by Julia A. Sherman and Evelyn Torton Beck. Madison: University of Wisconsin Press.

Spelman, Elizabeth V. 1988. *Inessential Woman: Problems of Exclusion in Feminist Thought*. Boston: Beacon Press.

Stacey, Judith, and Barrie Thorne. 1985. "The Missing Feminist Revolution in Sociology." *Social Problems* 32, no. 4 (April): 301–16.

Williams, Christine L. 1989. *Gender Differences at Work: Women and Men in Nontraditional Occupations*. Berkeley: University of California Press.

Gerald Handel

8 Case Study in Family Research

In a social science methods text published in 1950, Wilson Gee devoted a chapter to "The Case Method." Twenty years later, research methods texts devoted no more than a page or two to this topic, if they discussed it at all (e.g., Denzin 1970; Lin 1976; Phillips 1971; Simon 1969). The disappearance of the case study method from social science, and more specifically from sociology, is illusory, however. About the same time that the case study method was relocated from the table of contents to a brief citation in the index, another method was being increasingly written about that was, in effect, the case study in another guise. This was—and is—the method of participant observation.

Discussions of participant observation as a method seldom emphasize that the researcher is studying a single case; rather, they focus on the method's value for gaining firsthand knowledge of how a social unit is organized in terms of the members' own definitions of their reality and the processes that establish and change the unit. Participant observation is a method in which the researcher spends a great deal of time—over a period of weeks, months, or years—observing and, to a greater or lesser degree, joining in the activities of the group or organization he or she is studying. Participant observation has always been the method of cultural anthropologists, and it has long been one of the methods of sociologists. In recent years, a number of manuals, textbooks, and theoretical treatises devoted to this method have been published, supplanting what was previously an exclusively oral tradition of teaching it. Conspicuously absent from these works, however, is any discussion of families. One possible explanation is that very few researchers have managed to gain sustained observational access to families (though this fact does not fully explain why the few instances that do exist should not serve as textbook examples). Case studies of families, like other kinds of studies of families, have been more often based on interviews than on field observations. In brief, most participant observation studies are case studies, but not all case studies are participant observation studies.

What is a case study? Referring to the period between the first and second World Wars, the British sociologist Jennifer Platt wrote: "The idea of 'the case-study method' is one of central importance in methodological discussion in the interwar period" (1987, 1). In her effort to understand what American sociologists meant by the term, she examined a number of studies from that period and arrived at a constructed type whose features I extract from her prose account. A case study:

1. Entails the collection of intensive data about all aspects, including those which may be unique to the individual case;
2. Treats the case holistically rather than isolating variables;
3. Aims to provide data about personal experiences and their meaning;
4. Takes into account the history and social context of the case, thus making behavior intelligible;
5. Attaches special importance to the individual's own version of events, implying both that the researcher's preconceptions should not be imposed and that it is desirable that data should be collected in the subject's own words. (Platt 1987, 1)

An American philosopher of the social sciences, Paul Diesing, presented a discussion that overlaps (and expands on) the features that Platt identified. Diesing considered that it is useful to classify social research methods into four main types: (1) experimental methods; (2) survey methods; (3) formal methods; and (4) participant observation methods. (He regarded the psychologist's and psychiatrist's clinical method as a version of participant observation, and he often used the term *case study methods* interchangeably with the term *participant observation and clinical methods*.) Case studies, he stated, whether of a little community, factory, small informal group, family, city, mass movement, or large bureaucratic organization, are efforts to understand a whole human system in its natural setting. They are based on a holistic standpoint. Diesing noted:

> The holist standpoint includes the belief that human systems tend to develop a characteristic wholeness or integrity. They are not simply a loose collection of traits or wants or reflexes or variables of any sort. . . . This means that the characteristics of a part are largely determined by the whole to which it belongs and by its particular location in the whole system. . . . The contention that human wholes exist and determine their parts is not unusual and could be accepted by most social scientists. . . . The holist, however, believes not only that wholes exist but that his account of them should somehow capture and express this holistic quality. As Redfield says, it should be "knowledge that will preserve some of the holistic qualities of the things compared." . . . By "holistic quality" is meant not only the manifold interrelations among parts that appear in the original but also some of the unique characteristics, the distinctive qualities and patterns that differentiate this system from others. (Diesing 1971, 137–39)

These characterizations by Platt and Diesing are suitably descriptive of the family case studies to be discussed in this chapter. I will discuss a number of studies, which are similar to each other in the terms just discussed but different in other ways and which have one further characteristic in common that perhaps differentiates this chapter from others in the volume: most of the studies to be discussed are not based on a single case but on a small number of cases. This appears to be the most usual practice among family researchers who use the case study method.

My discussion will begin with *Family Worlds*, by Robert D. Hess and Gerald Handel, not only because, as one of the authors, I know it best, but also because it was one of the earliest of the post–World War II family research investigations in which case study was the major form of publication. Published in 1959, *Family Worlds* presents five case studies of families of northwest European ancestry; the case studies are preceded by a theoretical opening chapter and followed by a concluding comparative chapter and an appendix on method.[1] The conceptualization drew on sociological, psychological, and anthropological thought in a way for which we had no previous model.

Our opening statements in *Family Worlds* sketched our basic framework. We noted that there is a sense in which family is a bounded universe. Although a family's life extends into the wider community, parents and their young children also inhabit a world of their own making, their own "community of feeling and fantasy, action and precept." The prospective mother and father not only plan for the physical presence of a new member of the family; they also anticipate what the child will mean to them. Some of the child's activity will prove surprising, but mutual familiarity of parents and child will grow through the language, tones of voice, physical contacts, and other components that characterize their interaction. In time, the patterns of interaction will influence how the family members individually perceive their life together. By sharing an intimate daily existence, the family members become engaged in an ongoing process of negotiating uncertainty, dealing with conflict, and attempting to establish consensus, which may be more or less successful. The family's task is to provide a means for the individual members to be both separate and connected. Although families draw on the culture(s) in which they participate in carrying out this task, they do so selectively, and each family creates its own local version.

With specific reference to the book's aims, we went on to remark:

The psychosocial portraits we have sketched are intended to convey something of the particularity of American family worlds. These are American families, but the wider culture was not our primary interest. Rather, we tried first to find the family's boundaries, then to explore its psychosocial dimensions. When we looked at the culture, it was in order to take the point of view of a family looking out at it. The reader will recognize in these analytic sketches versions of middle and lower class cultural themes; again, our aim has been to illustrate what this feels like to actual individuals who shape a life in an intimate group. The case study is the method of choice for this purpose, and its aim is to amplify the richness of perception of American family life.

Depiction is not our sole aim, however. We are concerned with developing a framework for understanding the nuclear family as a group. . . . (Hess and Handel, 1959, 1–2)

This study was interdisciplinary in its conceptualization, unorthodox in its methods, and ambitious in its goals. The social context in which the study was conducted had a bearing on these characteristics, and so before describing the study in further detail, I will say something about that context.

Family Worlds—Background to the Study

Although today Robert D. Hess is a professor of education and psychology and Gerald Handel is a professor of sociology, both of us did our graduate work not in departments but in the Committee on Human Development, an interdepartmental degree-granting committee at the University of Chicago. *Family Worlds* was the product of work that we did after becoming staff members of the committee. The structure, atmosphere, and goals of the committee facilitated undertaking a study that had no model or analogue but involved framing a problem in an unfamiliar way and devising new study procedures.

The oldest of several degree-granting committees at Chicago, the Committee on Human Development was established to study the biological, psychological, and social factors influencing human growth and development. Founded as the Committee on Child Development in 1930 by professors of biology, child psychology, education, home economics, and sociology, the committee was renamed in 1940 to indicate its concern with the entire life span and life course. By the late 1940s, the faculty of the committee had become very diverse and were engaged in a variety of creative activities. The anthropologist-sociologist W. Lloyd Warner's teaching and writing on social class (Warner and Lunt 1941; Warner 1949; Warner et al. 1949) were influential in many directions. The anthropologist Allison Davis and the educator Robert J. Havighurst did studies of social class differences in child-rearing (Davis and Havighurst 1946), and Davis was also attempting to overcome middle-class bias in intelligence testing by developing intelligence tests that would be culture-fair to children of all social classes. Havighurst and the sociologist Ernest W. Burgess were beginning some of the earliest studies in gerontology;

they were joined by such colleagues as Bernice Neugarten, who in 1943 had received the second Chicago Ph.D. in human development. William E. Henry, in 1944 the third Ph.D. recipient, worked with Warner on a study of the meanings of radio daytime serials—"soap operas" (Warner and Henry 1946). Henry also was reconceptualizing the Thematic Apperception Test, a clinical psychology instrument invented by Christiana Morgan and Henry A. Murray (Murray 1943) at Harvard, into the thematic apperception *technique*, a specialized interview procedure for use in understanding symbolic and emotional life in groups as well as individuals (Henry 1951, 1956). In 1950, David Riesman, with Nathan Glazer and Reuel Denney, published his celebrated study of the changing American character, *The Lonely Crowd* (1950). Bruno Bettelheim was developing milieu therapy for treating emotionally disturbed children (Bettelheim 1955), while Carl Rogers was developing his theory and method of client-centered counseling (Rogers 1951).

Graduate students selected, from a large array in several departments, courses offered by these members of the committee as well as by other members and by faculty who were not members; courses were required in genetics and physiology. The expectation was that every student would create his or her own integration of the diverse materials being taught, although in 1948 a year-long core course was introduced to help. Perhaps the most general message communicated was that there was no one right way to study human development, nor in fact was there any preferred way, except that one's thinking should be broader than the teachings of a single department or discipline. As Havighurst wrote in a committee publication: "The graduate from Human Development must be an integrator and a creator, whether he be in practical work, in teaching, or in research" (1950, 30–31).

In the late 1940s and the 1950s, the study of child-rearing within the family was construed largely as the study of mother-child interaction, and this was true not only at Chicago but elsewhere as well.[2] The prevailing view was that child-rearing affected a child's personality, and child-rearing was understood largely in terms of mothers' practices with children, particularly weaning, toilet training, and methods of discipline. The baneful influence of mothers in generating psychopathology in their children was accentuated in the then current psychiatric concept of "the schizophrenogenic mother."

Totally unconnected either to the psychiatric discussions or to studies of ordinary child-rearing was an idea that pointed to a different way of proceeding. One of our own faculty members, the sociologist Ernest W. Burgess, in 1926 had coined a phrase that became a dictum: "The family as a unity of interacting personalities" (1968, 28). This was a prominent and widely disseminated concept for thinking about families and was akin to another foundation stone, Cooley's (1909) concept of families as primary groups in which the sentiments that constitute human nature are formed. Despite the great respect and reiteration that Burgess's concept received, one was hard put to find any studies based on it. Burgess himself did studies of engagement and marriage but not, so far as I know, studies that took his concept beyond the marital dyad. As late as 1950, the anthropologist Oscar Lewis wrote in the *American Journal of Sociology*: "Despite all the emphasis in the textbooks on the family as an integrated whole, there is little published material in which the family is studied as that" (1950, 471). Be it noted that Burgess's concept of *unity* was not used as a synonym for harmony. Rather, *unity* meant ongoing social interaction of whatever kind. As Burgess wrote: "The actual unity of family life has its existence not in any legal conception, not in any formal contract, but in the interaction of its members. For the family does not depend for its survival on the harmonious relations of its members, nor does it necessarily disintegrate as a result of conflicts between its members. The family lives as long as interaction is taking place and only dies when it ceases" (1968, 28). Although Burgess was mentioned only briefly in the preface to *Family Worlds*, his dictum was one of the guiding concepts of the study.

The Study

The overall goal of the Hess-Handel study initiated in 1952 was to understand how parents influence their children. To accomplish this goal, we judged it essential to obtain data from each member of the family—all the children as well as both parents. This methodology was innovative, and developing it was one of the three main initial aims of the study.[3] The methodology was applied in two different ways to the other two specific aims. One of these was the study of transmission of personality characteristics (specifically, aggression) between parents and children. This phase of the work resulted in a quantitative study (Hess and Handel 1956). The second was the study of what we called *family emotional structure*, which was further specified in the original proposal to the National Institute of Mental Health as follows: "Characteristic modes of family interaction will be examined in order to permit more adequate descriptions of families in terms of the kinds of relations between the family members. The study will be directed toward the characterization of families in terms of emotional organization." This aspect of the work resulted in a preliminary report (Handel and Hess 1956) and then in the volume of case studies under discussion.

Our initial language in the proposal was somewhat more psychological than sociological, speaking as we did of personality and emotion (unlike sociologists today, sociologists did not then study emotion), but we were also thinking in a way that developmental psychologists of that time were not, namely in terms of family members constituting a group with structure created out of the interaction among the members. Among the guiding concepts in the back of this author's mind were Cooley's concept of the family as a primary group, Burgess's concept of the family as a unity of interacting personalities, George Herbert Mead's concept of the relation of the self to the generalized other, and the concept of emotional climate that Lewin, Lippitt, and White (1939) and Lippitt and White (1943) had generated in their study of children's clubs. (Rather than mechanically apply to families their categories of "authoritarian," "democratic," and "laissez-faire," however, we thought it necessary to generate our own way of conceptualizing family emotional climate on the basis of our study of the actual empirical materials we were working with.) To understand socialization, we needed to understand the family as an operating group, and to do that, we needed to obtain the perspective of each member of the group.

After the two parents were interviewed jointly to explain the study and invite their participation and to gather some factual data (e.g., age of each member, birthplace, ethnic background), each person in the family was interviewed individually from one to three times. In addition, each family member told stories to a set of pictures from the Thematic Apperception Test. Although the TAT had been invented as a diagnostic instrument for clinical psychology, William E. Henry had shown (1951) how it could be used to study relations of individuals to a group, and we sought to adopt his logic and adapt it to the study of families in a way that had not been done before. Henry had taught that the TAT was not a test but a specialized form of interview to obtain information that a person cannot or will not tell about himself or herself. It seemed well suited for our purpose of comprehending the ties and conflicts among family members and for enlarging our understanding by providing information beyond what could emerge in the conventional discourse of the qualitative interview. Each family member also completed a set of incomplete sentences. Finally, each child wrote a short essay on "The Kind of Person I Would Like to Be Like," and each parent an essay on "The Kind of Person I Would Like My Child to Be."[4] All data-collecting sessions were in the family's home, which allowed for description of the dwelling.

The interviews were qualitative, conversational, and wide-ranging, although they could not, of course, cover every possible topic. The study was not designed to build up long-term relationships with the families in a way that would allow for an ever wider and deeper exploration of sensitive topics. Nevertheless, within the space of a few hours with each family member (less with the younger children), a range of material was sought that would make possible the realization of our goals. The interviews covered the following areas:

1. Each member's view of his or her family—what it is like, what the important things about it are
2. The family's daily life—each person's account of what the family does, including concrete happenings, feelings about what goes on, and the kinds of interactions that occur
3. Responsibility roles of each member—work, home, school, as well as church and voluntary organizations; also each member's feelings about his or her own roles and those of the other family members
4. Parents' families of origin and how they now see themselves in relation to their backgrounds; parents' goals for selves and children, as well as regrets and disappointments; children's own goals for themselves
5. How parents socialize their children; how children feel about how their parents deal with them

6. How the family members feel about one another, and how they believe they resemble or differ from one another
7. What problems each member feels he or she has in relation to himself or herself or in relation to other members[5]

Family interaction was interpreted by considering together all of the interviews and other materials obtained from all the members of a given family.[6]

The Hess-Handel project gathered data of the kinds just described from thirty-three intact families of northwest European ancestry, each with two or three children between the ages of six and eighteen. The age limits for the children were set on practical grounds, not theoretical. We were not prepared to use specialized techniques for obtaining information from very young children, and we regarded six as the youngest age at which interviews could readily be conducted; children older than eighteen were often not likely to be living with their parents. The specification of ethnic background was for the purpose of having a relatively homogeneous set of families so as to understand variation that was not a reflection of ethnic group differences. Social class variation, on the other hand, was deliberately sought, and families of working-class, middle-class, and upper-middle-class status were studied.

Our approach to this great mass of material was exploratory and essentially inductive. Together with research assistants who worked on the project for varying periods, we held case conferences in which we endeavored to understand each family as a unit. Although outlines of topics for analysis were prepared and revised over the course of this lengthy exploratory period, we were determined not to approach the material with a highly specified theoretical framework but to try to break through to a new approach that would deal with the group reality of families. We did have an orientation: to take the adumbrative sociopsychological ideas of Cooley, Mead, Burgess, Lewin, Lippitt, and White and integrate them with dynamic ideas of personality and child development to produce an analysis of families as groups that create their own corporate reality in a social and cultural context. Further, we wanted to show how each member of the family participated in the family's corporate reality. We were thus trying to produce statements that (1) described families as groups, each with its own corporate character; (2) accounted for each family member's particular and distinctive participation in the group; and (3) had generality that made the statements useful beyond the particular cases being described yet did not obliterate the particularity of actual families engaged in putting together an actual life. This tripartite objective was implicit in our work from the outset, but at first we were far from clear on how to accomplish it. What did become clear in the course of our discussions was that these objectives could not be reconciled with a publication format involving some kind of summary of findings from all thirty-three families. For a time, we were at an impasse.

The resolution of the difficulty was to recognize the case study as an essential procedure for publication. We selected for intensive analysis five families that varied in their social class position. The case studies together take up about 240 of the book's 300 pages. Preceding them is a theoretical chapter; following are a comparative chapter and a methodological appendix. The opening theoretical chapter, "The Family As a Psychosocial Organization," was in fact the last to be written. Although some of the ideas in it had begun to emerge during our case conferences, it was the intensive analysis of the five published cases that made it possible to develop these ideas in the focused form in which they appear. The chapter identifies five basic processes that "give shape to the flux of family life, coherence to the extended array of events, perceptions, emotions, actions, learnings, and changes which the members experience or undertake" (Hess and Handel 1959, 4). The processes are expressed briefly as follows:

1. Establishing a pattern of separateness and connectedness.
2. Establishing a satisfactory congruence of images through the exchange of suitable testimony.
3. Evolving modes of interaction into central family concerns or themes.
4. Establishing the boundaries of the family's world of experience.
5. Dealing with the significant biosocial issues of family life as in the family's disposition to evolve definitions of male and female and of older and younger. (ibid., 4)

While these five processes are no more than a beginning of a social psychology or microsociology of families, they do carry forward the undeveloped sensitizing concepts of Cooley, Mead, Burgess, Lewin, Lippitt, and White. They increase an understanding of how families function as primary groups, and they identify major categories of events and actions that contribute to whatever kind of unity of interacting personalities is established.

Had our discussion of these five family processes been published as a journal article rather than as a book chapter framing a set of case studies, its theoretical value might have been unaltered, but its communicative value would surely have been greatly diminished. Perhaps too, its theoretical value might have been less, for understanding does not consist in generalization alone. Knowledge and understanding increase both by generalization and by specification, and it is not clear how useful to readers an abstract account of the processes would have been without the case studies that not only illustrate the processes but also add case-by-case elaborations to them. Only by seeing actual cases is it possible to gain a clear perception of what the processes mean. For example, although the concept of family theme may be loosely apprehended without any specified knowledge, understanding is greatly increased by specifying some themes and by giving information portraying how the themes manifest themselves in family members' discourse, feelings, and actions. Only by the presentation and the working out of multiple instances can the full complexity of the phenomena to which the concept refers be made understandable.

There are many ways to think about families, but I believe the most fundamental activity of families is the creation of meaning. I see the five processes that we formulated as processes that partially explain and account for how families create meaning. A family is begun by adults who choose each other because each means something to the self of the other. Jointly they construct a world of meaning that not only governs their relationship but also makes intelligible the world outside it. The case study that aims at comprehensiveness is the best method, if not the only method, for trying to understand the breadth of meaning that any family generates.[7] In my judgment, this work is facilitated by comparing a few cases, although a longitudinal study of a single family would be sufficient to illuminate how some processes of meaning change over time. In graduate seminars on socialization and on family interaction, I have informed students of my willingness to sponsor a dissertation based on two cases.

Nothing whatsoever is known about how a marital dyad becomes a primary group when a baby is born. The general procedure would be for the student to find a couple as close to the beginning of pregnancy as possible, interview wife and husband repeatedly until the baby is born—focusing on each partner's own thoughts, feelings, and expectations and their joint conversations, as well as on all conversations with and incoming messages from others—and continue the interviewing for at least six months after the baby is born, supplementing it with observations in the home. Since nothing is known on this topic, a single case would be sufficient to generate initial concepts and to add to our knowledge, but a study of two cases that provide both similarity and contrast would make such a study easier to do. In the family field, I would argue for the merits of a comparative case study method as generally more useful than the study of a single case, but a single case studied by a gifted analyst could be productive.

Other Case Study Investigations

Oscar Lewis's volume of case studies of Mexican families, *Five Families* (1959), was published virtually simultaneously with *Family Worlds*. Lewis's purpose was to contribute to an understanding of what he called the *culture of poverty*, a distinctive subculture that can be found in lower-class settlements in many countries. He saw his method as innovative but particularly well suited to his purpose:

> The present study of five Mexican families is a frank experiment in research design and reporting. Unlike earlier anthropological studies, the major focus of this study is the family rather than the community or the individual. The intensive study of families has many methodological advantages. Because the family is a small social system, it lends itself to the holistic approach of anthropology. The family is a natural unit of study, particularly in a large metropolis like Mexico City. Moreover, in describing a family, we see individuals as they live and work together rather than as the averages and stereotypes implicit in reports on culture patterns. In studying a culture through the intensive analysis of specific families we learn what

institutions mean to individuals. It helps us get beyond form and structure to the realities of human life. . . . Whole family studies bridge the gap between the conceptual extremes of culture at one pole and the individual at the other; we see both culture and personality as they are inter-related in real life. (1959, 3)

In undertaking this work, Lewis was prompted by the conviction that anthropologists had to shift their focus from isolated, small-scale tribal societies to the peasants and urban dwellers of underdeveloped countries who make up almost 80 percent of the world's population. He pointed to the discrepancy between the accumulating economic and political knowledge about these countries and the absence of information about the outlooks, thoughtways, problems, and daily lives of those who live at the bottom levels of the social order.

Lewis's five case studies are based on knowledge acquired over a period of at least eight years of fieldwork. He had spent hundreds of hours in the families' homes and had also administered Thematic Apperception Tests, Rorschach tests, and other instruments, as well as conducting autobiographical interviews with each family member. The case studies do not, however, consist of integrated analyses of this enormous amount of material. Lewis chose, rather, to present the five families by giving an account of their activities over the course of a typical day. The days are actual days, not composites, and were chosen at random except that no day with an unusual event such as a fiesta, birth, baptism, or funeral was chosen. Some autobiographical material was woven into the accounts. Each case presents a morning-to-night account of activities within the household and accompanying conversations stenographically recorded by an assistant. The account of each family's day is an assemblage of mundane domestic activities, emotional responses to situations, evaluations of persons and events, and much else. A thematic unity to the volume is found in details that characterize the families' standard of living and in references to aspirations for social mobility, reflected in such diverse aspects as possessions acquired, jobs pursued, and choices of marriage partners.

Subsequently, Lewis devoted an entire volume to one of the five families, this time presenting the family through the autobiographical life histories of the father and his four adult children. His purpose was "to give the reader an inside view of family life and of what it means to grow up in a one-room home in a slum tenement in the heart of a great Latin American city which is undergoing a process of rapid social change" (Lewis 1961, xi.). He found a number of important methodological values in his procedure:

> This approach gives us a cumulative, multifaceted, panoramic view of each individual, of the family as a whole, and of many aspects of lower-class Mexican life. The independent versions of the same incidents given by the various family members provide a built-in check upon the reliability and validity of much of the data and thereby partially offset the subjectivity inherent in a single autobiography. At the same time it reveals the discrepancies in the way events are recalled by each member of the family.
>
> This method of multiple autobiographies also tends to reduce the element of investigator bias because the accounts are not put through the sieve of a middle-class North American mind but are given in the words of the subjects themselves. In this way, I believe I have avoided the two most common hazards in the study of the poor, namely, over-sentimentalization and brutalization. (Ibid.)

He did succeed in overcoming these hazards, but he did not recognize another. Apart from a brief introduction restating his concept of the culture of poverty and describing his research method, this five-hundred-page volume consists entirely of interview material. There is no analysis of any kind. Lewis stated, "The material in this book has important implications for our thinking and our policy in regard to the underdeveloped countries of the world and particularly Latin America [because it] highlights the social, economic, and psychological complexities which have to be faced in any effort to transform and eliminate the culture of poverty" (ibid., xxx). But his statement is too lofty in relation to the material. The implications of the material are simply not at all discussed.

An excellent integration of family case studies with an analysis of the main consequences of poverty and racial discrimination is achieved in Lee Rainwater's study of black families in a public housing project, *Behind Ghetto Walls* (1970). The study, based on three years of participant observation and repeated intensive interviewing by a large team of fieldworkers, examines the family relationships of poor black families, following in close detail and with penetrating insight the efforts of these families to adjust to a depriving and punishing social situation. After an introductory chapter on the setting, six case study chapters alternate with analytic chapters, and the volume culminates in a chapter, "Toward Equality," that offers policy recommendations that are formulated on the basis of the study's findings. The strategy of presentation is unique in the literature, and Rainwater explained it in the following terms:

> The case studies that are presented in alternate chapters below are intended not merely as illustrations or citations of data to support the generalizations made in the analytic chapters. We hope rather that they will allow the reader an opportunity to become acquainted with the complexity and multi-faceted quality of the information from which we draw conclusions, and to confront more directly the continuing nature of an individual experience in the Pruitt-Igoe community. Each case is based on a particular individual—the cases are not composites—and presents simply the edited and condensed transcripts of the field data as reported by the field worker. The case chapters have been located in the book so that each illuminates the dominant theme of the succeeding chapter, to help the reader focus both on analysis and on ethnographic description. But each case illuminates more than any single theme; each of them reflects the complex stuff of life with which we are here concerned. (Rainwater 1970, 16)

The cases are, in a sense, cases within a case, facets of a larger case, for the subject of the study as a whole is black family life in one particular housing project, and each pair of case chapter and analytic chapter illuminates a facet of the larger case.

Rainwater documented and analyzed the destructive processes within lower-class black families in their adaptation to economic deprivation and racial oppression. A different angle of approach to black family life is adopted by Reginald Clark (1983), whose goal was to understand how families affect their children's school performance. Taking issue with a prevailing view that father presence or absence in the home was a major factor, Clark decided to examine family interaction. From an initial group of sixteen low-income families, he selected ten on the basis of the achievement level of their twelfth-grade child and on parental composition. His ten families were thus divided: five successful students (three from one-parent and two from two-parent families) and five less successful students (two from one-parent and three from two-parent families). Over a six-month period he gathered data consisting of semistructured interviews, participant observation, and an attitude questionnaire. The general categories of data gathered were: (1) family theme and background; (2) early child-rearing and familial practice; (3) mental health: student values, attitudes, personality; (4) home living patterns; and (5) intellectuality in the home (Clark 1983, 17). Results of the study were presented in chapters organized on the basis of achievement level and family composition, each presenting case studies of the families. Thus, chapter 3, "The Family Life of High Achievers in Two-Parent Homes," consists of case studies of the two families of this type. Chapter 4 consists of case studies of the three single-parent families with a high achiever, and chapter 5 is an analytic chapter, "An Analysis of Dispositions and Life-Styles in High Achievers' Homes," that offers a rich array of findings. A similar sequence of chapters discusses the families of the lower-achieving students. Two concluding chapters draw out theoretical and policy implications.

The findings of Clark's study are too numerous to summarize here. However, examples of their diversity may suffice to indicate how the case study method, which aims at a searching comprehensiveness, makes possible a kind of understanding that is not attainable by other methods. For example, in the high achievers' homes: (1) parents engaged in cohesion-building family rituals; (2) the students had a sense of independence and a willingness to take responsibility; (3) parents perceived their own responsibility for helping children gain a fund of knowledge; (4) mothers were likely to monitor children's school assignments; and (5) parents tried to avoid acting out their job frustrations in the family setting (ibid., chapter 5). These examples suggest the breadth of the information that is built up in the case studies and that illuminates how low-income families contribute to the school achievement of the child. The comparable chapter on families of lower-achieving students presents findings of almost comparable diversity.

Clark's study presents a typology of cases. The typology is established in advance as part of the study design. In contrast, Joseph T. Howell's *Hard Living on Clay Street: Portraits of Blue-Collar Families* (1973) produces a typology as a result of the study. The author lived as a participant observer for a year in a white working-class neighborhood of Washington, D.C. His research led to his identifying two types of life-style among the working-class people in the neighborhood. The "hard-living" style referred to "an approach to life that is intense, episodic, and uninhibited. There is a strong emphasis on individualism, on being true to oneself" (1973, 6). "Settled-living" families were "usually church-going, teetotaling, politically and socially conservative . . . their life styles were more cautious and refined. Their marriages were stable. They were more concerned about what others thought" (ibid.). The bulk of the volume is devoted to case studies of two families, one hard-living and the other described as caught between hard-living and settled-living. For contrast, a much abbreviated case study of a settled-living family is presented in a few pages. Following the case studies is an extended analytic chapter presenting a systematic discussion of seven general areas in which hard-living and settled-living families are dissimilar: (1) heavy drinking; (2) marital instability; (3) toughness; (4) political alienation; (5) rootlessness; (6) present-time orientation; and (7) a strong sense of individualism.

Space limitations preclude a presentation of the methods and findings of other case study investigations, but the interested reader may wish to consult the following studies: Piotrkowski's *Work and the Family System* (1979); Cohler and Grunebaum's *Mothers, Grandmothers, and Daughters* (1981); and Jules Henry's *Pathways to Madness* (1971).

Discussion

The case study method in family research has been used for a variety of problems, and the case studies themselves have differed somewhat in the way they were done. All of the investigations described have in common, however, the assumption that the problem being investigated required a comprehensive view of the family as a functioning group. The view required could not be attained by lifting a few precut variables off the shelf and confining the study to those prechosen aspects. Further, data from the child members are as important as data from the adult members of the family. Each of the studies begins with a general idea of the problem and a general sense of direction, but there are no established ways of looking at whole families, and each study had the task of discovering its own subject matter. The subject matter emerges from the study in the form of observations and in the form of new concepts for comprehending the observations.

All of the studies discussed have been generally well received in the social science community. Nevertheless, they have also given rise to some disquiet. Each study was so unique in the way it was done that questions have arisen about whether such work can be considered science. Toward the end of a laudatory review of *Family Worlds*, Alan Kerckhoff raised this objection:

> The above should be sufficient to indicate that this reviewer believes Hess and Handel have made a considerable contribution to our understanding of family dynamics. However, this reviewer feels constrained to add a few less laudatory words as well. These in no way detract from the above, but they put it in what seems to be proper perspective. . . . This volume leaves this reader frustrated due to his feeling that other students of human behavior might analyze the same data and not come up with the same picture as did Hess and Handel. The very impressiveness of their product puts it beyond the realm of scientific method and stamps it as an artistic creation. (1959, 169)

Kerckhoff clearly implies that there is another kind of social science work that is scientific, not artistic. He does not say what that is, but it is a reasonable guess that he, like a great many other sociologists, would consider survey research to be the major scientific method in sociology, since the data are supposedly gathered (1) in a standardized way and (2) on a randomly selected sample, two conditions that permit statistical analysis and generalization of findings to a population.[8] This honorific view of survey research is widely held in sociology, but how tenable is it? Has anyone ever gathered a large quantity of survey data and then turned them over to five or ten different qualified survey researchers with no more instruction than to analyze the data and produce a report? Has any "Commission on the Objectivity of Survey Research" ever commissioned such a study and compared the five or ten resulting research reports? Perhaps it has been done, but I am not familiar with such an investigation. And there is some reason to believe that different survey researchers, handed the same set of survey data, would come up with different pictures. The likelihood of such an outcome has been communicated clearly by James A. Davis, an eminent survey researcher. Davis has written a chronicle of a national survey that he conducted as a study director at the National Opinion Research Center. Among the conclusions that he drew from his experience was the following:

> I think that this chronicle illustrates the ways in which survey analysis is much akin to artistic creation. There are so many questions which might be asked, so many correlations which can be run, so many ways in which the findings can be organized, and so few rules or precedents for making these choices that a thousand different studies could come out of the same data. Beyond his technical responsibility for guaranteeing accuracy and honest statistical calculations, the real job of the study director is to select and integrate. Of all the findings, only some should be selected for presentation, but which ones? . . . The answers must come from the study director's experience and his intellectual taste, his ability to simplify but not gloss over, to be cautious without pettifoggery, to synthesize without distorting the facts, to interpret but not project his prejudices on the data. These, I submit, are ultimately aesthetic decisions, and the process of making these decisions is much like aesthetic creation. (1967, 267–68)

Davis's statement makes abundantly clear that the surface of certitude in a survey research report is laminated to unseen layers of idiosyncratic judgment. He likened survey analysis as an art not to painting or sculpture, in which there are few limits to what can be done with the materials, but to architecture, which has more built-in constraints. Producing a case study is also governed by constraints: (1) there is a problem focus; (2) the researcher utilizes guiding concepts and ideas; and (3) within the constraints of problem focus and guiding ideas, the empirical materials are not infinitely interpretable, although assuredly there is no inevitable interpretation.

The creation of a case study is, in certain fundamentals, not different from the creation of a survey. The producer of a case study has the obligation to be honest in his or her handling of materials. In the effort to find and formulate coherence, there are inevitably data that do not fit within the pattern, and the researcher has to evaluate and decide whether these nonfitting data are important enough to include and call attention to or whether they are inconsequential. Beyond the question of honesty in handling data, there is a similarity in that both surveys and case studies produce more data than can possibly be integrated into a report. This superfluity necessitates selectivity. I know of no one who has taken up Kerckhoff's implied challenge and given a set of raw case materials to different social scientists to see how nearly alike their analyses would be. Becker believes that case study researchers who use the same theoretical framework and are interested in the same general problems would produce the same analyses, but to the best of my knowledge no one has put this proposition to the test (1970, 83). I think he overlooks the likely significance of individual judgment operating even within the constraints he specifies. Perhaps a "Commission on Objectivity" should compare the similarities of analyses of the same survey data with the similarities of analyses of the same case study data.

Doing a case study is an art, but in that respect it does not differ from other forms of social science research, and probably it does not differ from research in the natural sciences either. Research involves recognizing, identifying, and conceptualizing phenomena not previously known, or it involves finding connections or relationships that were not previously known. It involves assembling evidence and reasoning about the evidence. In these regards, all research is alike, and it requires some mental latitude.

But finally the question must be asked: How else can one study family functioning, if not by case study methods? There are, it is true, some experiments on families, but they deal with an extremely narrow range of topics. Is it possible to do surveys on families (meaning here units consisting of adults and minor children of diverse age) that meet the requisite conditions for survey research and that also have the family as the unit of analysis? Although there are many surveys of husbands and wives and some surveys of parents and adolescents, the analyses compare these status categories, not families. To the best of my knowledge, survey research has not been employed to study families as units, and it is not readily adaptable to this purpose, if adaptable at all. The only feasible way to develop wide-ranging knowledge of how families function is by using the case study method. The sociological profession would be doing itself a good turn by encouraging, cultivating, and fostering this scientific art.

Notes

1. A paperbound edition with a new preface was published in 1974 and a German translation in 1975. After keeping the work in print for thirty years, the University of Chicago Press allowed it to go out of stock indefinitely in January 1990. The German translation was in print for ten years.

2. Much of the literature of this period relating child-rearing practices to social class was reviewed and analyzed in Bronfenbrenner 1958.

3. Our work was among the earliest to recognize that socialization in families was a process in which fathers, as well as mothers, were participants.

4. This technique with children had been introduced by Havighurst, Robinson, and Dorr 1946. The idea of having parents each write a related essay was introduced by Hess and Handel for their study.

5. This summary is slightly modified from that presented in Hess and Handel 1959, 292–94.

6. Partisans of participant observation may find this procedure insufficient. The lack of observational data was judged a deficiency in an otherwise laudatory review by the anthropologist Jules Henry (1961). He went on to predict that ours would probably be the last study of this kind, to be succeeded by studies based on participant observation. I would agree that observational data are very important. It is also essential to note that although it has proved possible to obtain observational data on working-class and lower-class families, the only middle-class families that have allowed sustained in-home observation, to the best of my knowledge, are those that have produced a seriously emotionally disturbed child (Henry 1971) or have had a husband-father who sustained a heart attack (Speedling 1982). I would definitely encourage efforts to gain observational access to middle-class families, but until they are successful, the choice is to do studies based on interviews or to do nothing.

It is apposite to note here that it is commonplace in sociology to describe not only values, beliefs, and attitudes but also action on the basis of interviews, whether survey or qualitative. We were making an unusual inferential leap in attempting to say something about interaction on the basis of concurrent analysis of the interviews and projective tests from all the members of a family. In a later publication (Handel 1967), I tried to work out a more systematic procedure for concurrent analysis of the TAT stories obtained from all the members of a family, and I called this "the analysis of correlative meaning." Briefly, this involves interpreting each member's responses in the light of the other members' responses. In retrospect, even though the Hess-Handel procedure was less systematic, it can be considered a version of "the analysis of correlative meaning," applied to the entire body of materials that we had. The logic can be similarly applied to interviews alone, without accompanying projective test responses.

7. Becker has noted: "The comprehensive goal of the case study, however, even though it is not reached, has important and useful consequences. It prepares the investigator to deal with unexpected findings and, indeed requires him to reorient his study in the light of such developments. It forces him to consider, however crudely, the multiple interrelations of the particular phenomena he observes. And it saves him from making assumptions that may turn out to be incorrect about matters that are relevant, though tangential, to his main concerns. This is because a case study will nearly always provide some facts to guide those assumptions, while studies with more limited data-gathering procedures are forced to assume what the observer making a case study can check on" (1970, 76).

8. Elliot Mishler reported work showing that the administration of survey interviews is in fact much less standardized than is supposed. He cited four studies of the performance of experienced and well-trained survey interviewers; the studies found that anywhere from 25 percent to 40 percent of the questions were asked in a way that deviated from the prescribed wording or procedure. He added, "We do not know how typical these levels of 'incorrectness' and variation among interviewers are in 'routine survey research,' but it is not unlikely that the problem would be more serious in studies that rely on interviewers who are less carefully trained and supervised" (Mishler 1986, 18–19).

References

Becker, Howard S. 1970. "Social Observation and Social Case Studies."
 Pp. 75–86 in *Sociological Work: Method and Substance*, by Howard S.
 Becker. Chicago: Aldine.
Bettelheim, Bruno. 1955. *Love Is Not Enough. The Treatment of Emotionally Disturbed Children*. Glencoe, Ill.: Free Press.
Bronfenbrenner, Urie. 1958. "Socialization and Social Class through Time and Space." Pp. 400–425 in *Readings in Social Psychology*, edited by E. E.
 Maccoby, T. M. Newcomb, and E. L. Hartley. New York: Holt, Rinehart and Winston.
Burgess, Ernest W. [1926] 1968. "The Family As a Unity of Interacting Personalities." Pp. 28–34 in *Family Roles and Interaction: An Anthology*, edited by Jerold Heiss. Chicago: Rand McNally.
Clark, Reginald. 1983. *Family Life and School Achievement: Why Poor Black Children Succeed or Fail*. Chicago: University of Chicago Press.

Cohler, Bertram J., and Henry U. Grunebaum. 1981. *Mothers, Grandmothers, and Daughters*. New York: Wiley.

Cooley, Charles Horton. 1909. *Social Organization*. New York: Scribner.

Davis, Allison, and Robert J. Havighurst. 1946. "Social Class and Color Differences in Child Rearing." *American Sociological Review* 11:698–710.

Davis, James A. 1967. "Great Books and Small Groups: An Informal History of a National Survey." Pp. 244–69 in *Sociologists at Work*, edited by Phillip E. Hammond. Garden City, N.Y.: Anchor Books.

Denzin, Norman. 1970. *The Research Act*. Chicago: Aldine.

Diesing, Paul. 1971. *Patterns of Discovery in the Social Sciences*. Chicago: Aldine.

Gee, Wilson. 1950. *Social Science Research Methods*. New York: Appleton-Century-Crofts.

Handel, Gerald. 1967. "Analysis of Correlative Meaning: The TAT in the Study of Whole Families." Pp. 104–24 in *The Psychosocial Interior of the Family*, edited by Gerald Handel. Chicago: Aldine.

Handel, Gerald, and Robert D. Hess. 1956. "The Family As an Emotional Organization." *Marriage and Family Living* 18 (May): 99–101.

Havighurst, Robert J. 1950. "Human Development in 1949." *Human Development Bulletin* (January): 29–31. Committee on Human Development, University of Chicago.

Havighurst, Robert J., M. Z. Robinson, and M. Dorr. 1946. "The Development of the Ideal Self in Childhood and Adolescence." *Journal of Educational Research* 40 (December): 241–57.

Henry, Jules. 1961. Review of *Family Worlds*, by Robert D. Hess and Gerald Handel. *Harvard Educational Review* 31:361–62.

———. 1971. *Pathways to Madness*. New York: Random House.

Henry, William E. 1951. "The Thematic Apperception Technique in the Study of Group and Cultural Problems." Pp. 230–78 in *An Introduction to Projective Techniques and Other Devices for Understanding the Dynamics of Human Behavior*, edited by Harold H. Anderson and Gladys L. Anderson. New York: Prentice-Hall.

———. 1956. *The Analysis of Fantasy*. New York: Wiley.

Hess, Robert D., and Gerald Handel. 1956. "Patterns of Aggression in Parents and Their Children." *Journal of Genetic Psychology* 89:199–212.

———. 1959. *Family Worlds*. Chicago: University of Chicago Press.

Howell, Joseph T. 1973. *Hard Living on Clay Street: Portraits of Blue-Collar Families*. Garden City, N.Y.: Anchor.

Kerckhoff, Alan C. 1959. Review of *Family Worlds*, by Robert D. Hess and Gerald Handel. *Social Forces* 38:168–69.

Lewin, Kurt, Ronald Lippitt, and Ralph K. White. 1939. "Patterns of Aggressive Behavior in Experimentally Created 'Social Climates.'" *Journal of Social Psychology* 10:271–99.

Lewis, Oscar. 1950. "An Anthropological Approach to Family Studies."
American Journal of Sociology 55:468–75.
——. 1959. Five Families. New York: Basic Books.
——. 1961. The Children of Sanchez. New York: Random House.
Lin, Nan. 1976. Foundations of Social Research. New York: McGraw-Hill.
Lippitt, Ronald, and Ralph K. White. 1943. "The 'Social Climate' of Children's
Groups." Pp. 485–508 in Child Behavior and Development, edited by
Roger G. Barker, Jacob S. Kounin, and Herbert F. Wright. New York:
McGraw-Hill.
Mishler, Elliot. 1986. Research Interviewing: Context and Narrative.
Cambridge: Harvard University Press.
Murray, Henry A. 1943. Thematic Apperception Test. Cambridge: Harvard
University Press.
Phillips, Bernard S. 1971. Social Research: Strategy and Tactics. 2d ed. New
York: Macmillan.
Platt, Jennifer. 1987. "The Meanings of Case Study in the Interwar Period."
Unpublished paper, University of Sussex.
Piotrkowski, Chaya. 1979. Work and the Family System. New York: Free Press.
Rainwater, Lee. 1970. Behind Ghetto Walls: Black Families in a Federal Slum.
Chicago: Aldine.
Riesman, David, with Nathan Glazer and Reuel Denney. 1950. The Lonely
Crowd. New Haven: Yale University Press.
Rogers, Carl R. 1951. Client-Centered Therapy. Boston: Houghton Mifflin.
Simon, Julian L. 1969. Basic Research Methods in Social Science. New York:
Random House.
Speedling, Edward J. 1982. Heart Attack: The Family Response at Home and in
the Hospital. New York: Tavistock.
Warner, W. Lloyd, with Marchia Meeker and Kenneth Eels. 1949. Social Class
in America. Chicago: Science Research Associates.
Warner, W. Lloyd, et al. 1949. Democracy in Jonesville: A Study of Quality and
Inequality. New York: Harper and Brothers.
Warner, W. Lloyd, and William E. Henry. 1946. "The Radio Day Time Serial: A
Symbolic Analysis." Genetic Psychology Monographs 37:3–71.
Warner, W. Lloyd, and Paul S. Lunt. 1941. The Social Life of a Modern
Community. Yankee City Series, vol. 1. New Haven: Yale University Press.

Joe R. Feagin, Anthony M. Orum,

and Gideon Sjoberg

Conclusion

The Present Crisis in U.S. Sociology

In this book we have considered the nature of case studies at length and have shown various examples of case studies. To conclude the book, we wish to raise a few new issues and to repeat several others that have come up in the course of our discussion. We turn first to talk about a bifurcation that has become increasingly evident in the field of sociology—between "book sociology," on the one hand, and "article sociology," on the other. Sociology is not the only social scientific discipline that displays this bifurcation; it is evident in political science and to some extent in economics, though it is not as much in evidence in anthropology. Thus, even though we frame our discussion primarily in sociological terms, our general points, we believe, also have some bearing on the work now done in companion fields in the social sciences.

Two Sociologies?

Most memorable sociological research in the twentieth century has taken the form of case studies designed to probe one social phenomenon in depth. The general agreement, among sociologists of various perspectives, that *Street Corner Society, Tally's Corner, Union Democ-*

racy, and *Wayward Puritans* are sociological classics underscores this point. Book-length case study reports on important subjects have made up most of the distinguished core of the sociological opus from the beginning of sociology in the late nineteenth century to the present day. For much of this period, many articles in the mainstream sociological journals dealt with theoretical and substantive issues and used methodological approaches akin to those in the book literature. Until the mid-to-late 1960s, the array of articles in mainstream sociological journals reflected the diversity of research by sociologists, with the articles ranging from theoretical analyses and analytical essays to qualitative case studies and quantitative-statistical papers. For example, as late as 1964 an entire issue of the *American Sociological Review* featured five (and only five) major essay articles on evolution and change, including essays by Talcott Parsons, Robert Bellah, Wilbert E. Moore, and S. N. Eisenstadt (see Parsons 1964). Not one of these still seminal articles has any quantitative or positivistic apparatus, and not one could have been published in the *American Sociological Review* of the 1970s and 1980s. Yet they have lasting power and will be read long after recent issues of that journal have been forgotten, simply because they assess, with perspicacity and readability, major macrosociological issues.

Since the 1970s, sociology has polarized dramatically. There is now an article sociology and a book sociology. There are striking differences in style, methods, and subject matter between the two sociologies. Indeed, the texts and discourses of the two sociologies are to a remarkable degree nonoverlapping. In mainstream journals such as the *American Sociological Review, Social Forces, Social Science Quarterly,* and the *American Journal of Sociology,* little case study or other qualitative research has been published in recent decades; and very few classic analytic essays such as those by Parsons, Bellah, and Eisenstadt have appeared in recent years. In his article in this collection, Geis notes that words can usually capture the nuances of human feeling and experience better than numbers can, yet the sharp analytic essay seems to be dying as a sociological genre, at least in the mainstream sociology journals. Currently, mainstream journal-article sociology accents quantitative-statistical data interpreted in a hypothetico-deductive positivistic framework. A great number of mainstream journal-article sociologists are dependent on government or foundation grants, and most make use of official data—demographic data or survey data gathered under governmental or corporate funding auspices, a condition limiting the topics of and critical character of sociological research.

Book sociology, in contrast, is quite different. The majority of books written by sociologists in recent years focus on important contemporary issues. Even a cursory scanning of recent books by sociologists will reveal that most are focused studies of specific issues using either qualitative data or mixed research sources for analysis. The majority might be considered, broadly speaking, to be case studies, in that they are in-depth, multifaceted investigations of a single social phenomenon using some qualitative research methods. Book sociology accurately reflects the diversity of modern sociology, with a great variety of research and presentation styles being offered. It also appears to us that sociologists' reading of the mainstream journals is on the decline. And it is our impression that most sociologists now concentrate their reading in book sociology and in the specialized journals—such as those in theory, qualitative sociology, and urban sociology—that have developed as partial compensation for the dominance of quantitative positivism in the mainstream journals.

The Tragedy of Mainstream Article Sociology: Persisting Irrelevance

One of the most damning indictments of mainstream article sociology is that of Kai Erikson, who was discussed in the Sjoberg, Williams, Vaughan, and Sjoberg article in this volume. Reviewing articles in leading journals over the last several decades, Erikson concluded: "Many of the truly decisive happenings of our own time have passed with little or no comment from the sociological community. . . . [A future] historian would learn almost nothing about the pivotal events around which the flow of modern history turned" (1984, 306).

Most of what is published in the premier mainstream journals is irrelevant to a deep understanding of what is going on in this society, past and present. Erikson's apt comment needs to be extended beyond the dramatic historical happenings that he had in mind, such as the dropping of the atomic bomb on Hiroshima, to include many important questions about this society's basic institutions. It is not just the dramatic happenings that are often missed by the sociologists of the mainstream journals; the journal articles there tend to ignore an array of critical social problems, including environmental degradation, health crises, racial and gender discrimination, and worker exploitation by employers, to mention just a few. These and other important issues are difficult to research with the usual armchair research strategies of secondary analysis of survey and demographic data. And they are difficult to analyze if one works only with the small chunks of social life that can be assessed in short journal articles normed for character and length on the positivistic natural-science model. Most mainstream journal analyses are often not sufficiently macrosociological for their relevance to human experience to be clear to the nonspecialist sociologist, much less the intelligent layperson. As Sjoberg, Williams, Vaughan, and Sjoberg point out, the positivistic journal-article style is so tied to methodological individualism, such as the probability sampling (characteristic of survey research) that assumes individuals surveyed are independent and equal, that it can only with difficulty study stratified populations. These populations include those in bureaucracies and those in the systems of racial and gender stratification. Only rarely can such methodological individualism contribute deep insights into the character of stratified social institutions. This situation is made worse by the fact that in-depth, nonpositivistic field studies of critical stratification issues (such as the nature of the "capitalist class") are not likely to be funded by the government agencies that buttress institutionalized positivistic research.

The book-length case studies and focused essays that are the major carriers of the ongoing sociological research tradition have several advantages over the mainstream journal-article sociology. In the first place, they more often center on important issues, such as shifts in societal values, racism, age or gender exploitation, workplace troubles, environmental crises, and even the crises in sociology itself. They tend to make use of a variety of data sources to come up with a macrosociological or comprehensive view of the problem being analyzed. Typically the social units or dimensions under analysis are not so microsociological, specialized, or obscure that ordinary human beings cannot recognize and relate to them. Usually the analysis is clearly relevant to human experience, especially if it has involved the researcher's going into the field and talking to real people or observing people in real-life situations. The issues under discussion are likely to be of current interest as well. In contrast, most current journal articles are now about the past. By the time opinion and census surveys are processed through the statistical procedures and journal review protocols associated with positivistic-quantitative sociological analysis, the data analysis is usually no longer current. One result is that mainstream journal articles are less relevant to understanding contemporary problems and to facilitating policy discussion than they might be. Although book sociology can also involve analysis of old data, it can be more timely and provide coverage of the decisive issues and events of the present time. The universally recognized virtue of much book sociology is that it is readable and accessible to a much larger audience than mainstream article sociology, even including a much larger audience of sociologists!

Most sociologists and other social scientists admit they have learned much from case studies; many will note the insights they have gained from reading *Street Corner Society*, *Union Democracy*, or *Habits of the Heart*, even when they disagree with the arguments. And case study monographs are probably the major sociological source for textbooks in sociology. For example, the best-selling introductory sociology book in the late 1980s, *Sociology* by John Macionis, draws heavily on book sociology and nonsociological book sources, the majority of which are case studies or focused essays of a nonquantitative sort. Macionis rarely cited articles (especially post-1980 articles) in mainstream sociological journals in his presentation of the major topics of sociology. His book could easily have been written without any citations to recent research presented in the *American Sociological Review*, *Social Forces*, *Social Science Quarterly*, or the *American Journal of Sociology*, but it could not have been written without extensive citations to past and recent case studies in the core sociological tradition. Book sociology provides a much more central source of data and interpretation for writing about the modern social world. Macionis's textbook is not unusual in this regard; citations in most other introductory—and social problems—textbooks reflect the same dependence on book sociology and, more broadly, book social science.

Two Principal Advantages of Case Studies

A CLOSE READING

Two dimensions of case studies are accented throughout this book. There is the close reading of social life provided by the case study, and there is the attention to the broader social context. There is a strong tendency in current quantitative-positivistic work to make remote and to decontextualize the subject matter under study. Close-up sociology tends to be reported in books, whereas distant, once- or twice-removed sociology tends to be reported in the prestige journals. Close readings, usually characterized by richness and depth, are major virtues of the case study. Since the case study seeks to capture people as they experience their natural, everyday circumstances, it can offer a researcher empirical and theoretical gains in understanding larger social complexes of actors, actions, and motives. With the close reading, case studies can bring actors and agents into the sociological framework. There is a rough parallel between the mainstream positivistic research and an emphasis on the structural side of the structure versus agency dichotomy. Qualitative case study approaches can easily emphasize both structure and agents. Case study approaches make it easier to focus on the concrete actors involved in particular social situations. In the case of U.S. cities, for example, these actors would include developers and other major business actors, as well as the ordinary citizens. In the articles in this book, the case study researchers have usually given attention not only to the agents and actors but also to the institutions that shape, and are shaped by, the actors' concrete actions. Social systems do not develop out of an inevitable structural necessity, but rather in a contingent manner; they result from the conscious actions taken by individual actors who are, in part, constrained by those social systems.

The close reading of case study data by one or two researchers has a major advantage in that there is one central place through which the data are filtered. There is a distinct advantage to having all the information—all the contacts and interviews—in a study go through one or two brains. In this manner the interpretation of data can more easily take on a unified or holistic character.

THE CONTEXTUAL ADVANTAGE

A second advantage of most case study research is the contextual situating. Quantification is not the problem in the mainstream positivistic research. The problem is the way in which such methods are used. Taken alone, they cannot in principle give an adequate portrait of a social phenomenon because they cannot tell us much about the broader social context, the patterns or interrelationships among the individuals being analyzed. The methodological individualism of the standard demographic and survey research studies treats each person as part of a larger sum of individuals who are unrelated. As Snow and Anderson point out in their article, case study analysis has the tremendous advantage of focusing on a system of action and relations rather than on a one-time cross-section of isolated individuals. Individuals can be seen in relation to their contexts and their relationships to other individuals. In case studies, researchers try to arrive at a comprehensive understanding of the group under study by examining the group's members and their relations to one another.

In his article, Geis notes Charles Cooley's (1927) statement that the phenomena of life are often better distinguished by pattern than by quantity. Critical to case study analysis is a study of the patterned actions of related individuals. The study of patterns in action means a study of the contextualization of actions and processes. Yet contextualization, as Snow and Anderson point out, is more than a description of events and processes. It means articulating the relationship of the social phenomenon of interest to the surrounding world in which it is imbedded. The study of total complexes of social action is indispensable for much social analysis. We noted in the first chapter that action and belief are not fully understandable unless observed in context. As Clifford Geertz has written: "In order to follow a baseball game one must understand what a bat, a hit, an inning, a left field, a squeeze play, a hanging curve, and a tightened infield are, and what the game in which these 'things' are elements is all about" (1983, 69).

This insight can be extended to include a series of contextualizations. A case study such as that by Orum in Austin or by Feagin in Houston can permit a cubical analysis, an examination from six or more dimensions or contexts. A city can be examined in the local geographical and political context today, in the historical geographical and political context(s), in a national geographical and political context, and in an international geographical and political context. Each of these contexts can be considered in a way that enables us to understand better what this case is about. Although mainstream positivistic analysis can in principle examine data in context, this is rarely done, for a variety of methodological and political reasons.

On Doing Sociology: The Future

The current crisis in American sociology may be on the way to being resolved, for the dwindling interest in the mainstream sociological journals and the boycott, under way in some circles, of these journals may force the sociological power elites currently in control to give way. The sociological positivism of the profession's current ruling elite is a variant of what Paul Feyerabend has called (1975, 179) *critical rationalism*: develop precise hypotheses, use a careful falsification procedure, base your theories on quantitative-statistical measurement, and be objective (whatever that means). Much sociological education, graduate and undergraduate, has become perverse in its emphasis on this critical rationalism. Feyerabend's comments on modern physical science are directly applicable to the current situation in sociology and most other social sciences:

> Scientific education . . . simplifies "science" by simplifying its participants: first a domain of research is defined. The domain is separated from the rest of history . . . and given a "logic" of its own. A thorough training in such a "logic" then conditions those working in the domain; it makes their actions more uniform and it freezes large parts of the historical process as well. . . . An essential part of the training that makes such facts appear consists in the attempt to inhibit intuitions that might lead to a blurring of boundaries. (Ibid., 19)

Too much social scientific education simplifies social research by simplifying new social scientists. The domain of research is limited methodologically to positivistic rationalism, which in turn has provided the logic separating the field as social science from other "pretenders" to social science. And the domain of research is far too limited substantively, typically to what can be officially funded and researched by such positivistic methods. Training in the positivistic logic conditions those working in sociology and makes their actions more uniform. It also inhibits intuitions that might blur the methodological and official data boundaries.

One solution for modern sociological education is to refocus that education on fieldwork and case studies, putting budding (and established) sociologists back into contact with people in real-life situations on a regular and sustained basis. Case studies violate the logic of positivistic rationalism. They lend themselves to emergent theories and interpretations. They usually have an emergent, open-ended quality that facilitates the discovery of new theories of human behavior. Studying social life in situ and in diversity often adds the benefit of unanticipated findings and data sources. And this open-endedness links to a blurring of both methodological and disciplinary boundaries, so that case studies often have empirical and theoretical implications well beyond the boundaries of sociology.

For most of social science history, case studies have been the heart of social research and education. The hegemony of mainstream positivistic journal-article social science is but a temporary phenomenon. Yet it does have serious implications for the teaching of new sociologists at both the graduate and the undergraduate levels. To redress the current educational crisis, we must bring the case study back into undergraduate and graduate instruction. Students must be moved back into the field to observe, talk with, and interact with people in real-life situations. Adherents of the positivistic model emphasize testability and precision, but one can also emphasize other assessment procedures for making sense out of data, such as the contribution of research to the extension of the debate about a democratic social order or the contribution of research to the betterment of human life in other ways. The point of social science, as Karl Marx long ago reminded us, is not to study the world as philosophers in ivy-covered towers but to change the world for the better. This important point looms as central in many case study projects, and it must, we argue, be brought back into mainstream social science education and mainstream social science journals.

References

Cooley, Charles H. 1927. "Case Study of Small Institutions As a Method of Research." *Publications of the American Sociological Society* 22:123–32.

Erikson, Kai. 1984. "Sociology and Contemporary Events." Pp. 303–10 in *Conflict and Consensus: A Festschrift in Honor of Lewis A. Coser*, edited by Walter W. Powell and Richard Robbins. New York: Free Press.

Feyerabend, Paul. 1975. *Against Method*. London: Verso.

Geertz, Clifford. 1983. *Local Knowledge: Further Essays in Interpretive Anthropology*. New York: Basic Books.

Macionis, John. 1989. *Sociology*. 2d ed. Englewood Cliffs, N.J.: Prentice-Hall.

Parsons, Talcott. 1964. "Evolutionary Universals in Society." *American Sociological Review* 29 (June): 339–57.

Contributors

Leon Anderson (Ph.D. Texas, 1987) is Assistant Professor of Sociology at Ohio University in Athens. He is the coauthor (with David A. Snow) of a book on homelessness, *Down on Their Luck: A Case Study of Homeless Street People* (University of California Press, 1991). He has published on a number of issues pertaining to homelessness and has conducted research on both marginal and homeless families in rural Texas.

Howard M. Bahr (Ph.D. Texas, 1965) is Professor of Sociology at Brigham Young University. He and Bruce A. Chadwick were Co-Investigators on the Middletown III Project. In addition to the reports of the Middletown studies, he is a coauthor of *Social Science Research Methods, Life in Large Families, Old Men Drunk and Sober, Population, Resources, and the Future*, and *Recent Social Trends in the United States, 1960–1990*. He is presently writing a book on social change among the Navajo Indians and continues to dabble in Middletown studies.

Theodore Caplow (Ph.D. Minnesota, 1946) is Commonwealth Professor of Sociology at the University of Virginia. He was the Principal Investigator of the Middletown III Project. His present research interests include the sociology of world conflict, modernization and social change, and the sociology of complex organizations. He is the author of *The Sociology of Work, Two Against One: Coalitions in Triads, Principles of Organization, Toward Social Hope, Managing an Organization, Peace Games,* and many other books and articles. He is the senior author of several collaborative efforts with Howard Bahr and others, including *Middletown Families, All Faithful People*, and, most lately, *Recent Social Trends in the United States, 1960–1990*.

Joe R. Feagin (Ph.D. Harvard, 1966) is Graduate Research Professor at the University of Florida. He does research on public policy and inequality issues, particularly race and gender discrimination, and on urban and community development. A product of his urban case study research is *Free Enterprise City: Houston in Political-Economic Perspective* (Rutgers University Press, 1988). Some of his comparative urban research has appeared in *The Capitalist City* (Basil Blackwell, 1987), edited with Michael P. Smith. A current research study, funded by the Will C. Hogg Foundation, is probing the discrimination faced by successful black Americans across the nation and will be published, in a book tentatively titled *The Elusive Dream*, by Basic Books.

Gilbert Geis (Ph.D. Wisconsin, 1953) is Professor Emeritus of the Program in Social Ecology at the University of California at Irvine. He is a former president of the American Society of Criminology and the recipient of that group's Edwin H. Sutherland Award for distinguished research, as well as research awards from the Western Society of Criminology (Paul Tappan Award), the National Organization for Victim Assistance (Stephen Schafer Award), and the American Justice Institute (Richard A. McGee Award).

Gerald Handel (Ph.D. Chicago, 1962) is Professor of Sociology at the City College and the Graduate Center of the City University of New York. He has published in the areas of family interaction and childhood socialization. He is the coauthor (with Robert D. Hess) of *Family Worlds* (University of Chicago Press, 1959) and (with Lee Rainwater and Richard P. Coleman) of *Workingman's Wife: Her Personality, World, and Life Style* (Oceana, 1959). He is the editor of *The Psychosocial Interior of the Family*, 3d ed. (Aldine, 1985) and of *Childhood Socialization* (Aldine de Gruyter, 1988). His article "Abandoned Ambitions: Transition to Adulthood in the Life Course of Working-Class Boys," based on his current study of life histories of working-class men, will appear in *Sociological Studies of Child Development*, vol. 4.

Anthony M. Orum (Ph.D. Chicago, 1967) is Professor of Political Science and Sociology, and Head of the Department of Sociology, at the University of Illinois at Chicago. He has done research on the origins of the civil rights movement and on the political participation of black Americans and has written extensively in the general area of political sociology. His two most recent books are *Power, Money, and the People: The Making of Modern Austin* (Texas Monthly Press, 1987) and *Introduction to Political Sociology* (Prentice-Hall, 1989, 3d ed.). He is presently at work on a detailed historical study of Milwaukee, Wisconsin, that will form part of a much larger work on the rise, fall, and transformation of American cities.

Andrée F. Sjoberg (Ph.D. Texas, 1957) is Associate Professor in the Department of Oriental and African Languages at the University of Texas at Austin. She is the author of *Uzbek Structural Grammar* (Indiana University Press, 1963) and editor of *Symposium on Dravidian Civilization* (Jenkins Publishing Co., 1971). She has a lengthy essay published and several in press on a reinterpretation of Indian civilization and of Hinduism.

Gideon Sjoberg (Ph.D. Washington State, 1949) is Professor of Sociology at the University of Texas at Austin. He is the author of *The Preindustrial City* (Free Press, 1960) and (with Roger Nett) *A Methodology for Social Research* (Harper and Row, 1968). His recent publications have focused on the nature of social theory, bureaucracy, and human rights.

David A. Snow (Ph.D. UCLA, 1976) is Professor of Sociology and Head of the Department of Sociology at the University of Arizona in Tucson. He is the coauthor (with Leon Anderson) of a book on homelessness, *Down on Their Luck: A Case Study of Homeless Street People* (University of California Press, 1991), and is currently conducting research on social movement mobilization among the homeless across the country. He has published widely on social movement micromobilization, on framing processes in relation to social movements, on conversion processes, and on a host of issues relating to homelessness.

Ted R. Vaughan (Ph.D. Texas, 1964) is Professor of Sociology at the University of Missouri at Columbia. He is coeditor of *A Critique of Contemporary American Sociology* (General Hall, 1991). He has published extensively in social theory and human rights. His major project is on the latter topic.

R. Stephen Warner (Ph.D. California-Berkeley, 1972) is Professor of Sociology at the University of Illinois at Chicago, where he teaches sociological theory, qualitative methods, and sociology of religion. He is the author of numerous essays on theory and religion; (with Neil Smelser) *Sociological Theory: Historical and Formal* (General Learning Press, 1976); and *New Wine in Old Wineskins* (University of California Press, 1988), the focus of his contribution to this volume. A recipient of fellowships from the Guggenheim Foundation and the Institute for Advanced Study, he is at work on *Communities of Faith*, an interpretation of contemporary American religion, to be published by Basic Books.

Christine L. Williams (Ph.D. California-Berkeley, 1986) is Assistant Professor of Sociology at the University of Texas at Austin. She is the author of *Gender Differences at Work: Women and Men in Nontraditional Occupations* (University of California Press, 1989). Her current projects include a book on men in predominantly female professions and a study of noncustodial divorced fathers.

Norma Williams (Ph.D. Texas, 1984) is Associate Professor of Sociology and Social Work at the University of North Texas. She is the author of *The Mexican American Family: Tradition and Change* (General Hall, 1990). She is currently carrying out research on the Mexican American elderly. She has also published in race and ethnic relations, social psychology, and bureaucracy.

Index

sus nonrelativism, 33; and the unique versus the general, 33; data versus theoretical categories, 37; and methodological individualism, 37; and Meadian tradition, 38; and micro versus macro focus, 38; and utilitarianism, 38

University of Chicago: Committee on Human Development, 248

Urban case study: goals of, 85; multiple contexts in, 85; multiple levels of organization in, 85; as replicative, 85; and triangulation, 85; researcher's roles in, 88; demands of, 89; methods, 90; case selection and generalization, 91; problems encountered in, 91; high cost of, 102; as multi-disciplinary, 102; inference in, 124; generalization in, 143; and holistic research, 143; as longitudinal, 143; and comparative historical materials, 145

Urban entrepreneurs: and Austin growth, 126

Urban growth: Austin, 123, 126; factors of, 126–30; Houston, 131–38; economic, 134; and urban history, 135; and capitalistic development, 136; unplanned, 139; actors and institutions in, 140; and business elite, 141

Urban history, 135

Urban Real Estate Game, The, 133

Utilitarianism: and unit of analysis, 38

Validity, 19

Van Maanen, John, 184, 190

Vaughan, Ted R., 69; and Gideon Sjoberg, 31

Vienna Circle, 29, 30

Walker, Nigel, 200

Wallace, Anthony F. C., 13

Wallace, Samuel, 153

Wallerstein, Immanuel, 37, 40

Warner, R. Stephen, 183

Wattenberg, Ben, 97

Weber, Max, 40; The Protestant Ethic and the Spirit of Capitalism, 13

Wheeler Stanton: and David Weisburd and Nancy Bode, 216

Wheeler study, 216

White, Byron, 214

White-collar crime, 214–16

White Collar Crime, 208–9

Whyte, William Foote, 4, 15

Williams, Christine L., 234

Williams, Norma, 16, 65; and Gideon Sjoberg and Andrée F. Sjoberg, 57

Wilner, Patricia, 45

Wilson, William Julius, 60

Wirth, Louis, 44

Wiseman, Jacqueline, 153

Women of Suye Mura, The, 42–43

Wright, Erik Olin, 49

Writing: as method, 177

Yankee City, 82

Yin, Robert K., 165, 217

Young, Kimball, 206

Znaniecki, Florian, 61

www.ingramcontent.com/pod-product-compliance
Lightning Source LLC
Chambersburg PA
CBHW021810270326
41932CB00007B/125